The Silenced Majority

The Silenced Majority

Reed Pryor

LIBERTY HILL PUBLISHING

Liberty Hill Publishing
2301 Lucien Way #415
Maitland, FL 32751
407.339.4217
www.libertyhillpublishing.com

Paperback ISBN-13: 978-1-6628-4692-2
Ebook ISBN-13: 978-1-6628-4694-6

Dedicated to my three children
for the inspiration to make this a better world,
and me a better man.

Acknowledgments

Thank you to the love of a good woman. Without Lindsey's patience and understanding when work life and a home life were completely out of balance, this book could not have been completed.

Thank you, Kaitlyn, my uber talented daughter, for all of your wonderful help with the artwork. Your assistance was necessary to keep your father sane.

Thank you to my office staff for helping to organize and prioritize matters that were not in your job description.

Thank you to the influences of wonderful pioneers such as Bill Whittle, Andrew Wilkow and Alfonzo Rachel.

Contents

Chapter One:

The Dichotomy of the Brain

In this life I have learned some amazing lessons. One of the most amazing realizations that I have discovered has become one of my favorite premises for coaching young athletes. That premise seems even more relevant in the context of the current political landscape in the United States:

As emotions go up, logic goes down.

We have all been in a heated discussion with a spouse, a parent, a child, or a friend, where emotions begin to escalate into anger. The volume, cadence, and tone of our voice becomes increasingly angrier and seemingly more and more out of our own control. Suddenly the phone begins to ring. Then, as if the current discussion had never taken place, we answer the phone in a more melodious and loving tone. Reasonably, we can assume that if a person can intentionally turn those emotions on and off in that instance, they can do it in any instance. We simply cannot allow the illogical emotions of "this moment" to dictate actions that we will be forced to live with for the rest of our lives.

Take for instance the decision of a Midwestern man in the midst of a midlife crisis who has deemed it absolutely necessary to purchase a brand-new Ferrari on a Friday afternoon in May. With the fresh new-car smell fueling his childlike excitement, he starts the engine to take his new toy home. Intoxicated by the powerful torque of every depression of the accelerator, he maneuvers his finely tuned engineering marvel into a tooth-jarring pothole. Instantly he is shaken from his emotional state to find himself face-to-face with the logical consequences of his actions. Upon waking, the next morning, he is faced with the reality of the cost of tax, title, and licensing. That is the very moment buyer's remorse begins creeping its way into his conscious thoughts. In another month he will be forced to face the music, again, when he has to make the first installment on the loan. Five months later he will begin to realize the practical futility of his "emotional" purchase when his high-performance, low profile tires spin feverishly in the unexpected accumulation of two inches of snow. As happens far too often, when the initial emotion is long gone, he is left with only the logical consequences of his actions.

People in sales and people in positions of power will use emotion as a powerful tool for manipulation. In this hypothetical situation, imagine your sixteen-year-old child is learning to drive, and you must choose between two competing driver's education programs. The first program provides an expensive brochure complete with embossed lettering and a list of "safety promises" intended to put your mind at ease regarding the safety of your young driver. This group promises to provide a federally regulated vehicle equipped with seat belts, an airbag system, and side impact door beams. The vehicle is an electric car with zero emissions and an acceleration that is governed to prevent speeds over 65 mph. The owners of this program promise you that your young driver will never have to experience a single curve in the road and they are going to make sure that every penny of your program fees will be used to eliminate any hills or valleys. The cost of the program is only 70 percent of your annual income. The obvious problem with this driver's education program, aside from the abusive cost, is the fact that they cannot control the weather. Even on a straight road, with no hills, an ice storm can put your young driver in the ditch or into a pole. Nobody can ever produce absolute safety regardless of the cost.

The other driver's education program stands in stark contrast to the first. The instructor hands you a typewritten letter with a list of course objectives. Those objectives include learning to control the vehicle, learning to navigate hills and curves, and learning to use good judgment when it comes to driving in inclement weather. The cost of the second program is $400 for the summer. In lieu of a safety guarantee, this program comes with an insurance waiver that points out the possible risks and asks you to acknowledge those risks in advance.

Both programs want safety for their customers. We can all agree that we absolutely cannot control every external influence on a person's life. Instead of making false promises about safety, why don't we teach people to protect themselves responsibly? One worldview includes roads with no curves and no hills, and this view would allow government to confiscate as much money as possible to straighten all of the roads and eliminate all of the hills. The other worldview would rather teach people how to navigate curves and hills, how to maneuver their vehicle in all kinds of weather, and teach them the judgment to understand what conditions are unsafe for driving. The problem with the first worldview is that eventually it will snow—and that is something that money and the government cannot predict or control. It is not my place to tell you which driver's education program is right for you. That is the best part of living in this great country of ours. You have your own personal freedom to choose.

In this book I will encourage you to create a platform from which you create your own logical belief system. With a strong foundational belief system, you will be less likely to be manipulated by emotional deceit. First, we must understand the science behind the dichotomy of the brain.

Utilizing this science, I am going to attempt to explain why certain people are Liberal/Democrats, while other people become Conservative/Republicans. I assure you it is not my intention to offend anyone. In a sense, we are all "out of our minds." You see, the brain is split into two hemispheres, both with completely different functions.

The left hemisphere of our brain handles tasks such as reading, writing, speaking, arithmetic, reasoning, and understanding. Basically, this is the logical side of the brain. Studies show that when we speak or perform arithmetic calculations, activity increases in the left hemisphere of our brain. Another characteristic of our left hemisphere is that it tends to process information sequentially, one process at a time.

In contrast, the right hemisphere of our brain excels in visual perception, understanding spatial relationships, recognizing patterns, music, emotional expressions, and so forth. It is also good at making inferences. For example, when primed with a sequence of words such as "foot," "cry," and "glass," the right hemisphere of our brain will relate these words and automatically associate them with the word "cut." Our left hemisphere knows all these words individually but is unable to quickly make inferences from them. The right hemisphere of our brain also lets us perceive the sense of self. Basically, this is the emotional side of the brain, and it is very in tune with our own personal well-being. Unlike the logical side, our right hemisphere tends to process information as a whole.

In a normal brain, any information that enters will be allowed to cross back and forth between the two hemispheres for interpretation. The two halves of the brain work interdependently, and information is not being processed solely on one side or the other. Having said that, one hemisphere is usually dominant in certain functions. This is called lateralization. It appears it is this one-sided dominance that helps to determine a person's political affiliation.

The Liberal tends more toward an emotional basis for their decision-making processes. The decision has to make them "feel good" while delivering a message of hope, understanding, and nurture to the people around them. The self-interest groups tend to migrate toward the Liberal political stance, because the party recognizes the importance of "self." Due to this right-sided brain lateralization, as emotion goes up, logic goes down. To my dear Liberal friends, it is important to keep in mind that logic and intelligence are not the same things. Having a strong lateralization to the right side of the brain does not indicate a lack of intelligence. Instead, it merely means the Liberal tends to think more with their heart.

On the other hand, the Conservative tends more toward a logical basis for their decision-making processes. The decision has to be "calculated" while delivering a message of strength, control, and comforting confidence to the people around them. The "betterment of the whole" stance makes this logical group migrate toward the Conservative political stance. Due to this left-sided brain lateralization, as logic goes up, emotion goes down. To my Conservative friends, it is important to keep in mind this does not mean that you don't care about people. It simply means that you are willing to make small, calculated sacrifices for a greater majority to see benefit.

It is for this reason that Liberals and Conservatives can be involved in the same conversation and argue that the other side makes *no sense*. I assure you that both sides make sense to themselves. However, they are literally speaking two different languages, and the message gets lost in translation. The politicians have made a living on this language barrier. The two parties have masterfully marketed to their own individual party for years. The Liberals will tout tolerance, fairness, and civil liberties to stir an emotion in the Liberal followers. The Conservatives will quote laws, statistics, calculations, and will explain in detail why their stance is logical to the Conservative followers.

The problem occurs when the politicians use this tool to cause divisiveness. They use this divisiveness to create a diversion that will allow for themselves to be self-serving. They want us to argue about who cheated or failed first. It is the chicken-and-egg argument on a continual loop. Meanwhile, they create policy and benefits for themselves that do not serve the best interest of the people of this great nation. The next time you hear information from the party that you don't relate to, take a minute to remember that they are looking at the problem from a completely different perspective.

There are predictable shortcomings when a country is governed by emotion. Instead of following my heart, I choose to lead my heart. There are many in this world who would advise you to "follow your heart," but if you are not leading your own heart, then someone or something else is. The Bible says, "The heart is deceitful above all things," and it will pursue that which feels right at the moment. In other words, the heart is not to be trusted.

> "You will continue to suffer if you have an emotional reaction to everything that is said to you. True power is sitting back and observing everything with logic. If words control you, that means EVERYONE ELSE can control you. Breathe and allow things to pass."
>
> —Bruce Lee

Politicians have learned the art of speaking for prolonged periods of time without actually saying anything, while simultaneously avoiding self-incrimination. It is this "art" that also allows them to selectively use the most effective weapons of emotional warfare. To them it is the equivalence of choosing which weapon to use in a duel to the death. After one instance in which Loretta Lynch had successfully stonewalled a House committee's questions about the probe into Hillary Clinton's email server, the GOP lawmakers were clearly irritated.

> "The reality is here that the Left has been very good at using words. They perpetrate monotonic polysyllabic obfuscations, semantic gymnastics, and verbal circumlocution; and nobody really understands what the real truth is. They are gifted at that; and it is 'Rule' or 'Ruin' with them."
>
> —Trent Franks (R-AZ)

After hearing Franks's amazing response to Lynch's exceptional level of reticence, I thought to myself, this may be the most intelligently diplomatic way to ever accuse someone of executing a cover up with elaborate bull$h!t. The words rolled off his tongue as easily as someone saying their own name during an introduction. I was so impressed with this one sentence that I literally transcribed it into written form and practiced saying the words over and over again. Not once was I ever able to duplicate the tuneful sound that so freely flowed from his mouth. I hate to admit it, but I also had to use a dictionary to breakdown what he had actually said. The word "perpetrate" means to carry out or commit a harmful, illegal, or immoral action. "Monotonic" refers to the tone of her voice, implying that it either never decreases or never increases. Of course, "polysyllabic" refers to the use of words having more than one syllable. "Obfuscation" is the action of making something obscure, unclear, or unintelligible. This one word perhaps best describes the art form known as political jargon. Just when I thought he had summed it all up, he impressed me even more by pairing the words "semantic gymnastics." A semantic dispute is a disagreement that arises if the parties involved disagree about the definition of a word or phrase, not because they disagree on material facts but rather because they disagree on the definitions of a word, or several words, essential to formulating the claim at issue.

The term "semantic gymnastics" would best describe Bill Clinton's contending statement that "there's nothing going on between us" as truthful because he had no ongoing relationship with Lewinsky at the time he was questioned. Clinton then famously said, "It depends upon what the meaning of the word 'is' is." Finally, Representative Franks used the phrase, "verbal circumlocution," which means the use of many words where fewer would do, especially in a deliberate attempt to be vague or evasive. To this day I have never heard a greater sentence utilized to describe the way politicians speak to their constituents and to each other. To those who are unaware, the art of obfuscation can give the appearance of someone with superior intelligence and trustworthiness.

Once these politicians have gained the blind trust of a few willing followers, these unaware participants become ripe for emotional manipulation and expanded roles of usefulness to the person pulling at the heart strings. Anyone unwilling to fall into the conformity of groupthink will be persecuted for their presumed intolerance. When guilt is ineffective, the manipulators will resort to gaslighting. Gaslighting is a form of psychological manipulation in which a person or a group covertly sow seeds of doubt in a targeted individual, making them question their own memory, perception, or judgment, often evoking in them cognitive dissonance and other changes such as low self-esteem. They promote the perception that you are the only one who doesn't think like them and you are all alone in your crazy worldview. The fear of isolation can be a very strong motivation to comply.

Other emotionally manipulative tools include:

Cognitive dissonance: the state of having inconsistent thoughts, beliefs, or attitudes, especially as relating to behavioral decisions and attitude changes.

Conflation: the merging of two or more sets of information or ideas into one.

Conjecture: an opinion or conclusion formed on the basis of incomplete information; conjecture is the act of connecting dots that do not exist.

Contextomy fallacies: quoting out of context (sometimes referred to as contextomy or quote mining); this is an informal fallacy and a type of false attribution in which a passage is removed from its surrounding matter in such a way as to distort its intended meaning.

Deflection: most people inadvertently commit logical fallacies in presenting an argument, but regrettably they are often deliberately used by politicians, the media, salespeople, and others to manipulate and fool people and by those in power and authority to deflect, denigrate, or dismiss criticism. These people feel they are above reproach.

Double standards: a rule or principle that is unfairly applied in different ways to different people or groups.

False binary choices: this insidious tactic has the appearance of forming a logical argument, but under closer scrutiny it becomes evident that there are more possibilities than the black-or-white choice that is presented. These binary choices do not allow for the many different variables, conditions, and contexts in which there may exist more than just two possibilities. It frames the discussion misleadingly and discourages rational, honest debate. Many times, the Left will use this tactic to force someone to choose between two evils, in an effort to chastise the decision maker regardless of their choice.

False equivalence: a logical fallacy in which two incompatible arguments appear to be logically equivalent when in fact they are not. This fallacy is categorized as a fallacy of inconsistency. False equivalencies are absolutely necessary to maintain the global victimhood status of the Democrat Party.

Presentism: an uncritical adherence to present-day attitudes, particularly the tendency to interpret past events in terms of modern-day values and concepts. Presentism is the tendency to unfairly judge the actions of people in history according to the values of today.

Presumption: an idea that is taken to be true and is often used as the basis for other ideas, although its veracity is not known for certain.

Psychological projection: a defense mechanism people subconsciously employ in order to cope with difficult feelings or emotions. Psychological projection involves projecting undesirable feelings or emotions onto someone else, rather than admitting to or dealing with the unwanted feelings. "Projection" is a theory in psychology in which humans defend themselves against their own unconscious impulses or qualities (both positive and negative) by denying their existence in themselves while attributing them to others. The politicians have turned this into an art form.

In many instances the person involved in the act of projection is accusing someone else of doing exactly what they themselves are doing.

Once these politicians have created an emotional affinity to themselves, their agenda, or their ideology, the willing participant is ready for an expanded role as a useful idiot. Beware of the useful idiots, they are everywhere.

Beware of the Useful Idiots

"It was during the Soviet Union's heyday that Joseph Stalin introduced the political term "useful idiot" to describe that category of citizens who embraced and upheld Muscovite policy with innocent intentions. The term has been used to refer to Soviet sympathizers in Western countries.[1] "Useful Idiot" is the accepted term used to describe someone who is a propagandist for a cause whose goals they are not fully aware of and who is used cynically by the leaders of the cause. Today the Old Soviet Guard has been replaced with an American Deep State. The Deep State is comprised of both Republicans and Democrats, and they have an unquenchable thirst for power. With the advent of a government union and no term limits for the elected officials, it is nearly impossible to take these people out of their positions of power. Furthermore, it is unlikely that Congress will pass legislation that will self-regulate or place limits on their own power; therefore, the idea of term limits being enacted by Congress is out of the question. So, the only hope the common man has of breaking up this monopoly is a Convention of States.

Thankfully America's visionary founders planned for this problem and equipped the Constitution with a solution. The Article V Convention allows the American people to term limit Congress without needing congressional approval. This process, which allows the states to circumvent Washington, was designed specifically to rein in abuses of power coming from members of the House and Senate. However, you can be assured that the Deep State will not take this action lying down. The Deep State will resist any form of populism. Populism can use ideas of both the left and the right that earn the trust of the common man. Populism is the result of someone using the common man to win elections. Most recently we have seen the Deep State attack the populist approach of Donald Trump with every ounce of their being. In addition, this same Deep State was responsible for cheating Bernie Sanders out of a nomination in favor of Hillary Clinton, the Deep State's chosen candidate to replace their poster child, Barack Obama. In the 2020 election it is looking more likely that the Deep State may have duplicated their efforts against a Bernie Sanders nomination despite the fact that they also despised Donald Trump. With regard to an unpredictable Bernie Sanders candidacy, the Deep State has to be reminded that "when ancient cartographers were drawing up their maps of the known world; they would often write into the margins of the great unknown the phrase 'Here Be Dragons,' they literally drew serpents in the waters where they dared not sail."[2] This expression was used to describe areas on the map that were considered to be dangerous or unknown. With a Bernie Sanders candidacy, there definitely were dragons—big dragons.

The common man has recognized the Deep State for what it is, and as a country we are faced with the choice of conforming to their candidate or else we are left with two candidates who are on opposite ends of the populist scale. We were put here by a lot of well-meaning bureaucrats that claim they want to help the people, but it is obvious that what they really want is to keep their jobs and their power. Using Saul Alinsky's "*Rules for Radicals*" as their guidebook, they have literally created the monster known as the current political landscape. You might say that these Deep State operatives became the useful idiots of the far-left faction of the Democratic political party and they never knew it. Barack Obama was influenced by Alinsky and followed in his footsteps as a Chicago-based community organizer. When Barack Obama said, "We are five days away from fundamentally transforming the United States of America," little did we know that every policy stance, every social reform, and every executive order signed was another step further and further in the direction of a completely centralized government that was hell-bent on feeding itself power while slowly eliminating individual liberties. Intentional or unintentional, the results have been a full-on progression toward Socialism in the United States of America. Fueled by emotional manipulation and the promise of free stuff, the radical Left arm of the Democratic Party has created an army of useful idiots to carry water for them. There are eight levels of control that must be obtained before you are able to create a social state. Although this list has been erroneously attributed to Saul Alinsky, there are still questions regarding the actual author. Some have suggested that it is a passage from a book titled *Communist Rules for Revolution*. As you read through this list, it may frighten you to see how many of these levels have already been obtained.

1) Health care: Control health care, and you control the people. Despite the fact that there is no mention of the word "health care" in the United States Constitution, the federal government is becoming more and more involved in the control and regulation of the health care system in America.

2) Poverty: Increase the poverty level as high as possible. Poor people are easier to control, and they will not fight back if you create dependency by providing everything for them. (In 2016 there were 40.6 million people in poverty, according to the US census).

3) Debt: Increase the debt to an unsustainable level; that way you are able to increase taxes, and this in turn will produce more poverty. (As of November 1, 2017, the official debt of the United States government was $20.5 trillion. That amount of debt equated to $62,703 for each person living in the United States and represented 105 percent of the entire

US gross domestic product. A debt of $20.5 trillion represents 570 percent of all federal tax revenues collected in a single year. These figures are taken from *Just Facts News*)

4) Gun control: You must remove the citizens' ability to defend themselves from the government. Through gun control, and ultimately confiscation, Socialist countries have been able to create a police state.

5) Welfare: By controlling food, housing, and income, welfare is utilized to take control of every aspect of the citizens' lives. The Reverend Jesse Jackson declared, "It should be an 'honor' for Barack Obama to be called the food stamp president." (Under Barack Obama 52.2 million people were on welfare, according to the US Census Bureau.)

6) Education: Take control of what people see, hear, read, and listen to. It is this control that allows you to make the people incapable of critical thinking. By taking control of what children learn in school, you may create more useful idiots. Bernie Sanders praised Castro for bringing literacy and education to Cuba. A radio caller who had called into a radio talk show took offense to that praise. The caller suggested that what Castro was doing would be better described as "reeducation" rather than an actual education. She further argued, "What good is it to be able to read and write if you can't read what you want, write what you want, say what you want, or do what you want?" (Our education system is essentially a Soviet-style government-run monopoly that could only be loved by the likes of Lenin and Stalin. The government decides where your kids go to school, what curriculum they'll study, and even develops long-term educational plans just like the Communists devised five-year plans. This information was taken from *CNN Living*).

7) Religion: Remove the belief in God from the government and schools. (On June 25, 1962, the United States Supreme Court decided in *Engel v. Vitale* that a prayer approved by the New York Board of Regents for use in schools violated the First Amendment by constituting an establishment of religion. This information was taken from an online news journal called *Religion & Politics*.)

8) Class warfare: "If ever there was a device more suited to 'divide and conquer' I would have no idea what that would be. This is best done by eliminating the middle class for the purpose of dividing the people into two convenient categories: the wealthy and the poor. In other words, it is designed to create a 'victim' class and a 'villain' class. This type of warfare causes greater discontent from the poor people and it makes it easier to gain the support of the poor in an effort to take more and tax more from the wealthy."[3] In the last thirty years of politics there may not be a single politician more focused on this class discrepancy than Bernie Sanders. Congressmen win elections and reelections by turning many against the few.

"Every empire in the history of the world has collapsed from within. These collapses occurred, because they failed to protect the elements of control that insured their nation's vitality, prosperity and unity. In many instances these failures were fueled by voters choosing security over personal liberties. The people blindly welcomed authoritarianism in place of the individual rights that were put in place to protect their ability to make their own decisions, protect their own property and their rights to defend themselves against further reductions in their personal freedoms."[4]

In addition to foreign adversaries, the Marxists influences, from within our government, have embraced every opportunity to manipulate perceptions so they can cultivate propagandists in the media and construct an ever-growing army of useful idiots. Think for yourself.

> "If everybody is thinking alike, then somebody isn't thinking."
>
> —George Patton

The greatest remedy against the manipulation of your own emotions is to have a logical platform on which your belief system is founded. When you prioritize God, country, and family—in that order—the pillars that support a healthy logical foundation are freedom, the right to private property, and the rule of law.

Freedom

As a constitutional republic, we have a unique freedom in the United States that other countries simply do not have. While many people at the far left of the American political spectrum criticize the foundation of this country and claim that the rest of the world is laughing at us, it is no secret why the lure of freedom attracts millions of migrants every year. It is that Constitution that provides individuals certain unalienable rights, such as the right to bear arms, a right that "shall not be infringed." It is always the desire of the radical left to make determination on who gets to enjoy those rights. They want to regulate a certain age, or a certain mental fitness, and they want to determine who is mentally fit. They want to make the rules, interpret the rules, judge those rules, and ultimately determine when and how to enforce those rules. In other words, *they* get to determine who gets freedom and who does not.

What if this authoritarian group decided there was a set of criteria that determined whether you could express your opinions verbally or in writing, which were desirable only to their own agenda; would anyone vote to allow this group to stifle First Amendment rights? What if women weren't allowed to speak about gun issues, because women are rarely the shooter in a mass shooting? Those are the views of the leftists with regard to men speaking out about abortion issues. How would society change if this radical group controlled whether or not people under the age of eighteen could express ideas or opinions publicly? Where would we be if this group were allowed to make a determination on someone's mental fitness for posting on social media; based, of course, on this radical group's personal belief system? This is why red flag laws for gun ownership should never come into existence in this country. You see, once you start down the slippery slope of taking away Constitutional rights, or even limiting them for some but not others, then the authoritarians can use that precedence for *all* Constitutional rights. That is exactly what the far-left wing of the Democrat Party wants. To that point, contrary to the belief that our Constitution is an antiquated document written by a bunch of racist white men, these men were intuitive enough to provide us with the Bill of Rights. Within those ten amendments is the Second Amendment, the one right that ensures that nobody, foreign or domestic, is able to take away our rights or our freedoms. So let the rest of the world laugh. They do not have what we have. It is complicated, and at times it is messy, but nobody ever said that freedom was *free*.

Unfortunately, the freedoms provided to the citizens of this country are often used as manipulative tools to coerce people into compliance with some group's way of thinking. This authoritarian group will create situational cognitive dissonance to make you feel as though you are limiting someone else's freedoms with your own political beliefs. If you are limited to personal freedom as your only logical defense against emotional manipulation, then you stand the chance of being called a hypocrite. Simply put, I don't need the government, or anybody else for that matter, to tell me how to live my life according to their beliefs; and everybody else is feeling the same way about their own personal beliefs.

> "Conservatives want you to live the life you choose... Liberals want you to live the life they choose. Do what you want...just leave me alone."
>
> —Scott Baio

The Right to Private Property

When the pillar of freedom is weaponized against you, it is important to have the other two pillars of your foundation to lean on. The right to private property is a cornerstone of conservative values. Socialist economists are critical of private property. Socialism stands against the institution of private property because they feel it is the basis of all social troubles. Socialists want the whole population to control the property rather than an individual so that more attention can be paid to collective social interests. The very notion that someone would vote a group of people into a position of authority for the purpose of taking something from someone who rightfully earned that possession (through blood, sweat, tears, and financial sacrifice) is ludicrous. This concept is particularly disturbing since these groups inevitably find ways to exploit, corrupt, and depreciate everything they touch, including our tax dollars. In many cases these people have worked tirelessly to achieve their successes in life. Through hard work and personal merit their persistence has accounted for an accumulation of equity in both hard and soft assets. Nobody has the right to take these assets simply because the prejudice exists that all wealthy people have in some way stolen what they have achieved, and therefore, these successful people have a greater obligation to contribute than someone who has not worked as hard and is somehow deemed less fortunate.

> "What exactly is your 'fair share' of what 'someone else' has worked for?"
>
> —Thomas Sowell

The Rule of Law

And finally, I do believe in the rule of law. I derive these rules from the Bible, the Declaration of Independence, and the United States Constitution. I believe in constitutional law and do not believe that it is outdated. I believe that if society abided by the Constitution according to its original intent instead of bastardizing the interpretation to fulfill some private agenda, the world would be a much more civilized place to live. I do, however; believe in Federalism with regard to the tenth amendment. It is clear that the Founding Fathers intended for the states to make their own laws with regard to issues that are not clearly covered in the United States Constitution. For instance, I don't care where transgender individuals choose to urinate. It would be absurd to deny them a place to perform this natural human necessity. However, transgender bathroom issues are mentioned nowhere in the Constitution; therefore, it is incumbent upon the states to make their own rules on this issue, as long as the people involved do not infringe on the rights of others while performing this natural human act.

Unfortunately, there are millions of people in this country that view the Constitution as an outdated principle. It is their belief that the Constitution should be a living document that changes with the times. They believe the Constitution is a document that should conform to their fleeting desires. This group of radicals also believes in a centralized government that controls everything. They are so intolerant of dissenting thoughts and ideas that they are willing to bring about civil unrest to achieve their radical objectives.

"While we have been concerning ourselves with freedom, the preservation of private property and playing by the rules of dignity, collegiality and propriety, the radical Left has been, for the past 60 years, engaged in a knife fight where the only rules are those of Saul Alinsky and the Chicago mob. The Left has been engaged in a war against America. To them, it has been an all-out war where nothing is held sacred and nothing is seen as beyond the pale. It has been a war they've fought with violence, the threat of violence, demagoguery and lies from day one.

I don't find anything dignified, collegial or proper about lying about what really happened on the streets of Ferguson in order to ramp up racial hatreds, because racial hatred serves the Democratic Party. I don't see anything dignified in lying about the deaths of four Americans in Benghazi and imprisoning an innocent filmmaker to cover your tracks. I don't see anything 'statesman-like' in weaponizing the IRS to be used to destroy your political opponents and any dissent. Yes, being articulate and polished makes for an electable candidate, but in no way do those qualities make a person the least bit dignified, collegial or proper. The problem is that, through all these years, the Left has been the only side fighting this cultural war. Saul Alinsky's book is such pure evil that he mentioned Lucifer as 'the first radical known to man who rebelled against the establishment and did it so effectively that he at least won his own kingdom.' It seems only fitting since the radical Left believes it is better to reign in hell than serve in Heaven."[5]

"So, to my friends on the Left, I wish we lived in a time when our President could be 'collegial, dignified and proper.' However; these aren't those times. This is war. A war to save our country from a culture that seeks to destroy it from within."[6]

For too long we have allowed the Left to gaslight us into believing that their cultural ideology has been embraced by the majority of citizens in this country. They are wrong. The true majority is a sleeping giant. I have dedicated this book, and my life, to waking this silent majority before we become the *silenced* majority.

Chapter Two:

Tolerance Is Not the Best Indication of Love

The United States is world-renowned for being a country of tolerance. Unfortunately, what has been deemed to be one of the country's greatest attributes has also become one of the country's greatest vulnerabilities. For those who wish to exploit the generous nature of this country, tolerance has become a potent weapon. However, for those who wish to destroy this country from within, tolerance has become a seemingly invincible weapon. Oftentimes in the face of blatantly un-American ideologies, practices, or policies from our ideological adversaries we are guilted into kowtowing to these practices to avoid the ensuing accusation of hypocrisy for deviating from our own rule book. Being shackled to a policy of uncontested tolerance has made the entire country subservient to a slew of undesirable masters. Masters such as the most radical followers of Islam. It makes us obedient to masters who would subvert the Constitution for the chance to promote communism. It is this tolerance that makes this country vulnerable to the mob tactics of Saul Alinsky. Leftists in the Democrat Party promote themselves as the party of tolerance. If someone thinks differently than they do, they brand that person as "evil." They preach the ability to be free-spirited, independent thinkers and then punish people if they actually think independently. These same leftists are on constant attack and then vilify anyone who defends themselves against the attack. What is worse is the fact that they have a fan base of people willing to cheer as they steal our liberties.

Unlike the capitulation of our government officials, the majority of individuals in this country understand the perils of unconditional tolerance. A true friend would never be tolerant of another friend's drug addiction and claim to do so out of love. It is for this reason that I believe tolerance is not the best indication of love. In fact, someone who truly cared for and loved another would be willing to sacrifice that relationship to save their friend from long-term harm. Being willing to endure the discomfort of risking your own friendship or career to save another is a true indication of love. We need representatives in government to understand this. We need them to be impenetrable in the face of these harmful ideologies. Many times, they will kowtow to these inappropriate requests for tolerance to avoid political ramifications. Ironically, it is this unwillingness to sacrifice their political popularity that makes them undesirable at the election booth. Unfortunately, you have to stand for something or you'll fall for anything.

It is this very premise that makes Saul Alinsky's rules for radicals so effective. Alinsky never identified as a Socialist or a Communist, but he was a self-professed radical on the extreme left side of the political aisle. The teaching of Saul Alinsky was influential in the political ideology of many community organizers and Democratic politicians including Hillary Clinton and Barack Obama. Unfortunately, community organizing only seems to benefit the organizer, and rarely if ever benefits the community.

In his book *Rules for Radicals*, Alinsky laid out his organizing philosophy in detail. Within it, he made a list of rules or "power tactics" that were designed as a basic guideline for organizers and community activists. In my opinion, Saul Alinsky was just as conflicted in his own thoughts as the political left when it comes to policy stances. They are like sheets in the wind, depending on whom they are standing in front of at the time. According to Alinsky, the radical "will bitterly oppose complete Federal control of education. He will fight for individual rights and against centralized power...The radical is deeply interested in social planning, but just as deeply suspicious of and antagonistic to any idea of plans which work from the top down. Democracy to him is working from the bottom up." Having said that, here are his rules, followed by my observations:

1) Power is not only what you have, but what the enemy thinks you have.

Power is derived from two main sources: money and people. Have-nots must build power from flesh and blood.

The first takeaway from this rule is that Saul Alinsky chooses to use the word enemy when describing those who would concern themselves with his assets. If ever there was a doubt that this has been a cultural war, this rule demonstrates this point emphatically. His first rule also clearly identifies power as the true objective. Without power, or the perception of power, these radical movements have virtually no leg to stand on. Giving credence to their false claims of power is the only thing that actually empowers them. By denying the existence of their power, the enemy is reduced to threats and physical violence, which violates one of their own rules and creates sympathy for their enemy. Finally, the fact that they derive their power from money and people indicates that to them, ideological recruitment is necessary for growth. These people are quite literally willing to build power from flesh and blood, but it is never their flesh, and it is never their own blood. So, what is the antidote to Alinsky's first rule? The answer is quite simple. Reject the existence of their perceived power. Our elected officials need to start playing to win, instead of playing not to lose.

2) Never go outside the expertise of your people.

It results in confusion, fear, and retreat. Feeling secure adds to the backbone of anyone. A favorite tactic of the left is to substitute a consensus opinion for actual facts. They use this tactic, successfully, in the absence of expert answers. If they can make the general public believe that a majority of people consent to their own beliefs, then they argue that their response is somehow logical.

> "Facts do not cease to exist because they are ignored."
> —Aldous Huxley

Fortunately, for the time being, the only "expertise" of the radical left in today's society is to shout down their enemy by using mobs and the threat of violence. The days of logic, reason, and rational debate have come and gone, and they have been replaced with ANTIFA thugs swinging padlocks on chains and blinding people with chemicals. This Nazi "brown shirt" equivalent gains its "feeling of security" and "backbone" from the sheer numbers that can be bought and paid for by George Soros and other radical globalists with money. Despite efforts from pundits in the media such as Don Lemon, Chris Cuomo, and others from CNN and MSNBC to paint this group as being an antifascist group, the American people know the truth. While their name says "antifascists," their actions are antithetical to the cause. It is time for the State Department to label this group what they really are, a domestic terror group. As I call for the antics of this group to come to an end, I am doing so for their own safety. ANTIFA has already pushed the envelope of violence too far. It is only a matter of time before the citizens of this country respond, in kind, with violence of their own. We see this type of retaliation every week on the sports fields of America. One team gets overly aggressive while the referees remain complicit. Eventually, the game erupts into an all-out melee. If the antics of ANTIFA are allowed to continue, it will not end well.

3) Whenever possible, go outside the expertise of the enemy.

Look for ways to increase insecurity, anxiety, and uncertainty.

In order to defeat the enemy, you must truly understand the opposition. These radicals intend to endlessly question the ability of their enemy, stir up fear, and malign their character. They will relentlessly attack the enemy until they are completely fatigued. Ultimately that fatigue will magnify any fears that they have.

As I have read this particular rule several times, I have looked at it from many different perspectives. As a doctor, oftentimes I'm faced with questions that cannot be answered immediately. It is never inappropriate or unnerving to reply, "I don't know, but give me some time, and I will get back to you." Conservative politicians need to avoid the temptation of answering hypothetical questions. The left will always use these recorded sound bites, out of context, to vilify their opponent. With the advent of Internet search engines there are virtually no topics that are outside of our own expertise, given enough time to do the research. In fact, most people in today's society would rather have a politician take their time and get it correct than to flounder over a question that they are unsure of. We have more respect for the attendant in the plumbing aisle that sends us to another store for the part we need, rather than attempt to sell us the wrong part simply because that is all they have. We will applaud their honesty and reward them with our loyalty the next time we need a part.

4) Make the enemy live up to its own book of rules.

If the rule is that every letter gets a reply, send 30,000 letters. You can kill them with this because no one can possibly obey all of their own rules.

This rule, specifically, demonstrates the conflict inside of Alinsky's own mind. Here he is creating a set of rules, one of which admits that no one can possibly obey all of their own rules. The writings of people such as Alinsky, and other radicals, are littered with contradictions like this. Assuming this rule was a legitimate threat to hold someone to their political promises or practices, the remedy is straightforward. Always under-promise and over-perform. It is impossible to break a promise that was never made.

5) Ridicule is man's most potent weapon.

There is no defense. It's irrational. It's infuriating. It also works as a key pressure point to force the enemy into concessions.

> "Fear of ridicule begets the worst cowardice."
> —Andre Gide

"The ruthless criticism of all that exists" was the philosophy of Karl Marx. Ridicule is only man's Achilles's heel if that man has a fragile ego. It is impossible to force someone into concessions through ridicule if the man is capable of finding humor in his own faults. Modest criticism of oneself through self-deprecation is the easiest way to steal the punchline from your enemy's lips. As the anonymous saying goes, "If you lose one sense, your other senses are enhanced. That's why people with no sense of humor have an increased sense of self-importance."

6) A good tactic is one your people will enjoy.

They'll keep doing it without urging and come back to do more. They're doing their thing and will even suggest better tactics.

7) A tactic that drags on too long becomes a drag.

Don't become old news.

8) Keep the pressure on. Never let up.

Keep trying new things to keep the opposition off balance. As the opposition masters one approach, hit them from the flank with something new.

9) The threat is usually more terrifying than the thing itself.

Imagination and ego can dream up many more consequences than any activist.

10) The major premise for tactics is the development of operations that will maintain a constant pressure upon the opposition.

It is this unceasing pressure that results in the reactions from the opposition that are essential for the success of the campaign.

Rules six through ten dictate that the attacks on your enemy must be new, imaginative, and more importantly, they must be relentless. These antics remind me of a lesson my mother once taught me during an absolute hissy fit from a friend's child. In the middle of all the petulant screaming my mother leaned in and calmly told me, "There can be no show if there is no audience." It was not my child, but I realized instantly that this child had three different adults jumping through hoops to appease her. It made me wonder how many times this child had resorted to this tactic to get her way. Would she still be playing these games if the adults around her had stopped paying the price of admission to attend this show? One thing is sure. If you don't inspect what you accept, be prepared to expect just about anything. These petulant Alinsky tactics can only survive if the victims of these assaults continue to give them energy.

11) If you push a negative hard enough, it will push through and become a positive.

Violence from the other side can win the public to your side because the public sympathizes with the underdog.

There is no doubt that retaliatory violence in response to the violent acts performed by ANTIFA would be met with extreme criticism from the sympathetic mainstream media. While journalistic integrity may never be restored in this country, it is imperative that the citizens of this country retain their own integrity. The mantra of "taking the high road" is not just a catchy phrase uttered on a debate stage by people such as Hillary Clinton, as she simultaneously begins her low blow assaults. It is this position of lawfulness that separates us from them. Let them break their own rules as the public sympathizes with the "good guys."

12) The price of a successful attack is a constructive alternative.

Never let the enemy score points because you're caught without a solution to the problem.

I can only imagine that Saul Alinsky is agonizing in hell over this particular rule. The radical left has no solutions. In fact, in many cases they are the problem. They have ridiculous proposals for government programs but have no solution for how to pay for them. The numbers never add up. They accuse their enemy of denying science while nearly everything they offer defies data, statistics, math, biology and even physics. Most citizens of this country, regardless of political party, share the same goals. While we may disagree on how to achieve those goals, the goals are mutually shared. The Democratic Party has been hijacked by this radical leftist group, and a huge faction of the party has yet to realize that. It is getting to be more and more difficult to find mutual ground for agreement. The Democratic Party has been infiltrated by a group of Marxists, and for the first time in history, those Marxists are no longer hiding their identities or their identity politics. We cannot allow them to continue dividing us based on race, gender, age, income, or any other metric they can devise in an effort to pit us against each other. They would have us all fighting for crumbs so they can perch an elite group of people in one far away location to determine who gets those crumbs, while they make plans to steal the whole loaf. The Democrats have convinced themselves that they can run your life better than you can. This is your alarm clock. It is time to wake up before it is too late. I have no desire to fundamentally change America.

The march toward Marxism has been going on in this country since the early 1930s. Before the 21st century that march was silent and relatively slow, but today a new radical group has emerged, and they are, thankfully, loud and impatient. It reminds me of the story of the young bull and the old bull standing on the top of the hill. The young bull says to the old bull, "Let's run down there and screw one of those cows." The old bull holds the young bull back and says, "No, let's *walk* down and screw them all." You see, Bernie Sanders, Alexandria Ocasio-Cortez, and her crew represent the reckless young bull. Meanwhile, Elizabeth Warren, Nancy Pelosi, and Chuck Schumer represent the old, patiently tactful bull trying not to make a lot of noise that will scare the herd. So what is the moral of the story? We the People are the cows.

13) Pick the target, freeze it, personalize it, and polarize it.

Cut off the support network and isolate the target from sympathy. Go after people and not institutions; people hurt faster than institutions.

The best deterrent to this tactic is to stick together. This may prove to be the most difficult tactic to overcome since they have virtually separated us all into neat little compartments for their isolationist approach to identity politics. A healthy debate can still be had when both sides have shared goals. Unfortunately, the left does not share my goals. I will never accept the killing of a fetus, particularly when there is a heartbeat. I will never be satisfied with an open border society. I will never accept federal gun confiscation plans. I will never allow the silencing of a voice from being heard, simply because that voice doesn't share a particular political view. But the one thing that I despise the most about the political left is this infatuation with making your political opponent out to be an evil or villainous person without any evidence to that point. When you believe you are dealing with pure evil, then you have no value for their opinion or their very existence. The left feels justified even when this hatred turns to violence on a baseball field filled with Republican legislators. This manufactured "resistance to evil" gives the perception that no matter what the "evil" person says, they are justified in resisting them. This well-manufactured hatred has been propagated by the mainstream media, professional athletes, musicians, and the Hollywood elites. This hatred has made normally rational people fight tooth and nail to prove ridiculousness. Just recently, this hatred has caused rational people to argue that "walls don't work." I've got news for you; walls work 100 percent of the time. In fact, if you find a wall that does not work, the wall experts that I have spoken to have said, "Build a bigger wall."

So, my advice is to step back, take a deep breath in, remove the emotional influences for one second, and think rationally, logically, and scientifically about what your goals are for this country. Ask why you *think* that way. Are you fighting for what's best for you or your political party, or are you fighting for what's best for this country?

Remember their tactics are feckless against someone who understands that these attacks are initiated by another human who has similar, if not greater, character faults. It reminds me of John chapter 8:3–11 in the Bible, when the scribes and the Pharisees attempted to paint Jesus into a corner:

> The scribes and Pharisees brought to Him a woman caught in adultery. They made her stand before them and said, "Teacher, this woman was caught in the act of adultery. In the law Moses commanded us to stone such a woman. So, what do you say?"
>
> They said this to test Him, in order to have a basis for accusing Him. But Jesus bent down and began to write on the ground with His finger.
>
> When they continued to question Him, He straightened up and said to them, "Let him who is without sin among you be the first to cast a stone at her." And, again He bent down and wrote on the ground.
>
> When they heard this, they began to go away one by one, beginning with the older ones, until only Jesus was left, with the woman standing there. Then Jesus straightened up and asked her, "Woman, where are your accusers? Has no one condemned you?"
>
> "No one, Lord," she answered.

Likewise, the radicals implementing Alinsky's tactics understand their own vulnerabilities. Deep down they know that they are in no moral position to judge, but their desperation and arrogance drives them to do it anyway. We could all learn a lesson from this passage.

> "I don't want you to think like me. I just want you to think."
>
> —Monria Titans

Chapter Three:

The Origins of Political Correctness

What if it was all an illusion, all of it? The residual claims of systemic racism, the bigotry, the greedy corporate owners, the unfair work environment, the catastrophe of climate change, the mass hysteria over the exaggeration of gun violence—*all* just an illusion to propagate the need for *more* government interventions into our lives? The collective message from the left is that we are all victims of some oppressor, and the only solutions to be had are to vote more Democrats into office and raise the tax rates. Every newly elected Democratic politician picks up where the last one left off. Each dedicated; to ringing the bell of oppression. Stop! Shut off the echo chamber messaging system and take a look with your own eyes. The world is not ending, and they have everyone fighting ghosts from the political past. The Democrats have convinced the public that they are drowning in a flood. Only when people shut themselves off from this messaging do they realize that if they would just stand up, they are standing in a puddle that doesn't even begin to get their feet wet. The only reason they are wet is because the Democrats had them stomping mud in the middle of that puddle. A recent Gallup poll revealed that a record high 90 percent of Americans are satisfied with their personal lives. A person would never conclude that from the messaging you receive from the Democratic Party. Just like the emotional tug you receive from media advertisement; the goal of the Democratic Party is to sow discontent. The Democrats move to convince people that the average person doesn't have enough and that people are entitled to so much more.

I took a poll on social media that asked if the responders thought hate or fear was the greatest threat to our society. Of those polled, 61 percent responded that hate was the greatest threat. These results were predictable since we have been programmed by the leftists to believe that hatred is evil. In fact, there are social media memes dedicated to "Stop the Hate." I would argue that not all hate is bad. For instance, I hate when I see a child who is clearly being neglected by their parents. I hate true racism, and I hate true sexism. However, we must ask ourselves what drives that hate. I believe the answer to that question is fear. Hate on its own is innocuous: we can hate good things, and we can hate evil things. I believe that feeling is quite normal. Fear, on the other hand, can drive people to do things that they normally wouldn't do. It creates a situation of panic and irrational thought. I hate when people drive like maniacs around me; however, when my family is in the car with me, the maniacs driving around me create an overwhelming fear inside of me that turns into road rage. The outward reactions then become darker and somewhat more desperate. Yes, I am more apt to physically respond to fearful events that put the safety of my family at risk.

The radical left has made a living on this fearmongering. When a leftist claims that something is not good for American values or that something is un-American, they are not referring to us or even our personal quality of life. They are referring to their own agenda, and their twisted view of America. To manipulate us into their way of thinking, they will stop at nothing, and fear is one of their favorite tools. The left controls speech and actions of others through political correctness. This concept, which was originated to prevent marginalizing or insulting groups of people, has actually created fear and resentment in those who are constantly reprimanded for expressing themselves in a manner that does not adhere to the left's confusing and ever-changing standards. You might say that political correctness has marginalized those who are unable to keep up with its ever-evolving rules. "This Liberal ideology was intended to bring greater equality and freedom, but has been subverted by some who believe that they, and only they have the right to rule over their fellow citizens because of their superior knowledge, education, and intelligence (all, of course, subjective conclusions) and has become a means of control (not liberation) enforced on those who are not part of this small, minority, elitist group."[7] Nothing is more exhausting than the constant pressure of policing every word that we speak; for fear of persecution.

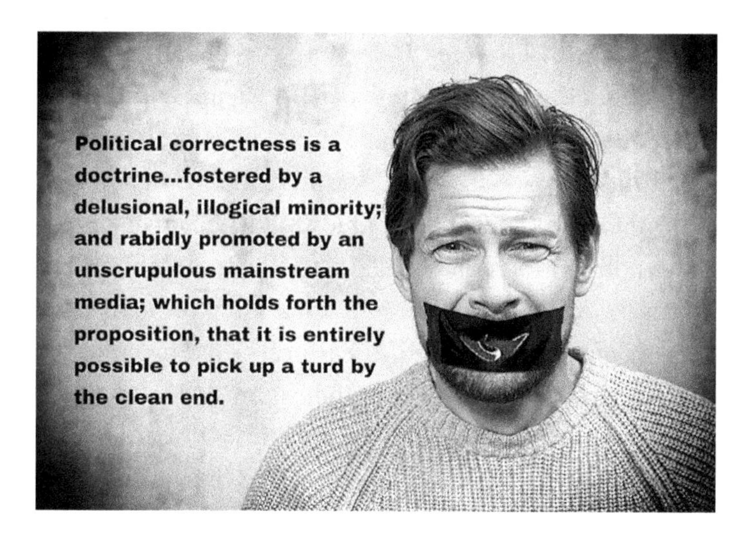

Early usage of the term "politically correct" by leftists in the 1970s was as self-criticism. It was meant more for irony than as a serious political movement. In today's world the old George Carlin list of seven things you can't say on television is officially down to only four things, but now there are 15,000 things you can't say in private conversation.

The first real influence in my conservative pilgrimage came to me while searching for speech material on YouTube. While searching the keywords "Best Speech Ever" for coaching motivation, I came across a post-election speech by Bill Whittle regarding the loss by Mitt Romney to Barack Obama. I became so moved by Bill's passion and ability to emphasize relevant matters that I began to search out more and more of his materials. It is for that reason that I decided to transcribe his YouTube video titled "The Narrative: The Origins of Political Correctness" and add it here with all the glory and honor to him, of course. I couldn't have said it better:

> Rodney King, a black man, was the victim of a severe beating at the hands of white policemen, and in the early 90s he was one of the most famous people in America. What about a man by the name of Kenneth Gladney? He too was beaten. King is famous, and Gladney is almost an unknown because King's beating, which was both criminal and appalling, fit a narrative while Kenneth Gladney's did not. Mr. Gladney made the mistake of attending a town hall meeting with Representative Russ Carnahan. President Obama, facing criticism of his radical health care reforms, promised Congressional Democrats that, quote, "If you get hit, we'll punch back twice as hard." Now part of that punching back strategy was to have members of the Service Employees International Union attend these townhall meetings in defense of Obamacare. Well, three of them wearing SEIU T-shirts saw Mr. Gladney handing out flags that bore the American Revolution slogan "Don't Tread on Me." Now when Mr. Gladney offered one of the SEIU members a flag, the man replied, "What kind of n***er are you

to be giving out this kind of stuff?" The three SEIU members proceeded to knock Mr. Gladney to the ground and repeatedly punch and kick him. Now let me answer the question that this left-wing union member asked. This American patriot, Mr. Gladney, is the kind of person that runs counter to the narrative. Racial protection, racial sensitivity and victimology only apply to those blacks and minorities that follow the narrative. That is why you'll never see Mr. Gladney on the cover of *Time, Newsweek*, or *The New York Times*. Now, what do I mean when I use the term, "the narrative"?

For that, let's turn to MSNBC. Greg Guttfeld and the *Hot Air* are trying to keep alive a remarkable story. There is a segment that ran on MSNBC at 10:45 a.m. on August 18, 2009. A man at a pro–health care reform rally wore a semiautomatic assault rifle on his shoulder and a pistol on his hip. The Associated Press reported that about a dozen people in all at that event were visible. Also, there were questions about whether this gathering had racial overtones. I mean, here you have a man of color in the presidency and "white people are showing up with guns strapped to their waist." And the gentleman with the assault rifle representing the angry ugly face of white racist America coming to lynch the black president, the man whose face we never see, but whose rifle and handgun are used to make the case...who is this horrible bigot? Oh, it's this man (an unidentified black man). And what is his hateful racist lynch mob reason for attacking the president of color? "I'm absolutely, totally against health care in this way, in this manner, stealing it from people. I don't think that's appropriate."

So why was he edited out? Why, in fact, did MSNBC producers choose to cut away from his face and hands but keep his rifle and handgun in the video clip to gin up stories of armed white mobs at townhall meetings ready to lynch a black president because of racial hatred? He was edited out because not only didn't he fit the narrative, he was edited out and the American people were lied to by MSNBC because he ran counter to the narrative. Just as that other American patriot Kenneth Gladney ran counter to the narrative. So what exactly is the narrative? These two men are *not* politically correct. Now, we've all heard that term, but what does it mean, where did it come from? Most people think it started in the 90s or perhaps even the 60s, but no. Its origins go back to World War I. Prior to the Great War, Karl Marx predicted that the workers of the world, united by class consciousness, would arise as one and overthrow national identities and bring about the paradise on Earth of world Communism. They considered this not theory but science, accepted fact, and war would be the trigger.

War came. The biggest, most appalling, most horrific war imaginable came, but Communist revolution only came to agrarian backwards Russia, which was practically a futile country, and not to the modern capitalist industrialized nations like England, Germany, and the United States—as communist science had assured the world that it would.

Now, as the dust settled on the Great War, a group of Marxist philosophers decided to form an institute, a think tank, to analyze what had gone wrong. It was originally to be called the Institute for Marxism, and would be similar to the Marx Engels Institute in Moscow, but some worried that the Institute for Marxism might be a little too, um, well actually a little too honest. So, they decide instead to name it the Institute for Social Research. Based at Frankfurt University in Germany, the Institute for Social Research opened its doors on July 22, 1924. Over a short period of time this Marxist brain trust became known simply as the Frankfurt School. The Frankfurt School's problem was very simple. The workers seduced by the material successes and general prosperity provided by capitalism were too blinded. That is the word they often used. Too blinded by this prosperity and relative well-being to recognize their class consciousness and bring about the Communist revolution. Someone else would have to be the vanguard—but whom? While these Marxist intellectuals were trying to figure out who the new vanguard of the revolution was going to be, another problem arose. Nazism was on the rise in Germany. Many of these intellectuals were Jewish Communists making them doubly unwelcome in Hitler's Third Reich.

In 1934 they moved the Institute for Social Research out of Frankfurt and took refuge in America, specifically at Columbia University, in New York City. The Institute for Social Research remained at Columbia until 1951, when it returned to Europe. Presumably

> it wasn't very far from the Columbia School of Journalism, which awards the Pulitzer Prize. It was while it was here in America that the institute, still informally known as the Frankfurt School, did its most important work. The great insight gained by the Frankfurt School was to divorce Marxism from economics and marry Marxism to the culture. The fruit of this fundamental change in strategy is known as "Critical Theory."[8]

Critical Thinking vs. Critical Theory

Critical thinking is a tool that is used to systematically and logically solve a problem.

Critical theory is a tool that uses systematic criticism of someone else's idea, not for the purpose of solving any problems but rather to "prove" fault in the other person's idea, hoping that (by default) others will seek an alternative option.

> "Throughout history...one of these was responsible for creating light, whereas the other has only created darkness."
>
> —Anonymous

"Now the theory of critical theory is simply to criticize. I know it sounds silly when you put it so plainly, but really that's all there is to it. You see, the Frankfurt School found their new vanguard for the revolution against Western Civilization, and it was going to be the dispossessed. The beauty, the genius of critical theory was twofold. First, each area of critical theory could appear to be unique and self-contained. For example, feminism could attack the Western Culture from the perspective of its oppression against women; and that oppression must be unique to Western Culture. No mention was made of what the ancient Chinese, or the Aztecs, or the Persians or anyone else; how they had treated women. Only the oppression of women in the West was on the table.

"Likewise, African American studies would only criticize American slavery; as if slavery were unique to America. The genuine horrors of American slavery and its consequences was a powerful weapon against traditional culture; as was the example of Rodney King. To quote the black African king Ghezo, who said, 'The slave trade is the ruling principle of my people; it is the source and the glory of all their wealth. The mother lulls the child to sleep with notes of triumph over an enemy reduced to slavery.' You see, a quote like that shows the economic incentive of a black culture to sell other blacks into slavery purely for economic gain. Quotes like that show that there's a little more than white English-speaking guilt to go around. It runs contrary to the narrative, and it has to be suppressed in schools. It is 'Politically Incorrect.

"Preeminent psychologist and Frankfurt School co-founder Erich Fromm argued there were no real sexual differences between men and women, and that the roles they played in traditional Western Culture were simply that; roles assigned to them by the culture. Under this guise, gender studies could launch critical theory attacks, and claim that all of the oppression of homosexuals or women throughout history was due merely to Western Culture and the patriarchy of dead white men. Dead white men laid the philosophical foundation for the United States of America. If capitalism had triumphed where Marxism had failed; the only way left to bring down this edifice of success and prosperity was to go to the root morality that it was based upon, and attack it from all sides.

"They use gender studies, radical feminism, African studies, Native American studies, and the deconstruction of classical literature; to show racism or sexism, or whatever other useful 'ism,' for philosophies that didn't even exist at the time of their writing. All these programs do is inculcate and aggravate a sense of rage, separatism and victimology. Then assign, to the only culture that actually tries to eradicate these injustices, the sole onus of their origins.

"I said that critical theory was a brilliant strategy in two ways. The first being, that it launched multiple, apparently unconnected attacks against the dominant culture, but the real source of its power and genius is that the criticism NEVER demands an alternative. What might have been better? What might have worked in its place? What alternatives have been tried successfully in the past? The answer is nothing. That's because they have nothing. There is no logic, no history, and no factual underpinning to their dreams and philosophy. Everything they believe in has proven to be wrong. It has been drowned in oceans of blood and tears; but why should mere fact trump ideology? One of the main pillars of the Frankfurt School, Max Horkheimer, famously wrote, 'Logic is not independent of content.' Yes, it is. YES, IT IS! Even the idea of facts, logic, reason and history are under attack which is why Rachel Maddow will spend thirty minutes making fourth grade jokes about 'tea baggers,' because that infantile snark is all she has against common American citizens who are quoting Hamilton, and Jefferson, and Adams chapter and verse. People who are referring to the various clauses of the United States Constitution and asking where these new federal powers draw their Constitutional legitimacy? You can't argue with that. You can't even let that come out. No, let's make 'tea bagger' jokes and let's mock the rubes instead.

"America, the Frankfurt School's bastion of racism and sexism, fought a civil war and lost 360,000 Union dead to eliminate the shameful heritage of slavery. America has elected a black president and run a female for vice president twice. Is there so much as a single black mayor in all of Europe? Are there even any black people living at all in China? None of that matters. It's off the narrative, in the same way that Kenneth Gladney is off the narrative. The narrative being that President Obama's radical socialization of

American health care and, in fact, the entire economy is opposed only by a small group of rural, white, ignorant, paid, gun-toting lunatics driven by a racial hatred for a black president. That is the narrative; and it will be maintained. Even if it means MSNBC producers and executives have to work throughout the night (or over the weekend) finding the footage they need to tell the story and excising those black faces and hands that inconveniently get in the way.

"I understand that Mr. Gladney brought a lawsuit. Good for him. If I was the unnamed black patriot from the MSNBC story (I can't find the name, because the media never deemed it worthy to report it), then I would sue MSNBC for defamation of character and for using me as a pawn to tell the exact opposite story I was there to tell myself. You know, there is a line in the movie *Serenity* that I often think of these days, and that line is, 'You can't stop the signal.' The truth will get out. The Left has been telling these lies for almost a hundred years now in order to resurrect a political philosophy that has killed no less than 100 million people; and still will not die.

"Do I think that Contessa Brewer, Rachel Maddow, and the producers at MSNBC are part of a vast Frankfurt School conspiracy? Of course, the answer is no. Contessa Brewer does not strike me as a person who was hired for her deep historical perspective. But that's the power of the narrative, you see. It's now so deeply and widely embedded in the culture that its simply what people believe. And if there were any real journalists left in the world, we'd have heard more about the Frankfurt School; but the signal will get out. The *signal* will get out even if it's just through the efforts of a few of us, sitting here in our basements, writing in our pajamas."[8]

Through political correctness the leftists ultimately plan to erode, piece by piece, the foundation of the United States Constitution. It is their belief that if they can demonstrate a lack of morality in the dead old white men that wrote the Constitution, then the Constitution itself must also be immoral. The leftists know that socialism is incompatible with the United States Constitution; therefore, the only way to progress this country into their Marxist dream is to eliminate the Constitution itself. Once this incompatibility is removed, the leftists will push to have socialism replace capitalism. They will, of course, use critical theory to argue that since capitalism has faults, by default, the only other viable option is socialism. They will ignore the faults in socialism to do so.

The remainder of this book will be dedicated to highlighting the most politically charged issues in American politics. The book will display the emotional lies these critical theorists use to sway the emotions of everyday Americans. After learning about the true origins of these divisive problems, the reader will be presented with bold solutions, founded in constitutional principles.

Chapter Four:

Illegal Immigration

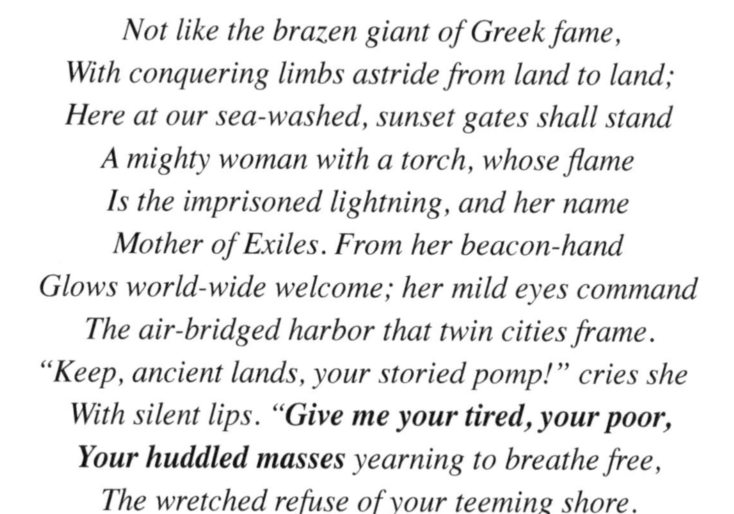

Not like the brazen giant of Greek fame,
With conquering limbs astride from land to land;
Here at our sea-washed, sunset gates shall stand
A mighty woman with a torch, whose flame
Is the imprisoned lightning, and her name
Mother of Exiles. From her beacon-hand
Glows world-wide welcome; her mild eyes command
The air-bridged harbor that twin cities frame.
"Keep, ancient lands, your storied pomp!" cries she
With silent lips. ***"Give me your tired, your poor,***
Your huddled masses *yearning to breathe free,*
The wretched refuse of your teeming shore.
Send these, the homeless, tempest-tost to me,
I lift my lamp beside the golden door!"

***The New Colossus,* by Emma Lazarus**

Since the first federal "public charge" rule was established by Congress one year earlier, in 1882, it was by no coincidence that Emma Lazarus, an immigrant herself, would pen a poem encouraging the United States to accept all immigrants, regardless of their ability to stand on their own two feet, assimilate, or contribute to society. The Immigration and Nationality Act declares "any alien likely at any time to become a public charge" as inadmissible to the country. Likewise, those immigrants who have received public benefits within their first five years in the United States are considered to be deportable. It goes on to say that "any alien who, in the opinion of the consular officer at the time of application for a visa, or in the opinion of the Attorney General at the time of the application for admission is likely, at any time, to become a 'public charge' is excludable."

Although President Franklin D. Roosevelt focused mainly on creating jobs for the masses of unemployed workers, he also backed the idea of federal aid for poor children and other dependent persons. By 1935, a national welfare system had been established for the first time in American history. In 1886 when the plaque inscribed with *The New Colossus* was added to the Statue of Liberty, those philosophical words could not account for the future introduction of a federal welfare system.

The Emotional Lie

"Our growth as a nation has been achieved, in large measure, through the genius and industry of immigrants of every race and from every quarter of the world. The story of their pursuit of happiness is the saga of America. Their brains and their brawn helped to settle our land, to advance our agriculture, to build our industries, to develop commerce, to produce new inventions and, in general, to make us the leading nation that we now are."[9] When immigration activists and Democrat politicians discuss the topic of immigration, they often conflate legal immigration with those immigrants who illegally cross our borders, overstay their visas, or abuse our asylum laws. Particularly with regard to the asylum laws, these activists will conflate legality in an effort to give the illusion of a moral high ground. Many of the 2020 Democrat candidates promised to decriminalize border crossings in an attempt to create an open border society. In their eyes, the consequences of the current immigration laws are devastating. These laws force large numbers of people to remain in other countries where they may experience economic deprivation, unsafe conditions, or separation from their family in the United States. They will tell you that the immigration laws are immoral constructs that arose primarily due to racism. In fact, they will tell you that I.C.E. agents and border patrol agents are immorally acting out some institutional form of racism. In their opinion, the elimination of immigration restrictions would benefit the majority of people who wish to move to the United States, end unnecessary suffering, and benefit the country.

The Secure Fence Act of 2006 authorized and partially funded the construction of 700 miles of fencing along the Mexican border. President Bush stated that the Act would "help protect the American people" and would "make our borders more secure." He said it was "an important step toward immigration reform." The Secure Fence Act passed the Senate by a vote of 80–19 on September 29, 2006. Those in opposition to the border wall will tell you that the border is a "fixed perimeter that defines a stark binary. It is a place of violence and insecurity, one that cleaves apart 'us' from 'them.' But the borderland of south Texas was historically, and continues to be, a site of racial pluralism and resistance to white supremacy. This land is not rooted in an English colonial history; it eludes the neat categories that both, conservatives and liberals, exploit. Its identity is shaped by a multitude of cultures and races. And the fluidity of border life has long represented an affront to the administrators of a nation that from its inception have drawn a bright, brutal line around racial groups."[10] They believe that this wall is a monument to a national identity that excludes and marginalizes them. Activists have literally called the wall racist and immoral.

Another emotional lie told in the last few years is that "walls don't work." Critics argue that the wall is expensive and ineffective.

"They will argue that this is a humanitarian crisis that is all about refugees seeking lawful entry into the United States to flee violence and poverty in their own countries. These people would rather see an option that is less expensive, less disruptive and less controversial. They call it a 'smart wall.' The vision, as laid out by its bipartisan political supporters, is to build an ocean-to-ocean technological barrier made up of a patchwork of tools like drones and sensors to help surveil and identify unauthorized individuals crossing the border, specifically in remote stretches of land between established ports of entry."[11] Perhaps the greatest emotional lie being told is that Donald Trump has put children in cages at the border and has inhumanely separated these children from their parents.

The Truth

The convoluted topic of immigration, illegal immigration, and border security in the United States has created a philosophical disconnect between the legal citizens of the country and their supposed representatives. A poll conducted by Gallup in 2020 found that 66 percent of Americans believe the level of immigration to America should either be maintained or decreased. Meanwhile, a poll conducted in 2017 found that 73 percent of Americans "support a new requirement that incoming immigrants must be able to support themselves financially." It is no secret that certain establishment politicians avoid legislating immigration restrictions because the migrants represent a cheap labor force. Ignoring illegal migration and migrants who overstay their visas only serves to undermine wage growth and employment opportunities for the legal citizens of this country. The cascading effect of this political dereliction causes irreparable damage to the entire economy.

Other political operatives, particularly in the Democrat Party, rather than ignore the subject of migration, have decided to exploit the idea of flooding illegal migrants into the country. With the dream of importing their own voter base and manipulating the census, they are creating their own majority in the House of Representatives. "The illegal immigrant population is as high as 29.5 million, far more than the 11 million accepted by experts and the government, according to an explosive new report from three Yale University experts. 'Our results lead us to the conclusion that the widely accepted estimate of 11.3 million undocumented immigrants in the United States is too small. Our model estimates indicate that the true number is likely to be larger, with an estimated 95 percent probability interval ranging from 16.2 to 29.5 million undocumented immigrants,' said their report published by *PLOS One*, an academic journal. 'The mean estimate based on our simulation is 22.1 million, essentially double the current widely accepted estimate,' they wrote."[12]

It is true that legal immigrants have contributed to our growth as a nation. However, the fiscal cost of illegal immigration to this country is a topic that most politicians would prefer to overlook. Activists will tell you that these undocumented migrants are still stimulating the economy because they pay some form of taxes. According to a recent study by the Federation for American Immigration Reform (FAIR), the fiscal burden of illegal immigration to this country and its taxpayers is nearly $135 billion per year, with only an estimated $19 billion recovered in the form of taxes. That is an annual loss of $116 billion.

Unfortunately, the costs do not end there. The Border Patrol expects to pay $1.2 billion annually in humanitarian costs border-wide. In addition, illegal immigrants have incurred more than $700,000 in medical care costs annually to cover sick migrants who have to be transported to the hospital upon arrival. US Immigration and Customs Enforcement (I.C.E.) agents have to be paid to round up the illegal immigrants that go on to commit additional crimes in this country.

According to the Pew Research Center the national net amount of remittance payments in 2017 from migrants in the United States to recipients in their home countries was $143 billion. That is $143 billion dollars that will never make it into the American economy. So much for the claim that immigrants are stimulating our economy.

Financial ramifications are not the only cost to this country. Time and resources are utilized as well. "All individuals apprehended by the U.S. Border Patrol are subject to an immigration inspection; which includes interviewing the subject to establish identification, capturing biometric information (i.e., photographs and fingerprints), entering information into a Department of Homeland Security case tracking and processing system, and checking biographic and biometric records against multiple databases for previous immigration encounters and removals. The U.S. Border Patrol also checks multiple crime and terrorist databases, including the National Crime Information Center for wants, warrants and criminal history; and the TECS database for possible 'lookouts.'"[13] TECS is the principal system used by officers at the border to assist with screening and determinations regarding admissibility of arriving persons. In combination with suspicious activity reports (SARs) these records act as a screening tool relevant to the anti-terrorism and law enforcement mission of the Customs and Border Patrol agents.

Although terrorism remains a major national security risk at our sovereign borders, the true existential health risk to our nation is the never-ending flow of illegal narcotics crossing over our borders.

"Mexican drug trafficking organizations are the largest foreign suppliers of heroin, methamphetamines, and cocaine to the United States, according to the U.S. Drug Enforcement Administration. Mexican suppliers are responsible for most heroin and methamphetamine production, while cocaine is largely produced in Bolivia, Columbia, and Peru; and then transported through Mexico. Mexican cartels are also the leading manufacturers of fentanyl; a synthetic

Opioid many times more potent than heroin. Illicit drugs, as well as the transnational and domestic criminal organizations that traffic them, continue to represent significant threats to public health, law enforcement, and national security in the United States. Drug poisoning deaths are the leading cause of injury related deaths in the United States. They are currently at their highest ever recorded level, and have outnumbered deaths by firearms, motor vehicle crashes, suicide and homicide. In 2016, approximately 174 people died every day from drug poisoning."[13]

Currently 300 Americans die every week from heroin, and 90 percent of the heroin in this country can be tracked to its origins south of our border. The amount of fentanyl seized by Immigrations and Customs Enforcement in 2017 alone was over 2,300 pounds. That amount of fentanyl is enough to kill every American citizen by overdose. "It is important to understand the magnitude and distribution of the economic burden of prescription opioid overdose, abuse, and dependence to inform decision makers in this country who are responsible for choosing approaches to address this epidemic. The total economic burden is estimated to be $78.5 billion. Over one third of this amount is due to increased health care and substance abuse treatment costs. Approximately one quarter of the cost is borne by the public sector in health care, substance abuse treatment, and criminal justice costs."[14] The border also serves as a conveyor of smuggled firearms, weaponry, dangerous materials, infectious diseases, and human trafficking.

While the Centers for Disease Control requires all legal immigrants to be vaccinated, there are no vaccination requirements for illegal immigrants, temporary visa holders, or visitors to the United States. "The Department of Homeland Security says we now face 'increased risk of life-threatening incidents and impact to public health,' and entire family units are released with 'unknown vaccination status and without a standard medical examination for communicable diseases of public health concern.'"[15] Among those showing up sick at the border, some are suffering from illnesses not generally seen in modern American society, including mumps, measles, and tuberculosis, as well as others with influenza and scabies and other skin diseases. It is even possible that Ebola may enter the United States through our southern border. Recently, over 100 African migrants were apprehended at the border, and several were from a region in Africa where the Ebola virus is spreading.

"Diseases like Los Angeles' typhoid problem don't just spring from nowhere. Someone introduced them. Pretending there is no disease among and from illegal immigrants is public health malpractice. It would be tragic to allow the undoing of the decades-long tremendous gains in public health in eradicating the prevalence and spread of infectious disease."[15]

"The trip from the Northern Triangle of Central America to the United States is a dangerous one, largely controlled by criminals for whom smuggling is big business. The proceeds of that smuggling go to fund other criminal organizations that are undermining the rule of law in Mexico and the United States.

"Human smuggling is the facilitation, transportation, attempted transportation, or illegal entry of a person or persons across an international border, in violation of one or more countries' laws, either clandestinely or through deception, whether with the use of fraudulent documents or through the evasion of legitimate border controls. It is a criminal commercial transaction between willing parties who go their separate ways once they have procured illegal entry into a country. The vast majority of people who are assisted in illegally entering the United States and other countries are smuggled, rather than trafficked. International human smuggling networks are linked to other trans-national crimes including drug trafficking and the corruption of government officials. They can move criminals, fugitives, terrorists, and trafficking victims, as well as economic migrants. They undermine the sovereignty of nations and often endanger the lives of those being smuggled."[13]

Thanks, in part, to legal loopholes there has been a shift in the demographics of the migrants entering America illegally. Nearly 60 percent of all aliens apprehended at the border were unaccompanied alien children and aliens traveling in family units. The larger majority of those unaccompanied alien children and family units were from the Northern Triangle of Central America, which includes El Salvador, Guatemala, and Honduras.

"By law [Section 235(c)(2)], the Department of Homeland Security is required to turn all of those unaccompanied alien children from non-contiguous countries (that is every country other than Canada and Mexico) over to the Office of Refugee Resettlement in the Department of Health and Human Services within 48 hours of the point at which they were identified as unaccompanied alien children, for prompt placement in the least restrictive setting 'that is in the best interest of the child.'

"Generally, most are released to a parent or other family member in this country, the majority of whom do not have lawful status in the United States. This legal requirement makes the United States government a de facto co-conspirator with the smuggling organizations. Not surprisingly the countries of El Salvador, Guatemala, and Honduras have exploited this loophole."[13]

Transnational MS-13 gang members originating from El Salvador have exploited the, unaccompanied alien children, loopholes to bring gang members into the United States and to recruit others who had already entered.

"Today, a smaller percentage of MS-13 members are believed to be here illegally, because some are now U.S.-born. Others have obtained green cards, been given a Temporary Protected Status, or have been granted a Deferred Action for Childhood Arrivals (DACA). When the gang leadership decided to launch a more concerted effort to enlarge in the United States, it was able to take advantage of the Obama administration's catch-and-release policies for unaccompanied minors apprehended at the border to move in younger members from Central America.

"Family unit apprehensions at the border have increased nearly 375 percent. This was noted after a federal judge in California blocked a policy that would force Central American migrants to wait in Mexico while their asylum cases proceed in the United States. It was the latest of several court rulings blocking attempts to discourage migrants from entering the United States. The continued release of family units will only increase the draw of people to the United States border."[13]

If only these judges, feigning moral superiority, understood the dangers of their enticing legal policies. Since 1997, "pull factors" like the *Flores* settlement agreement has been significantly expanded on by federal judges with loose border proclivities and is now interpreted to mean that all minors in detention cannot be held for more than 20 days.

Nearly 66 percent of all migrants successfully making the trek across these countries will be the victim of violence. One in three women will be sexually abused. Migrants and refugees walk for hours in high temperatures, on unsafe routes to keep from being caught. They travel on overcrowded transportation without food, water, or ventilation for hours. "The Dangers Awareness Campaign is an urgent 'call to action' to community groups, the media, parents and relatives in the United States and Central America to not put the lives of children at risk by attempting to illegally cross the southwest border."[13]

Beginning in 1985, immigration activist groups began a series of lawsuits against the federal government over its perceived mistreatment of alien minors in detention facilities. The most notable of these cases was that of a 15-year-old Salvadorian girl named Jenny Flores. The 1997 *Flores* settlement led to the government agreeing to set immigration detention standards for unaccompanied alien children, particularly regarding facility conditions and the timing and terms of the child's release. The Clinton administration was well aware of what it was doing when it signed this agreement. They knew that they were loosening the rules governing asylum. It is for this reason that the number of apprehended aliens who claim "credible fear" (the first step in applying for asylum) has skyrocketed by 67 percent. In response, the Trump administration implemented new guidelines for a zero-tolerance policy toward illegal entry without inspection. After detaining the accompanying adult, the government could either put the children in a shelter or release the entire family into the interior of the country and hope that they don't simply disappear. This "catch and release" into the interior of the country policy was executed time and time again by the Obama administration.

The first of these two options were heavily criticized by the media and the Democrat party as having placed "children in cages" and was decried by critics as a policy of "family separation." Conveniently, the Democrats selectively ignored the deplorable conditions migrants faced in detention facilities under the Obama administration. Instead, the mainstream media attempted to link leaked photos of filthy conditions taken in 2014 to the Trump administration. Truth eventually prevailed, and the photos were rightfully attributed to a timeline when Barack Obama was the president, but it never stopped the false accusations.

"In response, President Trump issued a memorandum directing the Attorney General and the Secretary of the Department of Homeland Security to develop a proposal that increases the efficiency of our asylum system in order to better address the humanitarian crisis at our southern border. Specifically, the memorandum called for fees for asylum applications, certain 'work permit' restrictions, and a 180-day limit for adjudicating asylum claims.

"Pursuant to current law, family separations typically occur in cases in which an adult claims asylum after illegally crossing the border. In these cases, adults are usually detained for longer periods than the government is legally allowed to hold children (20 days), resulting in the separation of children from adults that the government decides to hold as their pending asylum claim is adjudicated."[16]

President Trump then signed an executive order that sought to keep families together by prioritizing the adjudication of cases involving detained families and encouraging facilities be made available to house families together. Additionally, Senator Chuck Grassley co-sponsored two bills to prevent family separations. The Keep Families Together and Enforce the Law Act and the Protect Kids and Parents Act would require families be kept together during their immigration proceedings, except in certain cases involving aggravated criminal conduct or in which there is a clear threat of harm to the child. Unfortunately, some of the migrant families arrested at the southern border weren't actually families.

"Approximately 30% of rapid DNA tests of immigrant adults who were suspected of arriving at the southern border with children who weren't theirs revealed the adults were not related to the children. In some incidents where Immigration and Customs Enforcement told the adults they would have to take a cheek swab to verify a relationship with a minor, several admitted the child was not related and did not take the DNA test."[16] Do we have an obligation to return these children to adults that may have ill intentions, or so that they can be re-hired to accompany another adult across the border in an attempt to circumvent the loopholes in our immigration laws? In those instances, it seems that "family" separation may be the safest option for the children.

Attorney General William Barr issued a ruling that limits the ability of migrants to use alleged "threats against family members" as grounds for asylum in the United States. The Trump administration is also working to push its policy of having those who want to claim asylum undergo the process in Mexico instead of crossing into America first. Border Patrol agents noted a 30 percent average reduction in arrests of migrants along the southwest border within two weeks of implementation of the United States-Mexico "Remain in Mexico" policy for asylum seekers.

The processing facilities at the border were designed to house single, adult males. They were not designed to accommodate large numbers of family units and unaccompanied children. There is no circumstance in which a migrant child should be housed with an unrelated adult. "DHS has historically separated children from accompanying adults at the border and transferred them to the custody of Office of Refugee Resettlement officers for reasons that include: an inability to confirm a parental relationship, 'reason to believe the adult was participating in human trafficking or otherwise a threat to the safety of the child', or where 'the child crossed the border with other family members such as grandparents without proof of legal guardianship'."[13] The *Flores* agreement has enticed smugglers to place children into the hands of adult strangers so they can pose as families and be released from immigration custody for the purpose of either getting the child into the United States quickly or as a decoy to get the adult into the country by using the child.

"U.S. Border Patrol agents have identified cases in which children are possibly being 'recycled' and forced to repeatedly undertake the treacherous journey from Central America to the United States. While in an interview process, an officer noticed several inconsistencies that led him to suspect that the child and the alleged parent were not related. With continued questioning, Border Patrol agents, Office of Field Operations officers, and Homeland Security Investigations agents were able to gain enough evidence to determine that the child had been 'recycled' in at least two prior instances.

"Transnational criminal organizations continue to profit from individuals, utilizing loopholes in our immigration system, to commit fraud. These groups have no concern for the welfare or safety of the children and family groups being smuggled to the Southwest Border. The U.S. Border Patrol has continuously warned about the existence of this type of illicit activity and exploitation of minors."[17]

Acting Commissioner of Customs and Border Protection Mark Morgan told a Senate committee that 5,800 "fake families" were uncovered while entering the United States illegally in 2019. With only 20 days to make a determination, the U.S. authorities, he said, "do not have the time to determine" if migrant children are with their parents or human traffickers. Morgan added, "As long as our laws are the way they are, you are going to grab a kid; because that is your passport to the United States."

Border authorities have begun to increase the biometric data they collect from children under the age of 13, including fingerprints, despite privacy concerns and government policies that restrict what can be collected. With a DNA-proven 30 percent fraud rate in family unit claims, there is a shocking possibility that children will be smuggled back into Central America only to be paired up again with other adults in fake families. Documenting or tracking this "recycling" process would be impossible without fingerprints or other biometric data.

In addition to human trafficking at the border, "activist Jaco Booyens said sex-trafficking in the United States is a more prevalent issue than most people realize. Booyens is an activist and filmmaker who has fought child sex-trafficking since 2001 through his organization, '***Share Together***,' a non-profit that fights child sex-trafficking around the world. 'President Donald Trump has unequivocally done more to help end sex-trafficking in the United States than any other president,' Booyens said.

"U.S. law enforcement is under-resourced, and there are even states where the special task force for sex-trafficking consists of one person. In states where this is the case, authorities lean on local police departments to deal with trafficking. The police departments do not have the manpower or the resources to tackle this massive problem. Booyens suggested, 'it should be under the Justice

Department, or some other department, where it can: have its own earmark funds appropriated, its own support for local tax forces, and special divisions within the FBI.' Additionally, according to Booyens 'There needs to be awareness so children don't fall into the trap. Then, there needs to be a serious effort to rescue those already trafficked.'

"The foster care system in this country is a disaster that predators and traffickers understand and take full advantage of. The largest rising trend is family members willing to traffic their own children. Children are often lured from their homes by predators. Unfortunately, the United States has broken women down into sexual objects. The sex-trafficking activists blame this on a number of factors, but all agree that Hollywood, pornography and social media are the largest influences."[18]

Another loophole that encourages the entry of unaccompanied alien children is the William Wilberforce Trafficking Victims Protection Reauthorization Act of 2008. This Act distinguishes unaccompanied alien children entering from contiguous countries versus those arriving from non-contiguous countries. An unaccompanied alien child from a contiguous country can be returned, to Mexico or Canada, if the alien has not been trafficked and does not have a credible fear of persecution. Meanwhile, unaccompanied alien children from other countries are promptly placed in the least restrictive setting that is in the best interest of the child. The overwhelming majority of these children are released to sponsors inside of the United States who are family members, many of whom are not legal citizens. They are released to these family members to await their immigration hearings. You may recall the news stories accusing the Trump administration of "losing" migrant children.

"These children are not 'lost.' Their sponsors simply did not respond or could not be reached when a 'voluntary' follow-up call was made. While there are many possible reasons for this, in many cases the sponsors cannot be reached because they themselves are illegal aliens and do not want to be reached by federal authorities. This hits at the core of this issue. In many cases, Health and Human Services has been put in the position of placing illegal aliens with the individuals who helped arrange for them to enter the country illegally. This makes the immediate crisis worse and creates a perverse incentive for further violation of federal immigration law.

"The processing of unaccompanied alien children places the Office of Refugee Resettlement in a no-win situation: Either take time to adequately vet potential sponsors in the United States, and be accused of (and run the risk of being sued for) using delay tactics to release those unaccompanied alien children to willing sponsors in the United States. Or fail to adequately vet potential willing sponsors, however, and be blamed for the inevitable exploitation of, or harm to, at least some portion of that unaccompanied alien children population.

"Judge Hanen presiding over four similar cases noted that the human traffickers, who smuggled minor children, were apprehended short of delivering the children to their ultimate destination. In all cases, a parent, if not both parents, of the children was in this country illegally. That parent initiated the conspiracy to smuggle the minors into the country illegally. He or she also funded the conspiracy. In each case, the DHS **completed the criminal conspiracy**, instead of enforcing the laws of the United States, by delivering the minors into the custody of the parent living illegally in the United States. In response to this Court's inquiry about this policy in the instant case, the Government responded with a copy of the 1997 *Flores v. Reno* settlement agreement and a copy of a portion of the Homeland Security Act. No other explanation was offered — no doubt because there is no explanation. The DHS has simply chosen not to enforce the United States' border security laws."[13]

This simply encourages parents to have their children smuggled to the United States by criminals with impunity. There are many who are caught by the Border Patrol who are simply given a court date for their immigration hearings. The Department of Homeland Security has reported that 90 percent of those who are supposed to show up to court never do. These illegal immigrants simply run off to live in America with the hope that they are never caught. Allowing this behavior effectively makes the United States government a co-conspirator with the illegal immigrants who pay the smugglers.

"Only in United States immigration courts can litigants literally abandon their cases without fear of incarceration or removal, while litigants in nearly any other state or federal court risk arrest, contempt, and new charges for the same conduct. Federal law, 18 U.S.C. § 3146, imposes penalties of imprisonment for absconding from a U.S. district court or circuit court of appeals. Not so in federal immigration courts. Rarely, if at all, are aliens held accountable for their misconducts. U.S. citizens would be branded as felons and jailed for the same infraction of absconding from court."[13] Even more rarely are those who abscond from court ever found, much less removed. According to Democrats, "Nobody is above the law." Unless that somebody is an illegal immigrant.

In January of 2019, the Trump administration announced its "Remain in Mexico" policy with regard to its new Migrant Protection Protocols. Under this policy, any non-Mexican asylum seeker arriving by land at the US-Mexico border that passes a "credible fear" screening with a U.S. asylum officer (a first step in the process for requesting asylum) must return to Mexico to wait through the duration of their asylum hearing in the US immigration court system. The premise behind this policy is to avoid the pitfalls of the "catch and release" program. Of course, there have been legal challenges from the American Civil Liberties Union, the Southern Poverty Law Center, and several other groups. And of course, the Ninth Circuit Court of Appeals has granted an emergency stay, pending an appeal.

"Under the bilateral Migration Protection Protocols, or 'Remain in Mexico' policy, anyone returned must be fluent in Spanish, because they may have to reside in Mexico up to five years until a U.S. federal judge decides their asylum claim. Representative Veronica Escobar, a Democratic congresswoman, began sending staff to Mexico's northern border to find migrants returned from El Paso, Texas. The staff then began coaching the migrants to pretend they could not speak Spanish to exploit a loophole that would allow them to return to the United States.

"A Department of Homeland Security official aware of the situation said Democrats, non-profit organizations, and 2020 hopefuls 'are furious that these migrants' are not permitted to 'await their court dates in the United States, where they have the opportunity to disappear and slip into the interior, never to be seen again.'

"'Resources are being diverted into a foreign country in an attempt to reverse already-decided legal action, meaning these people were found inadmissible under a new program, and they must remain in Mexico. They're trying to subvert that,' the official said."[19]

"One of the most common arguments from advocacy groups with regard to the asylum claims from Central American migrants is that these migrants are fleeing violence. Groups such as the American Civil Liberties Union and the Southern Poverty Law Center cite 'gang brutality', 'gang violence', and fear of murder as reasons why the number of illegal border-crossing migrants has soared in recent years. After researching the figures, there is 'no obvious relationship between Central American homicide rates and the number of Central Americans apprehended illegally crossing our border in a year. In Honduras, for example, murder rates have fallen by over half. Guatemala saw a similar trend.

"An attractive job market in the United States is prompting more Central Americans to leave the poverty and insecurity of their home countries and head north, typically in groups of one parent and one child. Neither poverty nor insecurity is a basis for immigration relief in the United States for those who enter illegally. Loopholes in lax immigration laws are encouraging parents of unaccompanied alien children in the United States to pay smugglers to bring their children to this country.

"Finally, the presence of those parents in the United States would appear to undermine the claims of fear of their children who remained abroad until being smuggled into the United States. It is difficult to conceive of a scenario in which parents would willfully abandon children in a perilous situation in order to escape to safety themselves. However, if a foreign national parent residing in the United States were to believe, (correctly) that if he or she paid a smuggler to bring a child to the United States, that the child would be quickly reunited with that parent, it is only logical that the parent would do so."[13]

Most asylum seekers at the southern border, barring a bleeding-heart interpretation of facts, do not have a valid asylum claim. In order to seek asylum, the asylee must have a legitimate fear of persecution from their own government. To fear persecution from an individual, a gang, or street violence is not a credible reason to seek asylum. In fact, we have street violence and gangs in the United States. Many times, as is the case with the MS-13 gang members, this violence follows the migrant and creates a danger to our own citizens. Where does the American citizen migrate to avoid this imported violence?

Asylum laws do not allow the asylee to "shop" for the country of convenience. According to the United Nations asylum laws, the person seeking asylum must seek refuge in the next adjacent neighboring country. The asylum laws do not allow you to handpick the country with the most economic and social benefits to offer. If these people were truly seeking asylum, they would go to the US Embassy in their own country, or at a minimum they would attempt to enter this country through a designated port of entry.

You cannot blame the migrant for trying to enter the greatest country in the world. The real culprits in this issue are the Democrat Party, the American Civil Liberties Union, the Southern Poverty Law Center, and the Catholic Church. These groups incentivize the illegal migrants to make a dangerous trek across treacherous territory with promises of government programs and asylum. They do so with the hope of an eventual amnesty legislation that would lead to a path of citizenship and an imported group of new Democratic voters. We know this to be true based on demands by the Democrats to provide amnesty for current DACA recipients. The Democratic Party literally puts the bait on the hook for these migrants and then blames Donald Trump for killing the fish because he is driving the boat. It is not immigration that has failed America, but the American government that has often failed immigration.

> "There are enough laws on the books by Congress that are very clear in terms of how we have to enforce our immigration system that for me to simply through executive order ignore those congressional mandates would not conform with my appropriate role as president."
>
> —Obama (March 2011)

Since about 2000, there have been numerous efforts to address the situation of so-called Dreamers. The Dreamers are children who were illegally brought to the United States by their parents and who are therefore in this nation through no fault of their own. Many of these Dreamers have only known the United States as their home.

In late 2010 after the November elections, the Democratic-controlled House of Representatives passed "Dream Act" legislation to grant those children legal status with a potential path to citizenship if they met certain qualifications, but no action was taken by the Democrat-controlled Senate. After that failure and with no legislative action taken in 2011, President Obama created the Deferred Action for Childhood Arrivals (DACA) program in June 2012. On two separate occasions Barack Obama acknowledged that such an action was beyond his authority, but he did it anyway. The new program, created unilaterally through executive action, offered temporary protection from deportation for certain undocumented immigrants who were at least 15 years of age but under the age of 31 as of June 15, 2012. For the record, those defenseless "child" victims being "protected" by the Democrats and this program are between the ages of 23 and 39 at the time this book was written.

DACA allows eligible immigrants to request deferred action for two years, subject to renewal, and authorizes them to work in the United States. The Congressional Research Service notes that DACA recipients are not granted a lawful immigration status and are not put on a pathway to a lawful immigration status but are considered to be lawfully present in the United States.

Since DACA was established administratively rather than through legislation, Donald Trump gave Congress six months to develop and enact a permanent solution before he rescinded the executive action taken by Barack Obama. A compromise measure was negotiated to allow those individuals to apply for a new, merit-based green card through which they could eventually become US citizens, but House Democrats were unwilling, through compromise, to fully fund the border wall. When Congress failed to overcome their ideological impasses, Donald Trump attempted to make good on his promise to rescind the DACA program, but federal court orders through nationwide injunctions have, to date, required the government to continue the program.

In addition to DACA recipients, current law allows the Homeland Security Department to declare "Temporary Protected

Status" for individuals to legally remain in the United States if they cannot return to their country of origin due to civil unrest and violence, natural disasters, or other extraordinary reasons. According to the Congressional Research Service, the United States currently provides "Temporary Protected Status" to approximately 417,000 foreign nationals from ten countries: El Salvador, Haiti, Honduras, Nepal, Nicaragua, Somalia, South Sudan, Sudan, Syria, and Yemen. Trump attempted to end these protections for individuals from six of these countries, but that process is also on hold pending legal challenges.

The Congressional Budget Office estimates that any bill providing lawful immigration status to two million Dreamers and half a million Temporary Protected Status individuals would increase the federal deficits by more than $30 billion.

These so-called Dreamers began their time in the United States by breaking US immigration laws. Instead of penalizing them, the Democrats seek to pass legislation that rewards such behavior, with a special path to citizenship. The Democrats have no desire to address the root causes of the legal loopholes in US immigration laws that act as "pull factors" and have created a de facto system of "catch and release." Providing a meritless amnesty bill would only incentivize further illegal immigration and would surely exacerbate the crisis at the border. It would place the interests of those who violated US immigration law 8 US Code § 1325 (Improper entry by alien) above the interests of those who waited, or have been waiting, in many cases for years, to enter this country legally. Make no mistake. Giving citizenship to DACA recipients is only the first step in Democratic efforts to do away with borders in this country.

Oftentimes, if a person is willing to break the very first rule that they encounter, it is an indication that they are willing to break all of the rules. Donald Trump was ridiculed for saying that Mexico, by way of illegal immigration, was not sending their best. Of course, they conflated illegal immigrants with legal migrants with regard to their news narratives.

The federal, state, and local governments keep data to track the association between illegal immigrants and crime. "Local, state and federal statistics find that 'illegal immigrants are three times as likely to be convicted of murder as members of the general population and account for far more crimes than their 3.5% share of the United States population would suggest.' Illegal immigrants accounted for nearly 75% of federal drug sentences in 2014. 'It's difficult to contend that illegal aliens are more law-abiding than legal residents—at least when it comes to major crimes.' But the more disturbing fact was that 'approximately 2,430 illegal aliens are in prison just for homicide-related offenses' in California alone."[20] If not for their illegal presence in this country, thousands of crimes would not have been committed in this country.

"Tens of thousands of criminal illegals have been released by I.C.E. agents, and are at large in the country. In 2015, I.C.E. released almost 20,000 illegal immigrants that committed 64,000 crimes. It's even worse when one considers the fact that the Obama administration released '86,000 illegal immigrants who have committed over 231,000 crimes in just two and a half years.' Crime has increased among major cities that are 'immigration hubs.' Sanctuary city policies have hampered law enforcement in cracking down on crime."[20] The Democrat leadership and political activist groups claim that these migrants are fleeing their own countries to escape violence and crime. It appears that many of them have decided to bring that culture here to our streets and neighborhoods.

"While left-wing religious groups, tax-exempt non-profits tied or allied to George Soros, and the amnesty-shilling Catholic church scream 'No hate, no fear, everyone is welcome here' at the top of their lungs, American neighborhoods are being overrun by dangerous criminals and jihad plotters.

"Here are the facts that the pro-refugee advocates don't want you to know. They make billions of dollars off the federal refugee settlement racket. They are protected by the Open Borders, Inc. media, which routinely whitewashes the gob smacking financial self-interest of the 'Let Them All In' leeches. Finally, they are never held accountable when untold numbers of the world's most wretchedly violent and aggrieved refugees come here to sabotage the American Dream. These organizations work with the hostile United Nations and State Department social justice warriors to import thousands of new refugees every year with little to no input from the communities in which they are dumped. These open border advocates equate any and all criticism of the refugee program as racist, xenophobic hatred. Many of these refugees have absolutely no interest in assimilating themselves into our customs, measures and laws. Many of them have outright contempt for Western civilization. They're not here to strengthen our nation with their 'diversity.' They're here to destroy it.

"More than half of these foreign menaces came from Somalia. These refujihadis include Muslim translators, convicted weapons felons, confessed aiders and abettors of terrorism, stabbing spree vigilantes, and bombers; all sworn to wage war against infidels in the name of Allah. And they do it while fraudulently posing undercover as victims of political and religious persecution.

Abdul Razak Ali Artan resettled in Ohio. In 2014, he became a legal permanent resident. At Ohio State University, in 2016, he plowed his car into a group of students and then broke out a knife and stabbed innocent bystanders. Eleven people were injured before the police shot and killed Artan. Somali refugee Dahir Ahmed Adan went on a stabbing spree at a Minnesota mall in 2016. He was able to injure ten people before being shot and killed by an off-duty police officer.

"Open Borders Inc. propagandists will do what they always do when confronted with criminal nightmares that don't fit the Emma

Lazarus fantasy narrative. They will whitewash the story. They will tell you that the vast majority of refugees are law-abiding. They will claim that only xenophobes will dwell on the negative impacts. But an untold number of refugees are not just committing ordinary civilian crimes. They are Islamic oppressors masquerading as the oppressed.

"How many more horrifying reasons do we need to stop underwriting the United Nation's sovereignty-eroding agenda, and get our own house in order? Thankfully, a new asylum rule will require those who come to the southern border seeking asylum to first seek asylum in the first safe country they enter."[21]

Border Patrol agents noted a 30 percent reduction in migrant arrests within two weeks of implementation of the "Remain in Mexico" policy for asylum seekers. With this new regulation in place, asylum-seeking immigrants who pass through a third country en route to the US must first apply for refugee status in that country rather than at the US border.

Any alien who attempts to enter the United States across the southern border after failing to apply for protection in the first country outside their own country of citizenship or nationality is ineligible for asylum in the United States. This rule will decrease entry by economic migrants who seek to exploit our asylum rules.

We constantly hear Liberals say, "We care about people," but it is the policy of these Liberals that drives these people to make the most dangerous trek in the world. "*The Washington Post* reports the huge migration out of Guatemala and into the United States workplaces is driven by basic economics, despite Democrat's lockstep claims the migration is driven by fear of crime and abuse. 'The migration problem is a coffee problem.' Cultivating coffee was once a way out of poverty. As prices fall, growers are abandoning their farms for the United States. United States asylum laws are designed to protect people from fleeing persecution. The laws do not protect people fleeing a disastrous drop in coffee prices. But

Democrats insist the migration is a humanitarian problem, and that Americans are obliged to provide asylum to much of Central America."[22]

Everyone knows that the real reason Democrats promote illegal immigration is for the purpose of importing their own voter base. The Democrats have opposed re-instating the citizenship question on the census, in an effort to increase their representation in Congress. They do so with dreams of gaining majority control of the House of Representatives and the Senate. Control of both chambers of Congress would allow them to force an amnesty bill that would immediately increase their voter base by as many as the estimated 29.5 million illegal migrants residing in this country. Without a citizenship question on the census, those 29.5 million people are assumed to be citizens. With citizenship comes representation. That means, in a country of 330 million people, nearly 10 percent of our representation in the House is fictitiously based on a populace of illegal migrants. Essentially, of the 435 representatives in the House, nearly 43 of them are representing illegal migrants, and they shouldn't be there. Quite literally the Democrats have imported their own legislative majority in the House of Representatives.

"The Supreme Court's decision to leave the 'citizenship' question blocked could have profound political consequences. The new population counts from the 2020 census will determine, for the next 10 years, how many seats each state will have in the United States House of Representatives and how many Electoral College votes each state gets in presidential elections beginning in 2024. They also help determine how some $900 billion per year in federal money is allocated across the country for roads, schools, hospitals, health care and more."[23] Each census has an enormous impact on everyone living within our borders. Census data is used to decide congressional districts and how much money state and local governments get for infrastructure, social services, education, and housing. The proposed citizenship question has been controversial because experts and Latino advocacy groups have been united in their belief that it would result in an undercount of the Hispanic population. The Trump administration maintained that citizenship data was necessary to help enforce the Voting Rights Act.

Democrats, using the tactics of guilt, will accuse their opponents of being less than Christian for criticizing the immigration policies of the liberal left. The mere suggestion of turning away a migrant or reducing foreign aid is a sin in their eyes. While it is acceptable to forgive the person who breaks into your home, most people would not allow the intruder to stay. Most people in this country are more than happy to help people in need outside of our own homes. However; after one million times of having your home violated, how would these Democrats' attitudes change? Forced generosity is called theft.

The problem of illegal immigration is similar to an overflowing bathtub. When the Democrats see this problem, the first thing they do is collect more taxes so they can pay two people to mop up the water. Then they hire photographers and the media to come in and report what a great job they are doing with the mop up duties. Day in and day out, for years on end, the mopping and pandering continues. When the Conservatives see this problem, the first thing they do is *turn off the water*. Then they begin to clean up the mess. Maybe a media team will report the story, but odds are they won't.

The Solution

Article 4 Section 4 of the United States Constitution demands a National Border Wall. "The United States shall guarantee to every State in this Union a Republican Form of Government, and shall protect each of them against Invasion; and on Application of the Legislature, or of the Executive (when the Legislature cannot be convened) against domestic Violence."

"In 2012 Justice Scalia believed that even a state like Arizona had the right to enforce its sovereignty and not allow in illegal aliens. Scalia asked Obama's attorney general during an oral argument in *Arizona vs. United States*, 'What does sovereignty mean if it does not include the ability to defend your borders?' He was referring to even Arizona's right as an individual state to defend its own borders. 'The Constitution recognizes that there is such a thing as State borders and the States can police their borders, even to the point of inspecting incoming shipments to exclude diseased material,' said Scalia during litigation between the Obama administration and the state of Arizona. 'Are the sovereign States at the mercy of the Federal Executive's refusal to enforce the Nation's immigration laws?' Could anyone imagine the entire federal union, 'at the mercy of' a lower court judge's refusal to recognize this nation's immigration laws and its own long-standing judicial precedent on staying out of questions of entry at our border?"[24]

Everywhere that an actual wall has been constructed on the southern border of this country, illegal migration has slowed by 90 percent. Democrats will try to convince you that walls don't work. By contrast, I have personally spoken to several wall experts, and they have told me without fail, if the wall isn't working, build a bigger wall. A wall has already been approved legislatively. It is time that the Democrats fall into line and appropriate the necessary funds to complete the task. Video surveillance at the border is as ineffective as a shock collar on a hound dog. Once the dog sprints passed the boundary, the only thing the collar is good for is to deter the animal from coming back into your own yard. Unless you rig a drone with lethal weaponry, it is just as useless as the video surveillance. Congratulations, you have a photo of the person who broke into your country *after* they have broken into your country.

It is also time for Congress to create legislation that makes illegal entry into the country a felony. A slap on the wrist for a civil offense or a misdemeanor is no deterrent for criminal activity.

In addition, Mexico must formally be informed that every time an illegal migrant from a non-contiguous-country crosses through Mexico to unlawfully cross our southern border, we will hold the country of Mexico accountable for aiding and abetting the enemy in an act of war against our country. As a matter of international law, acts against the territorial integrity of political sovereignty of another state is illegal.

We must stand firm on our resolve to restore enforcement policies for our existing immigration laws. "Catch and release" can no longer be the border policy. Donald Trump already introduced policies that will close the asylum loopholes that created the crisis at our southern border. Legislation must be passed immediately that puts an end to chain migration. Additional legislation must be passed to put an end to the "diversity lottery" program. Our immigration process should be based on merit, and merit alone, a merit-based system that promotes the dignity of work and assimilation into America's rich civic and cultural heritage.

Ninety-three years after the United States Constitution was ratified, Congress passed the Immigration Act of 1882. Included within the act was a provision stating that incoming immigrants who were at risk of "becoming a public charge" would not be allowed to enter the United States of America. "If on such examination there shall be found among such passengers any convict, lunatic, idiot, or any person unable to take care of him or herself without becoming a public charge, they shall report the same in writing to the collector of such port, and such person shall not be permitted to land," the act reads.

The notion that attempts to impose reasonable restrictions on immigration is somehow rooted in racism and bigotry is absolutely absurd. This notion should be confronted at every turn. This immigration rule is based on the widely held belief that America, while generous of her opportunities, should only accept the best of the best into its fold. This country should not merely serve as a refuge for people who are suffering or merely seeking more opportunities. The migrant should have to prove him- or herself worthy to obtain entry. The Trump White House described a "public charge" rule that will help ensure that permanent residents and those seeking citizenship in America via a green card are more self-sufficient. The rule is also meant to take some of the burden off from American taxpayers.

All "sanctuary city" policies must be abolished with the firm understanding that any public official that promotes sanctuary policies will, from this time forward, be formally charged with "aiding and abetting" an illegal alien and will be subject to prison time. Thomas Homan said that the Department of Justice needs to file charges against municipalities that don't cooperate with federal immigration authorities and deny them federal funding if they do not comply. He also says that politicians should be held "personally accountable" for crimes committed by people living in the United States illegally and under the shield of sanctuary policies. There is no sanctuary from federal law enforcement.

Appropriately, Senators Lindsey Graham and Ted Cruz have introduced a piece of legislation called "The Justice for Victims of Sanctuary Cities Act." This act allows those harmed by illegal immigrants to sue sanctuary cities. According to Lindsey Graham, "There must be consequences for governments and entities that gamble with public safety, refuse to work with federal officials, and refuse to deal with felons here illegally. This legislation empowers individuals who are victims of these entities and governments' poor decisions." Ted Cruz said, "The American people are tired of seeing our federal immigration laws flouted and criminal illegal immigrants enabled to commit future crimes and escape prosecution. Sanctuary cities and their policies are a dangerous affront to the rule of law and only exasperate the crisis at our border."

Every state in the Union must, finally, update their antiquated voter rolls. There are voters registered in multiple states, there are illegal immigrants on the rolls, and there are dead people still on the rolls. Obama's administration did not enforce these update policies—and it is time. Legislation must be passed for some form of voter identification. Whether it be a thumb print on the ballot, an indelible ink mark placed on the individual on Election Day, or an identification card (paid for by the state), we need to know who is voting in our elections.

It is time for the Supreme Court to make a ruling regarding birthright citizenship and the proper interpretation as it was intended when the naturalization laws were written. Simply having a baby within the borders of a sovereign country cannot constitute citizenship. The founders never intended for that interpretation. It is also time to call on Congress to pass legislation declaring that only United States citizens are guaranteed the rights as defined by the United States Constitution; therefore, only United States citizens can vote. We the People are also calling on Congress to declare English as the official language of the United States. Assimilation is the key to determining if the migrant will try to fit in.

Theodore Roosevelt said, "In the first place we should insist that if the immigrant who comes here does in good faith become an American and assimilate himself to us, he shall be treated on an exact equality with everyone else; for it is an outrage to discriminate against any such man because of creed or birthplace of origin. But this is predicated upon the man's becoming in very fact an American and nothing but an American."

Roosevelt went on to say, "If he tries to keep segregated with men of his own origin and separated from the rest of America, then he isn't doing his part as an American."

Theodore Roosevelt spoke frequently on the premise of Americanism. He condemned the use of the hyphen "whenever it represents an effort to form political parties along racial lines or to bring pressure to bear on parties and politicians, not for American purposes, but in the interest of some group of voters of a certain national origin or of the country from which they or their fathers came." "The effort to keep our citizenship divided against itself" the colonel continued, "by the use of the hyphen and along the lines of national origin is certain to breed a spirit of bitterness and prejudice and dislike between great bodies of our citizens."

> "We have room for but one flag, the American flag. We have room for but one language here, and that is the English language, and we have room for but one sole loyalty and that is a loyalty to the American people."
>
> —Theodore Roosevelt

If *all* of these demands have been met, then the following DACA legislation should be passed: All current DACA residents will have to self-report within a given six-month period of time. Any DACA recipient that fails to report within the allotted time period will be considered an illegal immigrant and will be set for immediate deportation to the country of their parents' origin.

Those DACA recipients that self-report on time will be subject to a background check. They will be checked for criminal records. If they have a felony, a significant misdemeanor, or three or more other misdemeanors, they become ineligible for citizenship. If they otherwise pose a threat to national security or public safety, they become ineligible for citizenship. They will be checked to see if they meet certain education, employment, or military service requirements. If they have received a degree from a United States institution of higher education, completed two years in good standing of a bachelor's degree program or a career and technical education program, they would be found to be in good status for an opportunity to achieve citizenship. If they served in the United States military for at least two years, or earned income for at least

75% of the time they were authorized to work, they would not be considered a "public charge." They will be checked for their involvement in welfare programs to see if they have avoided becoming a "public charge." In addition, they will be assessed for their assimilation into the culture of the United States of America. These individuals must pass the English-language and civics test required for naturalization purposes. Once they are vetted, they will either be set for immediate deportation *or* they will be allowed to proceed through the naturalization process to become a United States citizen after they have paid the appropriate naturalization fees. If this particular group is provided naturalization, they do so with one *major*, non-negotiable stipulation. These people will be considered a new class of felons called a "Class I Felon" and will *never* be given the right to vote. As a country we must *never* grant mass amnesty to the millions of illegal immigrants who broke our laws and entered our country illegally. That includes amnesty for E-verify recipients. This DACA compromise should satisfy the fears of Republicans that amnesty is not an option, while satisfying the Democrats arguments that immigration law should humanely and realistically respond to the existence of undocumented immigrants without sacrificing safety or the rule of law.

Work visas must be monitored with intention. Too many times, these immigrants are allowed to simply overstay their welcome with zero consequence for their actions. A system of checks and balances must be established to monitor visa expiration dates, as well as the whereabouts of the visa recipients. Policies must be placed that hold not only the person in violation accountable but also hold the complicit administrators accountable as well. Until these co-conspirators are held to a legal standard, there will be an abuse of the visa work program.

It is also time to close the *Flores* "catch and release" loophole.

"The Department of Homeland Security is issuing a *Flores* regulation which will allow border agencies to detain migrants and children for multiple weeks; until their legal claims for asylum can be completed. The regulation replaces the 2015 court-ordered *Flores* rule which said migrants with children must be released after 20 days, even if officials suspect the migrants are ineligible for asylum. The new regulation says migrants with children will be detained in state-licensed shelters until their various claims for asylum are either approved or denied, according to the regulation.

"Officials expect the promise of family detention will sharply reduce the economic incentive for migration from Central America, Africa, and Asia, because it will prevent migrants from getting U.S. jobs to pay their smuggling debts to the cartel-affiliated coyotes. The new regulation replaces the so-called Flores court decision, made in 2015 by Democrat-nominated Californian Judge Dolly Gee. Her decision has enabled more than 433,000 poor 'family unit' migrants to walk through the border wall since 2018."[25]

Congress has repeatedly refused to close Judge Gee's huge loophole.

This policy of flooding the market with cheap, foreign labor shifts enormous wealth from young employees toward older investors. As cheap migrant workers flood in, the wealth gap widens. High-tech investments are reduced, state and local tax burdens increase, and education suffers. One party will use the consequences of their own migrant policies as an excuse to complain about wage gaps and inequality but ignore their own involvement in those outcomes. It must be increasingly more difficult to explain to their own constituents why they have such blatant disregard for federal immigration laws while allowing low- or no-skilled labor to directly compete with American workers. Their actions ultimately lower the average wage in this country, which is in contradiction to their demands for a $15 per hour minimum wage. They quite literally import poor legal and illegal immigrants into the country and then use the pay gap as an excuse for why they support *socialism*.

It is time to shut down a Federal Reserve program that profits off remittances sent to foreign countries by illegal aliens. There are an ever-increasing number of Democrat politicians that would like to see a marginal tax rate of 70–90 percent on a particular segment of American taxpayers. I wonder if that same group of politicians would legislate a 70–90 percent remittance tax on all of the remittance payments that leave this country. Currently, the annual remittance totals paid from immigrants in this country to parties in their native countries totals approximately $888,282,901, and the money is untaxed. Even at a 70% remittance tax, the United States would retain nearly $100 billion. Money received through a remittance tax would indeed stimulate the local economies and would help offset the nearly $138 billion that this country spends on illegal immigrants annually.

In 1986 Congress created criminal penalties for employers who knowingly hire workers who are in the United States illegally. The "knowingly" term has proved to be a huge defense for employers. The illegal migrant worker gets jail time, and the employer gets a stiff financial penalty and a slap on the wrist. Those rules need to change. We the people propose a new immigration whistleblower program. Under the guidelines of this program, any person who turns in an illegal migrant for deportation is awarded a $5,000 reward for every migrant reported. For every corporation reported for hiring illegal migrants, the reward becomes $20,000. For those who argue that there are too many illegal immigrants to discover over such a large area of land, there is always a way. Nobody is above the law, and that includes illegal immigrants.

In 1965 the United States passed reforms that ended the system of assigning different immigration quotas for each nationality. By doing so, the country, in accordance with the new Civil Rights Act of 1964, had ended its favoritism for northwestern European migrants. But that hasn't stopped the open borders societies and immigration activists from claiming that current immigration laws are devastating. They will tell you that the immigration laws are immoral constructs that arose primarily due to racism. In their opinion, the elimination of immigration restrictions would benefit the majority of people who wish to move to the United States, end unnecessary suffering, and benefit the country. But these people never mention the harm it does to the citizens of this country because they don't care. We have much to do, and the clock is ticking.

Chapter Five:

Racism Exists...But Is It Systemic?

"Racism is not dead, but it is on life support—kept alive by politicians, race hustlers and people who get a sense of superiority by denouncing others as 'racists.'"

—Thomas Sowell

"We must reject the idea that every time a law's broken, society is guilty rather than the lawbreaker. It is time to restore the American precept that each individual is accountable for his actions."

—Ronald Reagan

As a high school football coach, I was confronted and accused of racism by one of my athletes. It was a practice the night before our sixth game of the season. I had asked the third string running back to take his turn in the offensive rotation. He had missed most of the practices that season and desperately needed the reps. In spite of his obvious frustration, he headed toward the huddle, but not before making the declaration, "The only reason I'm not starting is because I'm black." The whole team went silent as they waited for my reply. Without hesitation I said, "That's an interesting observation considering the fact that the two men starting in front of you are also black. The difference is...they showed up to every practice... and they put in the work that was required." The sheepish look on the young man's face revealed in an instant his realization that he had gone to that well one too many times.

I knew it wasn't his fault. He had been "programmed." Programmed to believe that every individual failure could be effortlessly blamed on the color of his skin, and no one would dare to question the validity of the claim without facing judgment of their own. This powerful trump card was free, easily accessible, and immediately provided relief from the pain associated with personal accountability. The only problem is, without pain, there is no personal growth and no incentive for improvement.

> "I have a dream that my four little children will one day live in a nation where they will not be judged by the color of their skin, but by the content of their character."
>
> —Martin Luther King Jr.

The Emotional Lie

"Institutional racism, also known as systemic racism, is a form of racism that is embedded as normal practice within society or an organization. It can lead to such issues as discrimination in criminal justice, employment, housing, health care, political power, and education, among other issues.

"The term 'institutional racism' was first coined in 1967 by Stokely Carmichael and Charles V. Hamilton in *Black Power: The Politics of Liberation*. Carmichael and Hamilton wrote that while individual racism is often identifiable because of its overt nature, institutional racism is less perceptible because of its 'less overt, far more subtle' nature. Institutional racism 'originates in the operation of established and respected forces in the society, and thus receives far less public condemnation than individual racism.'

"Institutional racism was defined by Sir William Macpherson in the 1999 *Lawrence Report* as: 'The collective failure of an organization to provide an appropriate and professional service to people because of their color, culture, or ethnic origin. It can be seen or detected in processes, attitudes and behavior that amount to discrimination through prejudice, ignorance, thoughtlessness, and racist stereotyping which disadvantage minority ethnic people.'

Institutional racism is distinguished from racial bigotry by the existence of institutional systemic policies, practices and economic and political structures that place minority racial and ethnic groups at a disadvantage in relation to an institution's racial or ethnic majority...examples include public school budgets, restrictive housing contracts and bank lending policies...Other examples sometimes described as institutional racism are racial profiling by security guards and police, use of stereotyped racial caricatures, the under- and misrepresentation of certain racial groups in the mass media, and race-based barriers to gainful employment and professional advancement. Additionally, differential access to goods, services, and opportunities of society can be included within the term 'institutional racism.'"[26]

With rallying cries of "hands up, don't shoot," we have been told that we must confront systemic racism and police violence head-on. The election of a black president, it might be recalled, was supposed to be the breakthrough that led to a kinder, gentler America. Instead, it seemed to be followed by a more fractious period in race relations. In office just six months, Obama intervened in an incident in Cambridge, Massachusetts. In the absence of any facts, Barack Obama accused the police of "acting stupidly" in arresting a belligerent black professor at his home. The city was burned down because of the "hands up, don't shoot" lie. Evidence later revealed that the officer was acting in self-defense. That was the moment in America's history that Martin Luther King Junior's hard-fought legacy began to unravel and race relations changed trajectory.

The solution, according to Robert L. Johnson, co-founder of *Black Entertainment Television*, is to call for reparations. During a speech at the Roosevelt Room of the White House on December 12, 2018, Mr. Johnson said:

"When you see all the lagging statistics between Blacks and whites, you must ask yourself, 'Why?'

The only honest conclusion to the question of wealth and income disparity is simply that white Americans, due to 200-plus years of slavery and systemic racism, had an unjust head start in wealth accumulation, income, and educational opportunities that were denied to African Americans—and are still denied in many ways today.

When you accept that conclusion, the only thing left is to admit and acknowledge that the pernicious legacy of slavery is the primary factor in the wealth disparity and racial animosity and discrimination.

The system of slavery and its aftermath not only denied African Americans the right to accumulate any kind of wealth, but even more detrimental to the human spirit, it convinced African Americans that they were never intended to be economically and socially equal to white Americans. African Americans were left to believe that, for them, the American Dream, in a nation founded on capitalism and rule-of-law, was nothing but a cruel hoax.

So, I'm calling for reparations and asking for two things. First, that white Americans recognize that reparations are a payment to atone for the largest illegal wealth transfer in this nation's history; and second, to understand that the phrase equal justice and economic equality will ring hollow to black Americans until they are made whole."

Robert L. Johnson then claimed that he estimated, the amount of, reparations owed to be $14 trillion. He admittedly arrived at that number by using "mostly math with some justifiable assumptions." He then went on to assume that "a typical African American's net worth is $17,000, while the typical white American's worth is $170,000, which is a tenfold gap." By "assuming" gaps in home-ownership, cost of education, differences in savings and invest-ment, to "close all gaps...with payments over 30 years, it's going to be somewhere in the neighborhood of $357,000 per African American citizen. Multiply that by the 40 million individuals whose ancestors were enslaved, and you arrive at around $14 trillion."

Along with Robert L. Johnson's erroneous assumptions and far-fetched calculations, there has been another fallacy that was propagated by the *New York Times* in August of 2019. The *New York Times* attempted to rewrite US history with its public release of "The *1619* Project," which was launched in the *Times'* Sunday magazine. This project intended to reframe the country's history by ignoring 1776 as America's founding date. Instead, they claimed that 1619 was the founding date because it coincided with the year that 20 or more African slaves were brought to Jamestown, Virginia. The project's creator, Nikole Hannah-Jones, beamed with pride as she described the way her version of the story "de-centers whiteness."

James McPherson, dean of Civil War historians and Pulitzer Prize winner, said the *Times* presented an "unbalanced, one-sided, account" that "left most of the history out." In keeping with her smugness, Nikole Hannah-Jones was quick to dismiss any critics as "old, white male historians." She even went as far as to say that the project goes beyond Mr. McPherson's expertise regarding the Civil War. She wrote in the lead essay that for the most part, "black Americans fought back alone" against racism. No wonder she would rather not talk about the Civil War. Not to be silenced, Mr. McPherson quickly pointed out the hypocrisy of the project's "implicit position that there have never been any good white people, thereby ignoring white radicals and even liberals who have supported racial equality." He added that fellow historians have privately expressed their agreement.

In 2013 an organization called Black Lives Matter was founded in response to the acquittal of George Michael Zimmerman in the shooting death of Trayvon Martin. Self-described as a global organization in the United States, the United Kingdom, and Canada, this group claims their mission is to eradicate white supremacy and build local power to intervene in violence inflicted on Black communities by the state and vigilantes. They purport to do this by combating and countering acts of violence, creating space for Black imagination and innovation, and centering Black joy to win immediate improvements in Black lives. Holding to the same premise as Nikole Hannah-Jones, the Black Lives Matter organization operates under the assumption that there have never been any good white people. This is evidenced by the fact that their website claims they are "working for a world where Black lives are no longer systematically targeted for demise."

Finally, and perhaps the greatest lie of all, is the notion that affirmative action is in the best interest of people of color. Affirmative action refers to a set of policies and practices within a government or organization seeking to increase the representation of particular groups based on their gender, race, sexuality, creed, or nationality in areas in which they are underrepresented.

> "When people get used to preferential treatment, equal treatment seems like discrimination."
>
> —Thomas Sowell

The Truth

"Here we sit in the most tolerant, diverse country in the world just a few years after having twice elected a black president with the middle name 'Hussein,' and the people in charge of the media are breaking down into pools of self-pity because they want to scream racist at us even more than they already have. And again, let's not forget that the only way they can try to pretend America is racist is by way of massive hoaxes: the Very Fine People Hoax, the Covington Hoax, the George Zimmerman Is White Hoax, the Hands Up Don't Shoot Hoax, the Jussie Smollett Hoax, and the countless hoax hate crimes they spread over and over again without scrutiny."[27]

Contrary to the narrative, the white man did not sail to Africa and drag "Negroes" out of the jungle, kicking and screaming. And not one living soul in America today has been a slave or has ever owned a slave.

In the 1840s the Black African King Ghezo was quoted as saying, "The slave trade is the ruling principle of my people...it is the source and the glory of all their wealth." He was also quoted to say, "The mother lulls the child to sleep with notes of triumph over an enemy reduced to slavery." Quotes like that make slavery seem less about racism and more about economics. And quotes like that show that there is a little more than white, English-speaking guilt to go around. Messages like this run contrary to the narrative and have to be suppressed in the media and in the schools, because it is politically incorrect.

Other black tribes, stronger tribes, preyed on the weaker tribes and enslaved them. These enslaved individuals were then sold for profit on the Atlantic slave trade. This slave trade existed legally from the 16th century until it was made illegal in the United States in 1808. Nobody ever asks what may have happened to these people if they had remained in Africa as a member of these weaker tribes.

What would their lives and the lives of their ancestors look like in today's world? Nobody mentions the sacrifices that migrants make in today's world to migrate, willfully, to the greatest country on the planet. The concept of slavery is indeed atrocious, and at that time that guilt was shared by many countries in addition to the United States; however, the end result is legal citizenship in a country with the greatest opportunities on the planet.

In 1811, Paul Cuffee, "a black man who was a wealthy man of property, a petitioner for equal rights for blacks" began to explore the idea of black people returning to their native land as he was convinced that "opportunities for the advancement of black people were limited in America," and he became interested in African colonization. With the help of some Quakers in Philadelphia he was able to transport 38 blacks to Freetown, Sierra Leone, in 1815.

In 1816 Charles Fenton Mercer founded the American Colonization Society. The group was an early advocate of the idea of resettling American-born blacks to Africa. In all honesty, the group was composed of two groups: the philanthropists, clergy and abolitionists who wanted to free African slaves, and their descendants, and provide them with the opportunity to return to Africa. The other group was the slave owners who feared free people of color and wanted to expel them from America.

In 1821 under President James Monroe, and long before the Civil War, Liberia was purchased from Africa. The purpose of this land purchase was for colonization for those freed slaves that chose to return to Africa. Yes, the United States gave freed slaves a choice. The freed slaves had an opportunity to be repatriated to Africa or be emancipated. Liberia was a colony of the United States and was under constitutional law. The freed slaves were given an entire country. Obviously, some chose not to go. In 1847, Liberia declared independence from the United States. Unfortunately, Liberia has gone on to become the poorest country in the world. Those freed slaves that chose to remain in the United States may have grateful descendants today, because they currently live in a country with significantly greater opportunities than those that chose to be repatriated to Liberia.

In 1854 the Republican Party was founded with its primary platform dedicated to the abolition of slavery. In 1860, Abraham Lincoln was elected as the first Republican President of the United States. In 1861 the Civil War began.

"Most of us know that before the American Civil War there were so-called 'slave' states and 'free' states. If such a line as 'Mason Dixon' existed, slaves must have resided below it and free black people above it; with every man, woman and child in chains trying to escape to the North just as soon as they could.

"Genealogists speak of blacks who had been freed well before the Civil War. However; most African-American ancestors, around 90 percent, became free either during the Civil War or with the ratification of the 13th Amendment following the war. All of these freed people, and their descendants, continued to live in slave-holding Virginia, even during the Civil War. Their part of Virginia would join the Union as the state of West Virginia in the middle of the war, but they had no way of knowing this when they decided to remain there, rather than flee. The presence of freed slaves in the South and their decision to 'stay put' during the war were not as uncommon as imagined. This seemingly counterintuitive decision can be explained using numbers in plain sight, including those in the 1860 U.S. Census.

"In that raging year of Lincoln's election and Southern secession, there were a total of 488,070 free blacks living in the United States, about 10 percent of the entire black population. Of those, 226,152 lived in the North; and 261,918 in the South. A few months before the Confederacy was born, there were 35,766 more free black people living in the slave-owning South than in the North. And they stayed there during the Civil War. In fact, at no time before the Civil War (at least not after the first U.S. Census was taken in 1790 and future states were added) did free blacks in the North ever outnumber those in the South.

"There were other sources besides manumissions (formal acts of emancipation by slave owners), to be sure, including an increase in runaways and immigrants. Among the immigrants were free blacks fleeing the West Indies (often with their own slaves). Another important surge in the Southern free black population occurred when Napoleon Bonaparte sold his country's vast Louisiana territory to the Americans under its slave-owning president, Thomas Jefferson. With it, the U.S. acquired thousands of 'free people of color.' Still another group of free people of color migrated to New Orleans from Cuba, in the upheavals of the Napoleonic wars, doubling the size of the black population there."[28]

Millions of black people have migrated to this country during and after the Civil War. In addition, millions of white people have migrated to this country in that same time frame. Who is going to do the historic research to determine who is responsible for reparations and who is deserving of reparations? Are we also going to ask the descendants of slaves to pay reparations to the descendants of all the men, black and white, that lost their lives in a Civil War that was responsible for freeing the slaves? Why is it that nobody ever talks about that sacrifice?

There is no doubt that freed Southern blacks were "perversely incentivized to distinguish themselves from slaves. Throughout the region, repressive laws helped create the conditions for a vast underclass that for most free blacks meant living along a very thin line between slavery and freedom, debt and dependency, poverty and pride. In fact, many of those same laws would lay the groundwork for what would follow after the Civil War and Reconstruction during the Jim Crow era."[28]

On January 1, 1863, as the nation approached its third year of bloody Civil War, Abraham Lincoln issued the Emancipation Proclamation. The proclamation declared "that all persons held as slaves" within the rebellious states "are, and henceforth shall be free." In 1865, the slaves officially became free when the 13th Amendment was passed. The 13th Amendment was passed with 100 percent Republican support and only 23 percent support from the Democrats.

Also in 1865, William T. Sherman gave Special Field Order Number 15 promising former slaves 40 acres. That is where the phrase "40 acres and a mule" came from.

"It's a staple of black history lessons. The promise was the first systematic attempt to provide a form of reparations to newly freed slaves, and it was astonishingly radical for its time, proto-socialist in its implications. In fact, such a policy would be radical in any country today: the federal government's massive confiscation of private property—some 400,000 acres—formerly owned by confederate land owners, and its methodical redistribution to former black slaves. What most of us haven't heard is that the idea really was generated by black leaders themselves.

"It is difficult to stress adequately how revolutionary this idea was. As the historian Eric Foner puts it in his book *Reconstruction: America's Unfinished Revolution, 1863–1877*, 'Here in coastal South Carolina and Georgia, the prospect beckoned of a transformation of Southern society more radical even than the end of slavery.' Try to imagine how profoundly different the history of race relations in the United States would have been had this policy been implemented and enforced; had the former slaves actually had access to the ownership of land, property; if they had had a chance to be self-sufficient economically, to build, accrue and pass on wealth. After all, one of the principle promises of America was the possibility of average people being able to own land, and all that such ownership entailed.

"What exactly was promised? We have been taught in school that the source of the policy of '40 acres and a mule' was a Union General William T. Sherman's Special Field Order No. 15, issued on January 16, 1865. But what many accounts leave out is that this idea for massive land redistribution actually was the result of a discussion that Sherman and, Secretary of War, Edwin M. Stanton held with 20 leaders of the black community in Savannah, Georgia. The meeting was unprecedented in American history.

"Today, we commonly use the phrase '40 acres and a mule,' but few of us have read the Order itself. Three of its parts are relevant here. Section one dedicates 400,000 acres of land, along a strip of coastline stretching from Charleston, South Carolina to the St. John's River in Florida, to be redistributed to the newly freed slaves. Section two specifies that the sole and exclusive management of affairs for these communities would be governed entirely by the freed people themselves. Finally, section three specifies the allocation of a plot of not more than (40) acres of tillable ground to each family. The extent of this Order and its larger implications are mind-boggling, actually.

"Who came up with the idea? Here's how this radical proposal, which must have completely blown the minds of the rebel Confederates, actually came about. The abolitionists Charles Sumner and Thaddeus Stevens and other Radical Republicans had been actively advocating land redistribution 'to break the back of Southern slaveholders' power.' But Sherman's plan only took shape after the meeting that he and Stanton held with those black ministers. Stanton, aware of the historical significance of the meeting, documented a verbatim transcript of that discussion. Stanton recalled that 'for the first time in the history of this nation, the representatives of the government had gone to these poor debased people to ask them what they wanted for themselves.' Stanton and Sherman asked the local Negro community something that no one else had apparently thought to ask: 'What do you want for your own people?' And what they wanted astonishes us even today.

"The chosen leader and spokesman of these twenty thoughtful black ministers was a Baptist minister named Garrison Frazier, aged 67, who had been born in Granville, North Carolina, and was a slave until 1857, 'when he purchased freedom for himself and wife for $1,000 in gold and silver.' It was Frazier who bore the responsibility of answering the twelve questions that Sherman and Stanton put to the group. The stakes of the future of the Negro people were high.

"And Frazier and his brothers did not disappoint. What did they tell Sherman and Stanton that the Negro most wanted? Land! 'The way we can best take care of ourselves,' Reverend Frazier began his answer to the crucial question, 'is to have land and turn it and till it by our own labor...and we can soon maintain ourselves and have something to spare...We want to be placed on land until we are able to buy it and make it our own.' Four days later, Sherman issued Special Field Order No. 15, after President Lincoln approved it.

"What became of the land that was promised? The response to the order was immediate. When the transcript of the meeting was reprinted in the black publication *Christian Recorder*, an editorial note intoned that 'From this it will be seen that the colored people down South are not so dumb as many suppose them to be,' reflecting North-South, slave-free black class tensions that continued well into the modern civil rights movement. The effect throughout the South was electric. As Eric Foner explains, 'the freedman hastened to take advantage of the Order.' Baptist minister Ulysses L. Houston led 1,000 blacks to Skidaway Island, Georgia, where they established a self-governing community with Houston as the 'black governor.' By the way, Sherman later ordered that the army could lend the new settlers, mules; hence the phrase, '40 acres and a mule.'

"And what happened to this astonishing visionary program, which would have fundamentally altered the course of American race relations? Lincoln's successor, Andrew Johnson (a Democrat from North Carolina), and a sympathizer with the South, overturned the Order in the fall of 1865 and 'returned the land along the South Carolina, Georgia and Florida coasts to the planters who had originally owned it'—to the very people who had declared war on the United States of America."[29]

This reneging on a promise by Andrew Johnson was just the beginning of a whole history of atrocities perpetrated by the Democrat Party against the black population in America.

In 1868 the 14th Amendment gave citizenship to freed slaves. The Amendment passed with 94 percent Republican support and zero percent support from the Democrat Party. In 1870 the 15th Amendment was ratified. The 15th Amendment guaranteed citizens of the United States could not be denied the right to vote on account of race, color, or previous conditions of servitude. The 15th Amendment passed with 100 percent Republican support and zero support from the Democrat Party.

The Ku Klux Klan was founded in 1866 by ex-Confederate soldiers and other Southerners opposed to Reconstruction after the Civil War. In the waning years of Reconstruction, the Klan disbanded. Nearly 50 years later, in 1915, "Colonel" William Joseph Simmons revived the Klan after seeing D.W. Griffith's film *Birth of a Nation*, which portrayed the Klansmen as great heroes. In its second resurgence, the Klan moved beyond just targeting blacks, and broadened its message of hate to include Catholics, Jews, and foreigners.

In the 1920s, the Klan moved in many states to dominate local and state politics. The Klan devised a strategy called the "Decade," in which every member of the Klan was responsible for recruiting ten people to vote for Klan candidates in elections. In 1924 the Klan succeeded in engineering elections of officials from coast to coast. In some states they placed enough Klansmen in positions of power to effectively control the state government. Known as the "Invisible Empire," the KKK's presence was felt across the country. The KKK used violence and intimidation to influence marriage laws in this country as a way of preventing interracial relationships. The KKK also used intimidation and violence to discourage black men from running for public office in the Republican Party. During the 1924 Democratic National Convention the Ku Klux Klan gathered at what was known as the "Klanbake" in New York City. On the agenda for the Convention was a resolution to condemn the KKK for its use of violence and intimidation. The Democrat Party kowtowed to the intimidation of the Ku Klux Klan, and the anti-KKK plank was not included in that year's platform.

In 1916, Margaret Sanger opened the first abortion clinic. Sanger shaped the eugenics movement in America. Her views and those of her peers in the movement contributed to compulsory sterilization laws that resulted in more than 60,000 sterilizations of vulnerable people, including people she considered "feeble-minded, idiots and morons." She even presented at a Ku Klux Klan rally in 1926. In her autobiography she recounted, "In the end, through simple illustrations I believed I had accomplished my purpose." That she generated enthusiasm among some of America's leading racists says something about the content and tone of her remarks.

The "Negro Project" conceptualized by Margaret Sanger was implemented by a birth control group that has come to be known as Planned Parenthood. Sanger skillfully crafted her language of caring for children and women while at the same time blatantly spewing her repugnance for the "unfit," the "garden weeds," and the "human beings who should never have been born at all." In 1921, she wrote, "Today eugenics is suggested by the most diverse minds as the most adequate and thorough avenue in the solution of racial, political and social problems."

Jim Crow laws were state and local laws that enforced racial segregation in the Southern United States as early as the 1870s. These laws were enacted by white Southern Democrat-dominated state legislatures and served to disenfranchise and remove political and economic gains made by black people during the Reconstruction period. The Jim Crow laws were enforced until the Civil Rights Act was passed in 1964.

"Lyndon B. Johnson, a beer-swilling, blunt-speaking Texan, didn't shy from using what we refer to as the n-word. One sentence often attributed to LBJ, which has gained great fame on the internet, is this: 'I'll have those n*ggers voting Democratic for 200 years.' The line is often trotted out to allege that the Civil Rights legislation LBJ pushed and ultimately signed was motivated not by altruism, but a cynical ploy to lock up votes.

"The source of the '200 years' quote is Robert MacMillan, an Air Force One steward who said LBJ uttered this comment to two governors during a conversation on the Civil Rights Act of 1964:

"'These Negroes, they're getting pretty uppity these days and that's a problem for us since they've got something now, they never had before, the political pull to back up their uppityness. Now we've got to do something about this, we've got to give them a little something, just enough to quiet them down, not enough to make a difference.'

"The source of the quote was historian Doris Kearn Goodwin's biography of Lindon B. Johnson, and she was a pretty credible source. Lyndon B. Johnson's racist rhetoric toward African Americans is well documented, as well as his fondness for the use of the n-word. Numerous historians have LBJ on the record referring to the Civil Rights Act of 1957 as the 'n*gger bill,' a phrase that runs counter to altruism on civil rights."[30]

After all of the institutionalized bigotry of the Democrat Party becomes evident, we can see why the Democrats want you to believe that there was some huge party "switch" that took place. However, in order to believe that nonsense you would have to believe that all of the Democrats, at one time decided to put away their racist ideologies while simultaneously convincing all of the Republicans to suddenly become racist bigots. It did not happen.

Liberal groups such as Black Lives Matter and ANTIFA don't remove Confederate monuments to remove emotional torment for descendants of slaves. They remove these monuments to remove their own torments because these monuments serve as a constant reminder that the Democrat Party was the evil party of slavery.

"During testimony in front of the House Judiciary Subcommittee on Reparations, Burgess Owens blasted the Democratic Party 'for all the misery' they've brought to blacks, citing everything from the party's support of slavery, the KKK, Jim Crow laws, and abortion.

"'I used to be a Democrat until I did my history and found out the misery that that party brought to my race...Let's pay restitutions. How about the Democratic Party pay for all the misery brought to my race...' NFL legend Burgess Owens agrees with Democrats about reparations, except he believes the Democrats should be the ones who have to pay them."[31]

> "The demand for bigots in America greatly exceeds the supply."
>
> —Reverend C.L. Bryant
> (Former President of the NAACP)

"The NAACP compared the Trayvon Martin shooting to the lynching of Emmett Till, in 1955. Two young black men on their way to buy some candy being murdered for the crime of being black. Sirius XM radio host Joe Madison called the Martin shooting, 'nothing more than a modern-day lynching.' Well, he was right about that, an innocent person was tied to a tree, kind of a tree anyway, and destroyed before he could be tried...before any evidence was in...that's exactly what happened. Because the trial wasn't important, the world found George Zimmerman guilty. A poor black child murdered in cold blood on the way to the 7-11 to buy some candy. Stories like this are evidence of one of two things on the part of the media; either criminal fraud, or criminal negligence.

"I'm not here to retry this case, but I am here to skim and I mean skim the volumes of credible material, often in Trayvon Martin's own words, that every major news organization simply ignored in order to tell this story.

"Weeks and months after the event, presumably reputable news sources presented a narrative that was sold to the world as news... journalistic truth...the truth is still there; it's the journalism that's gone. So, let's put aside the sentiment for a moment, (we'll come back to the sentiment) and look at what we know. Daniel Patrick Moynihan once remarked, 'you're entitled to your own opinion, but not your own facts.' So, where to begin? Well, you could start with the media representation of the cherubic innocent boy and the scowling white-Hispanic racist assassin; everywhere, all the time. Meanwhile, social media images of, a not so innocent, Trayvon Martin with his middle finger in the air were ignored. Also ignored were the images revealing the brutal and bloody gouges on the back of George Zimmerman's head when the police arrived on the scene.

"Trayvon Martin was not the child portrayed on the magazine covers, or in the hoodie; and you can tell that George Zimmerman has hardly assassinated a defenseless child from a distance. So, what did the media know, or should have known about the two principles that they sat on in order to perpetuate this story? Well, let's start with Trayvon. That happy looking boy on the *People* magazine cover really came apart, especially after his father's second divorce. He became active in mixed martial art style fighting; texting, for example, that he wanted a rematch with an opponent, because, in his own words, 'the other guy hadn't bled enough.' Witnesses testified that he was on top of Zimmerman at the time of the shooting...raining down what were called, 'mixed martial art style blows.' We have screen grabs of Trayvon's texts (they are not airable here for extreme graphic content) that showed sexual aggression typical of hip hop culture in America today. Anyone reading those texts would not describe Trayvon Martin as a sweet young child. He was violent and highly sexualized.

"And then, things start to get even more serious, because a search of Trayvon's locker, at school, revealed a burglary tool and several pieces of stolen property including jewelry. Incredibly, well it would have been incredible at one time; Dade County school officials decided to list that as 'found property' rather than stolen property. If they had listed it as stolen property a police report would have been required; which would reflect badly on black crime rates in the school system. So, it was ignored. Nevertheless, Trayvon had been suspended several times for behavioral issues in the months leading up to the shooting.

"Then there is the issue of the candy and the iced tea. Now, we were told that Trayvon, an innocent child, simply went to the store to buy some candy and some iced tea. But it wasn't just any candy... and it wasn't iced tea...it was Skittles candy and a drink called Arizona Watermelon Fruit Juice Cocktail. The prosecution continually kept up this deception by referring to this drink as iced tea; and some have speculated that they did so to avoid the racial stereotype of black people and watermelon, but there is a much better explanation. Because if you take Arizona Watermelon Fruit Juice Cocktail, a bag of Skittles and add simple cough syrup; you get a cheap codeine-based drink called 'Lean.' There is an entire on-line subculture devoted to the use of Lean; which Trayvon was familiar with. We have screen grabs of him trying to score some codeine on-line, and instead being told he could make some 'fire ass Lean' using cough syrup, Skittles and Arizona Watermelon Fruit Juice Cocktail. It seems a bit of a coincidence to me that the only two items he picked up out of the entire 7-11 were two-thirds of the ingredients needed to make Lean. Now additionally, we have a report from his autopsy that reveals a form of liver damage, in this otherwise healthy young man (just a few days short of eighteen) that are consistent with the kind of trauma that excessive Lean usage does to an otherwise healthy liver.

"Now, most importantly the on-line subculture refers to a number of psychological symptoms associated with the use of Lean; the two most prominent being: extreme physical aggression and paranoia. And we could do this for hours.

"So, what about Zimmerman the arch racist who shot an innocent boy in cold blood? Well, he was raised alongside of two black children. Black members of his community testified, 'he was the only person of any race or color that came up and introduced himself when they moved into the neighborhood.' When a homeless black man named Sherman Ware was knocked down by the son of a Sanford police officer; George Zimmerman, and only George Zimmerman, was so outraged by this assault that he printed up fliers and continued to do so until the son of the policeman was charged with the assault on the homeless black man. The FBI told Eric Holder's Justice Department that a civil rights case against Zimmerman would fail, because, not only was there no evidence that he was racist...there was a preponderance of evidence that he was not. His was not a white 'gated community,' but a multi-cultural one, and one in which he seems to have been, pretty nearly universally, liked and admired.

"A breakdown of the times and distances between the video recording of Trayvon in the 7-11, the 911 call and the time of the shooting show that Trayvon was not being pursued by Zimmerman. He'd had ample time to reach his destination...about four minutes to go a hundred yards...Trayvon had actually gone about 30 yards in that time. He was waiting for Zimmerman. Now, maybe the Lean had made him paranoid and aggressive...we don't know...that's speculation. But what isn't speculation is that George Zimmerman was lying on the ground calling repeatedly for help (Why would he call for help if he was determined to kill this person?) with Trayvon Martin, who was several inches taller; astride him raining down mixed martial arts blows, and telling him he was going to die that night. And when Trayvon started bashing his skull against the cement; Zimmerman thought (pretty reasonably, in my opinion) that if he didn't act, he would indeed die that night. Which is why the police did not charge him (and refused to charge him) until the President and Attorney General of the United States brought overwhelming political pressure, in contradiction of all the evidence, for a prosecution.

"Now remember, no one in the jury was allowed to know about the Lean, the burglary, the altered mental state, the history of violence; none of it. And they acquitted George Zimmerman anyway. Those are the facts. How do we know this? Is it because of the in-depth reporting of the *New York Times*, the *Washington Post* or the *Miami Herald*? No. None of them were interested in any of this. Most of this comes to light through the internet, and among many dedicated researchers, especially the works of Jack Cashill at *American Thinker* and Sundance at the *Conservative Treehouse*. Now I know, some of you are snorting *Conservative Treehouse*? *American Thinker*? Typical right-wing liars, but the problem with that is; this is not speculation, it is Trayvon Martin in his own words...go look. It is screen grabs of his texts. It is his Facebook posts. It's the actual autopsy report. It's sourced...its evidence... it's called journalism. There's no journalism in places like the *New York Times*; these facts were available to anyone. That a few individuals could find them without resources and without pay proves that there's no journalism in places like the *New York Times*. You know the definition of tragedy is something terrible that didn't have to happen. Should George Zimmerman have gotten out of his truck that night? I think of all the people in the world saying no; he would be at the top of the list. And if it weren't for the political correctness, Trayvon Martin might have gotten charged with his earlier burglaries. Would that have scared him or his parents into changing his direction? No one knows.

"After the verdict; an artist created an image that appeared to depict Martin Luther King Jr. wearing a hooded sweatshirt. It was meant to connect Trayvon Martin with Martin Luther King; and of all the things in this wretched lynching of George Zimmerman, this is the most disgraceful. Why is there a Martin Luther King Day and not say a Jessie Jackson Day, or an Al Sharpton Day or a Louis Farrakhan Day? Well, Dr. King is revered, because he preached inclusion and non-violence. Martin Luther King thrilled us with his, 'I have a dream' speech; and the entire point, not only of the speech, but his entire life's work was summed up with these lines, 'I have a dream that my four little children will one day live in a nation where they will be not judged by the color of their skin, but by the content of their character.' The people that are pushing this narrative of a racist assassin and an innocent black child, the judge and prosecutors, and the worst kangaroo court in living memory did everything in their power to make certain that no one knew anything about the content of George Zimmerman and Trayvon Martin's character and only knew about one thing; and one thing only, and that is the color of their skin. To connect Martin Luther King to this travesty is an outrage and it's disgusting. It's perpetrated by outrageous and disgusting people. And if all of this political power and journalistic malfeasance can be deployed to sell a tortured lie as in the case of this little story, then what political power and journalistic malfeasance do you think might be deployed in making us buy a much larger one?"[32]

In this era of hype, pomp, and circumstance, it is of little wonder that an organization such as Black Lives Matter can perpetuate its propaganda, all while being predicated on a series of lies and omissions of exculpatory evidence. Black Lives Matter is an anti-police organization with neo-Marxist dreams of collectivism and the destruction of the nuclear family. To discover the underlying agenda of this group you need look no further than the founders: Alicia Garza, Opal Tometi, and Patrisse Cullors. In a revealing 2015 interview, Cullors admitted that she and Alicia, in particular, have an ideological frame. She claims that they are "trained organizers and trained Marxists." If you go to the Black Lives website you can read their list of demands to get a sense of how deep the transformation is that they are calling for.

As part of their mission, they list: "We disrupt the Western-prescribed nuclear family structure requirement by supporting each other as extended families and 'villages' that collectively care for one another..." The group became a "fiscally sponsored project" of a progressive non-profit in 2016. Representatives of the group were heard saying, "If we don't get our way, we are going to burn it down." The group has become a lot less about "black lives" and a lot more about Marxist propaganda.

Actor Terry Crews attempted to make a stand against the extreme "militant forces" within the Black Lives Matter organization and was immediately met with backlash from the left. On a CNN interview with Don Lemon, Terry Crews mentioned the black-on-black crimes where nine black children were killed in a single month, and the Black Lives Matter movement had said nothing. When Crews suggested that black people need to hold other black people accountable, Don Lemon went silent. When Terry Crews pointed out the hypocrisy of the black community chanting, "Black lives matter", with no actions taken other than to watch as black on black crimes continue in these communities, Don Lemon remained silent. Don Lemon then went on to lie and say that the Black Lives Matter movement was started because it was talking about police brutality, insinuating in some way that the only "black lives" that matter are those that are killed by the police. With disingenuous news coverage like this, it is no wonder that the black community is confused and angry. Can Don Lemon, Alicia Garza, Opal Tometi, or Patrisse Cullors name one socialist or communist country in the world that treats people of color with the same level of equality that they experience in a free nation such as the United

States? The short answer is, of course not. The Democrat Party, once again, has the black community acting against their own best interests.

The media in America is so anxious to propagate this narrative that they are often times willing to forgo seemingly reasonable follow-up questions for anyone making a claim of racism. When images of Jussie Smollett, with a noose around his neck, appeared in the news, not one journalist questioned why Smollett would leave the noose around his neck long after the alleged attackers were gone. Who would do that? Of course, it came as no surprise when it was discovered that Smollett had paid the attackers to perpetuate this hoax. All in an effort to push the narrative that Donald Trump and his followers were racists. When Bubba Wallace claimed that he had found a noose attached to his garage door, not one journalist asked if the rope was the door pull for the garage door. Of course, it was of no surprise, after an FBI investigation, that all of the drivers had the exact same "loop" for their door pulls and that they had been that way for years.

Video footage taken out of context of the Covington High School kids gave the appearance that MAGA hat–wearing juvenile delinquents were the racist norm in society today. Of course, full footage of the incident revealed who the true inciter was. Even the George Floyd footage that was aired for weeks before the actual police cam footage was exposed painted a sordidly different image from the true events that unfolded that day. When asked why the police cam footage was not released earlier, Keith Ellison (attorney general of Minnesota) said he wanted to "protect the prosecution of the case." Prosecutors and family members were disappointed with the state autopsy report because it revealed lethal levels of methamphetamines and fentanyl in George Floyd's system. The autopsy also failed to indicate asphyxiation as the cause of death, because there wasn't enough tissue necrosis in the neck region to warrant a cause of death determination. They were so disappointed that they requested an independent medical examination.

With Black Lives Matter and the media continuously perpetuating the narrative that "black men are being systematically targeted for demise," it has changed the way that black men have reacted when confronted by the police. In an ABC News interview with Michael Strahan, Jacob Blake spoke out about his encounter. When asked why he resisted being put in custody, Blake replied, "I resisted getting beat on." Blake then went on to say, "What I mean by that is not falling, not letting them put they [sic] knee on my neck. I didn't wanna be the next George Floyd," Blake said. "I didn't wanna die."

The officer on the scene, Officer Sheskey, and Jacob Blake ended up in a physical altercation on the ground, and Blake walked away from the officers. "I'm rattled, you know?" Blake said. "I realized I had dropped my knife, had a little pocketknife. So, I picked it up after I got off of him, because they tased me and I fell on top of him."

"I'm not really worried," Blake said. "I'm walkin' away from them so it's not like they gonna shoot me. I shouldn't have picked it up only considering what was going on, you know? At that time, I wasn't thinking clearly." After weeks of media reporting, that another "unarmed" black man had been shot by the police, it was finally revealed by Blake's own recollection that he was not unarmed.

In many instances, the rhetoric proclaimed by Black Lives Matter and the media has actually manufactured the crisis. This notion that men are being hunted by the police "for the crime of being black" has created an irrational fear in people of color. This fear, in turn, has changed the way that people behave in these situations and quite literally has created a self-fulfilling prophecy of sorts.

Another example sometimes described as institutional racism is racial profiling by security guards and police and the use of stereotyped racial caricatures. This notion that profiling by the police is racially driven is contrary to reason or common sense. If the person described in an armed robbery is a blonde, female midget with blue eyes, it would be preposterous for the police to stop people who clearly do not fit that description. Profiling is a useful tool for the police to narrow their search. Race just happens to be one aspect of the profile. How futile would it be if the victim described the criminal by saying, "The criminal was a gender-neutral individual with hair, who stood about five feet tall"? We would never solve another crime in this country.

After an entire summer of "seeded" riots, under the guise of "peaceful protests," Black Lives Matter issued a litany of demands. Demands that needed to be met if the country didn't want to see the "system burned down." After watching an entire summer of looting, rioting, and billions of dollars of property being burned to the ground, it was not difficult to envision a literal burning down of the system. Perhaps the most ludicrous of those demands was the call to defund the police. In a time when rioters on the streets were setting up "autonomous zones," destroying businesses, burning property, dismantling national monuments, and attacking federal buildings, the last thing an underfunded police force needed was less funding and less resources. Yet, it did not stop some mayors in some of the most liberal cities in America from doing just that. Of course, crime rates in those cities have increased at disastrous rates. People in those communities, including the black community, have called for a reinstatement of the policing resources to restore civility in their own communities.

To those looking on, from a bird's-eye view, it was evident that the riots and calls for defunding the police were all tactics to sow discourse during an election year. These anarchist techniques were clearly deployed to blacken the eye of the Trump administration with one clear vision in mind: remove Donald Trump because he was the greatest obstacle standing in front of their Marxist utopia. If racial division, a few dead Americans, and billions of dollars in damage was necessary to unseat an obstacle, then no damage was too much when you are willing to put party before country. Besides, a riled-up base is more likely to vote in an upcoming election. The ultimatum was simple: "Either vote in our candidates so they can install a system of government that will destroy this country from within, or we will destroy this country."

Finally, and perhaps the greatest lie of all, is this notion that affirmative action is in the best interest of people of color. As already described, affirmative action refers to a set of policies and practices within a government or organization seeking to increase the representation of particular groups based on their gender, race, sexuality, creed, or nationality in areas in which they are underrepresented. The problem with this concept, aside from ignoring merit, is that in many cases, these particular groups are not underrepresented at all. By the number, if 13 percent of the total population is black, then it is only reasonable that 13 percent of people working for a corporation or organization are black. But that is not what affirmative action is striving for. In fact, many times, affirmative action is calling for an over-representation as some form of compensation for past indiscretions. If anyone had ever called for only 13 percent of NBA players to be black, or only 13 percent of NFL players to be black, they would quickly be reminded of a merit-based program. However, the Rooney Rule in the NFL is constantly being changed with regard to black representation in the coaching ranks. According to a rule approved by the NAACP, multiple black applicants must be interviewed before hiring a new coach, regardless of their merit or their ideological fit for the team and that team's direction.

The phrase "affirmative action" first appeared in 1961, when John F. Kennedy created the Committee on Equal Employment Opportunity. Initially, affirmative action encouraged employers to hire "marginalized" people. With terms like that it is easy to see the underpinnings of the Democrat Party's true feelings. After declaring that the black members of society couldn't possibly be expected to compete in academics and in the workforce, it was determined that some program must be installed to make up for a "perceived" discrepancy in ability. It is staggering that after sixty-years, nobody has pointed out how racist that notion truly is. What is more racist...asking someone to apply for a college application or a job based on their skills, with the chance of rejection... or being told in advance that they cannot compete (due solely on the color of their skin); therefore, the application process will be modified to accommodate their shortcomings? The answer is clear. And affirmative action robs the black community of any sense of victory or pride, regardless of the final outcome. In essence, affirmative action represents the soft bigotry of low expectation.

Imagine playing a game of one-on-one basketball with someone who feels they are a far superior player, so they offer to give a handicap of eighteen points on the way to twenty-one. If the handicapped player scores three points before their cocky opponent reaches twenty-one, the person spotting the points will never let the supposed underdog forget about the eighteen-point handicap. And even worse than that, if the opponent finds a way to score twenty-one points before the recipient of the handicap can score three points, the defeat would be absolutely demoralizing. Regardless of the final outcome, the person receiving the handicap can never truly experience victory. There can be no pride in either outcome. Affirmative action serves to rob someone of their pride, or it creates a feeling of animosity in those that lost out on their rightful victory to make room for someone else based on diversity instead of actual merit.

> "We are more often frightened than hurt, and we suffer more in imagination than in reality."
>
> —Seneca

The Solution

The simple act of recognizing cultural and physical differences is not an instance of racism. Black, white, Asian, Hispanic—it does not matter what your skin color is, or where your heritage begins; we can all be proud of our culture. And we can celebrate our differences in the same light that we can celebrate our similarities. This cultural war was created in an effort to divide and conquer a nation for political gain. By conjuring up "ghosts from the past," there are certain factions in the political world that would like to see America divided over racial lines. These evildoers would have the country ignore any and all progress made over the course of the last 200 years in order to use that animosity against one another.

We must resist the misinformation being presented through critical race theory. If it was actual American history, it wouldn't be called critical race theory, with heavy emphasis on the word "theory."

Critical theory was, is, and will always be a Marxist tool to undermine the foundation of this country. They absolutely intend to destroy this country from within. A society riled up on emotion cannot use that same emotion to clearly see the truth. Only logic can do that.

The question isn't whether we should teach each other about cultural differences and learn about the history of slavery and racial injustices; the question is about what is being taught. If we do not learn from history, we are doomed to repeat it. Telling a group of children, employees, or government agencies that they are inherently racist simply because of the color of the skin they were born with is wrong. It is the definition of racism. Likewise, we shouldn't be trying to convince someone that they are not a victim of someone else's hate when those real instances occur. The discussion needs to be a dialogue with all voices and opinions being heard, but critical race theory demands a monologue, and anyone with a differing opinion is silenced or labeled a racist. That is not teaching; that is indoctrinating, and there is a huge difference. We cannot look at a person's skin and automatically assume anything. The concept known as critical race theory is pushing that agenda. They are quite literally teaching the idea that all white people are racist by nature. There is no denial that racism exists—we cannot change the evil that lives in a man's heart—but to make generalizations based on skin color or to assume that racism only goes one way, well, that is divisive, and it is a lie.

If advocates want to have a conversation to promote fairness, love, patience, and understanding one another, the American people are all in. But if they are swinging the pendulum 180 degrees the other direction (by blanket blaming an entire race of people based on skin tone and skin tone alone) to atone for the sins of people that no longer exist on this planet, then the American people will dissent. That doesn't make America racist; it just means they are not willing to pay for the sins of someone else. Let the individual be held responsible for the consequences of their own actions.

Individual racism does exist, but there is no evidence of systemic racism. There are programs that slap us in the face with stark reality for their divisive nature, but to say that we are a racist country does a disservice to the huge progress that we have made to right the wrongs of the past. If we focus only on the negative, we will attract more negative. If we focus on, and celebrate, the positive, then we will incentivize more positive. As a country we have the resources and the intelligence to recognize true racism when it occurs—and we can surely deal with those individual cases as they occur. We must all avoid broad brush-stroke assumptions about anybody—let alone an entire race of people.

The critical race theorists are practicing "presentism" by asking the people in the colonial days to be held to the social standards of today. There is a global guilt movement being utilized against the United States to crush the founders of this country because if the founders were flawed, then we can conclude that the system is flawed. What is the purpose? To change the current system into the only alternative: a Marxist nirvana. Critical theory of any kind is a Marxist tool designed to do one thing: attack Western culture. Why don't you hear about slavery in Europe, Asia, or the Middle East? Because they have already moved toward Marxism—there is no longer a need to criticize those regions. That is literally what critical theory means: to criticize; and the beauty is that the person doing the criticizing doesn't need to have an alternate or better solution, just criticize enough and demand change. In fact, if you criticize the people propagating the notion of systemic racism, they respond by calling you a racist. What is the sense of being named the "progressive" party if the progressives refuse to acknowledge progress of any kind? Ironically, these same progressives would struggle to name one socialist or communist country in the entire world that treats people of color better than they are treated in the United States.

Clearly, we cannot regulate the thoughts that go through a person's mind. Likewise, we cannot regulate the feelings that a person experiences after an interaction. Racism is an action (usually discriminatory) that is clearly a wrong against an individual. Actions like these can be resolved, regardless of who is in a position of power. There are legal actions available to people of all races for individual, case-by-case situations.

As a black man, Jesse Owens helped to shatter the beliefs of Aryan superiority in the presence of Adolf Hitler. Owens's gold medals in the 1936 Olympics in Berlin were, in themselves, a symbol of racial equality. Thirty-two years later, while Owens was in attendance at the 1968 Summer Olympics in Mexico, American athletes Tommie Smith and John Carlos stepped up on to the podiums to receive their medals. The crowd noticed that they had removed their shoes and were wearing black stockings. As the flag raising ceremony began, Smith and Carlos (each wearing a black glove on one hand) raised their fists in a Black Power salute and looked toward the ground, creating one of the most memorable moments and photographs in Olympic history.

A culture, even one as diverse and robust as the United States', cannot accommodate both the need for recognition of those cultural demonstrations and simultaneously be asked to recognize when it is conveniently appropriate to ignore cultural differences. It is impossibly unfair for a society to be asked to see any person, of any race, in only a positive light. That is the very definition of racism. However, this overcompensation for past indiscretions is exactly what is being asked of America in today's society.

We can no longer allow an individual to blame their independent failures on the color of their skin, just as we can no longer allow society to attribute a person's success solely on the color of their skin. This country elected a black man to be the president of the United States, and as such, he held the most powerful position in the entire world, not once, but twice.

There is little doubt that some misguided individuals will always maintain biases based on visualized differences, but it would be difficult to consider this the norm in today's society. Those people will always fear what they do not understand. Allowing that fear to morph into hate is the real crime. The word "racism" itself has undergone a transformational change, and not necessarily a change for the better. The word "racism" has become so subjective that the user can virtually use the term to describe any uncomfortable feeling experienced over a sweeping spectrum of subject matters. And anyone who dares to question the validity of its use will, of course, be deemed a racist. The power of the word makes it seem like the ultimate trump card, but "going to the well too often" has diminished its meaning. Claiming victimhood for every failure in life actually cheapens the moments when people are actually the victim.

For clarification, society needs to universally define racism as an objectionable mistreatment of a person based solely on the color of that person's skin. Simply saying that a person is black is not an act of racism. In fact, it is an accurate assessment of that person's profile. On the other hand, if an individual was denied a job, a loan, denied admission to a school, denied a position on a team, denied a seat in a restaurant or on a bus, or any other access that was normally public, because of the color of their skin, then that would be the definition of racism.

"It is not that whites are more intelligent, morally superior or more industrious than black Americans, which are the primary sociological attributes that cause people to succeed in life.

"African Americans are very industrious: They disproportionately work at some of the toughest and least rewarding jobs in the country. It's not a lack of morality, as African Americans have a deep moral fiber. They firmly believe in traditional Judeo-Christian morality and can be more conservative than whites in many ways. It's certainly not a lack of patriotism. African Americans are loyal to this country and have fought in our wars when rights for which we were fighting for others were denied to us here."[33]

> "Our preconceptions can dramatically alter the way we perceive the world."
>
> —Anaïs Nin

"WE DON'T SEE THINGS AS THEY ARE;

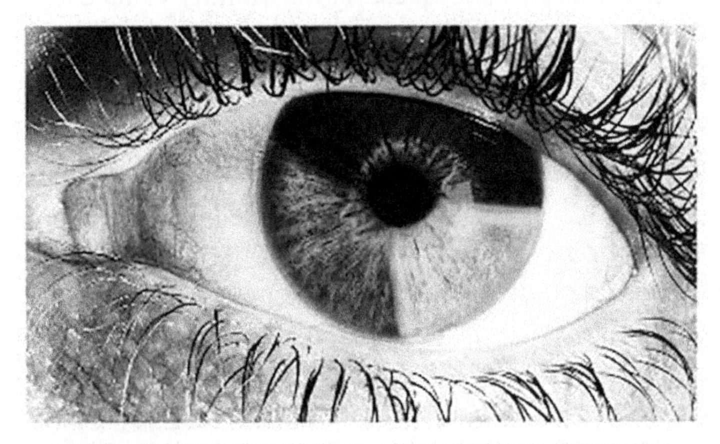

WE SEE THEM AS 'WE' ARE."

A man walks into the psychologist's office and immediately demands a Rorschach (ink blot) test. The doctor asks the man why he believes he needs such a test, to which the man replies, "All of my friends think I am a pervert." Interested in this hypothesis, the doctor proceeded with the test. After the doctor flipped the first card, the man described, "A naked woman." After the doctor turned the second card over, the man reported, "Two women kissing." After the doctor showed the third card, the man recounted, "A pair of breasts." After revealing thirty cards, and getting similar answers, the doctor slammed the cards on the table and declared, "Your friends are correct, you are a pervert." The man calmly responded by saying, "You are the one showing all of the dirty pictures."

In 1994, Joe Biden introduced a crime bill that was later signed into law by President Bill Clinton. The law included provisions to crack down on domestic violence and rape against women. It helped to fund background checks for gun purchases. And it encouraged states to back drug courts, which had attempted to divert drug offenders from prison into treatment programs. The law imposed tougher prison sentences at the federal level and encouraged states to do the same. It resulted in mass incarceration, more prison cells, and more aggressive policing, disproportionately affecting black and brown Americans. Retrospectively, many people considered this to be a racist bill and have accused Joe Biden of racism. The problem with this perspective is that the observer making this claim would have to be of the impression that black and brown Americans are the only criminals capable of doing drugs or committing acts of violence against women. It is this type of prejudice that indicates that "we don't see things as they are; we see them as 'we' are." Even if Joe Biden had secretly envisioned a mass incarceration of people of color, he clearly would have no control over who would commit those crimes after creating the bill. We clearly do "suffer more in imagination that we do in reality." Every rule in the law books of today's world were dedicated to not only giving black people a fair system, but in many ways, it has created an "affirmative action culture" to give an unfair advantage for the black community.

We all know smart people, and we all know stupid people. We all know motivated people, and we all know lazy people. Skin tone has absolutely nothing to do with any of that. But stupid, lazy people are never short of excuses—and that also knows no skin color. Like Thomas Sowell said, "When you are 'given' a job, instead of 'earning' a job...when you are 'given' a placement in college, instead of 'earning' your placement in college...when preferential treatment is no longer 'given,' then equal treatment feels like you have been discriminated against."

Perhaps the biggest step to removing racism from our system would be to eliminate affirmative action mandates. Let's ask the question: Are the people calling for equal treatment actually asking for equality? If so, let's make *everything* equal. It is time to remove the safety net that prevents any man from feeling the freedom and pride of accomplishment that can only be felt when it is genuinely earned. It is only when these provisions are removed that people will apply themselves academically and vocationally to their fullest potentials. Safeguards are the greatest robber of incentive and initiative. There are plenty of other opportunities such as the "Opportunity Zones" and the "Platinum Plan" created under the Trump administration that provide opportunity, security, prosperity, and fairness to people of all colors. The Platinum Plan in particular is a black empowerment program designed to give access to capital to people of color.

Just like in 1865 when Union General William T. Sherman asked the local Negro community, "What do you want for your own people?" and Garrison Frazier replied, "Land! The way we can best take care of ourselves is to have land and turn it and till it by our own labor...and we can soon maintain ourselves and have something to spare...We want to be placed on land until we are able to buy it and make it our own." Ownership and pride have not been replaced as a priority in all of those years. Notice that Garrison Frazier didn't want the land gifted to them. He wanted to be placed on land until they were able to "buy it and make it our own."

The next step to removing racism from our system is to clean up the current census procedures. After the 15th Amendment guaranteed citizens of the United States could not be denied the right to vote on account of race, color, or previous conditions of servitude and the 19th Amendment guaranteed women the right to vote, there was no longer a need to determine a person's race or gender on the United States census. So why are they still asking these questions? And why are Democrats so adamant about denying the citizenship question on the census? For all intents and purposes the United States census only serves two purposes: to determine representation in Congress and to determine how many voters are eligible. There literally is no need to determine a person's skin color when counting the people for the census, unless, of course, someone believes that one race or another may require additional welfare resources based on some preconceived notion that one race is superior or inferior to another. And there can be no reason to deny the citizenship question unless someone is trying to skew elections or misappropriate federal funds to states and cities that have harbored illegal immigrants in sanctuary cities and states. This census version of a shell game is all sleight of hand tactics to use corrupt policies for personal gain, and it must be stopped. Logistically, the United States census only needs to ask two questions: What is your birthdate? and, Are you a legal citizen of the United States?

Individual acts of racism will never be completely eliminated. We cannot change the evil that resides inside of a man's heart. Statistically, contrary to the media narrative and certain groups with an underlying agenda, acts of racism in America are declining. There are so few examples of unfairness that society has sunk to actually manufacturing stories of unfairness. And the media echo chamber makes the few actual cases appear to be of a much larger magnitude than they actually are. When a white man mowed down a white woman with his car in Charlottesville, the media declared it an act of racism. While they have a right to their own opinions, they do not have a right to their own facts.

Robert Johnson made claims that "reparations are to atone for the largest illegal wealth transfer in this nation's history." What he doesn't explain is how you can transfer wealth from someone who never had wealth to begin with? It is inconsistent claims like these that make reparations impractical. In the instance of slavery, white people were not the only owners of slaves. Half of the country, black and white, fought on the side to abolish slavery. Black men participated in the slave trade, and they too prospered from the ownership of slaves.

We recognize the injustices that were perpetrated, but the sins of our ancestors are their burdens. Our only obligation now is to ensure that that history is not forgotten and never repeated in America.

A congressional hearing erupted when *Quillette* writer Coleman Hughes trashed a bill to study slavery reparations as a "moral and political mistake." The House Judiciary Committee's Subcommittee on the Constitution, Civil Rights, and Civil Liberties held a hearing entitled "H.R. 40 and the Path to Restorative Justice." The audience booed after hearing Coleman Hughes say, "Black people don't need another apology. We need safer neighborhoods and better schools. We need a less punitive criminal justice system. We need affordable health care. And none of these things can be achieved through reparations for slavery."

He went on to describe reparations as not just divisive but an "insult" to "many black Americans by putting a price on the suffering of their ancestors." Hughes then went on to say, "Reparations by definition are only given to victims, so the moment you give me reparations, you've made me into a victim without my consent. The question is not what America owes me by virtue of my ancestry. The question is what all Americans owe each other by virtue of being citizens of the same nation."

Aside from the statistical impossibility of determining who did and who did not own slaves, there would be the daunting task of determining who migrated to this country after the abolition of slavery. It is estimated that nearly 8.7 percent of the 40 million blacks in America have migrated here after slavery was abolished.

It is not as simple as saying white people have to pay and black people get to receive a check. For lack of a better term, it is not that black-and-white.

In today's volatile society, even an act of reparations in this matter would be construed the wrong way. Someone would argue that it would be an admission of guilt and that any payment would not be enough. Others would say that the payment, by way of reparations, would be a symbol of white supremacists displaying their privilege and acknowledging their own superiority, while looking down their noses at the inferior victims during the transactions. There never was, never is, and never will be a suitable solution for those who want to claim victimhood, and it will forever cheapen actual claims by actual victims. There can no longer be a solution that won't be convoluted out of context. The current culture won't allow for it.

Instead, we must be a nation committed to the equal treatment of all of its citizens. That means no more preferential treatment to anyone based on the color of their skin. Additionally, we must destroy this narrative that racism is a one-way street. The current media narrative in this county has set up circumstances where there is an unjustified vitriol toward white men. With broad-stroking false claims that white men are the greatest existential threat to our society, there can be no healing. The media will spend countless hours covering hoax hate crimes but has no desire whatsoever to cover a truly disturbing rise in anti-Semitic hate crimes. Why not? Well, because those crimes are politically inconvenient. In other words, they are not committed against the correct people.

We must have equal rights for all in order to live up to our founding principles. "*We hold these truths to be self-evident, that all men are created equal, that they are endowed by their Creator with certain unalienable Rights, that among these are Life, Liberty and the pursuit of Happiness*." That all men are by nature equally free and independent and have certain inherent rights, of which, when they enter into a state of society, they cannot, by any compact, deprive or divest their posterity; namely, the enjoyment of life and liberty, with the means of acquiring and possessing property, and pursuing and obtaining happiness and safety. The people of this nation must serve to build a unified society and work toward social and economic harmony for all. Ultimately the goal is not for people to merely survive, but they also need to thrive.

Since the civil rights movement, this country has done more for black rights, gay rights, and women's rights than any other country in the world. Then the leftists hijacked this well-meaning civil rights movement to create anarchy, with one goal in mind. They aim to undermine the "evil" white men who wrote the Constitution so that Marxism can prevail and this global governance can finally begin. The Marxists want the black man to stand up and raise his fist in the air to indicate the power derived from the color of his skin but hypocritically judge anyone as racist for actually recognizing the color of his skin. And it is the Democrat Party that has embraced this political and cultural concept of Marxism.

"Black people…you are voting for the party that fought to keep the slave market legal. You're voting for the party that authored Jim Crowe. You're voting for the party that created the KKK. All the bigotry that has so deeply scarred America; was the Democrats. And you vote for them.

"Democrats haven't changed. They still want you to be dependent on the master. And they are still dependent on you. It's just that now, instead of using blacks to farm cotton, they now use blacks to farm votes. And you've been suckered into believing that this off-balanced circle of dependency is Democrats doing something for black folks. If Democrats do so much for you, why are you still so angry? Why are you still saying, 'we shall overcome,' as if it hasn't already happened? I'll tell you why overcoming hasn't happened for you. You've been suckered into voting for the party that you were supposed to overcome. The Democrats want you to believe that you are entitled to other people being deprived of their rights for your comfort. Democrats haven't changed, because that's what slavery is all about...depriving someone else of their rights for the comfort of someone else.

"Democrats have effectively conditioned many blacks to willingly participate in the Democrat's genocidal campaign against them via *Planned Parenthood*. Democrats be like, 'hey there my black sister, are you pregnant? We can abort that thing, and make someone else pay for it. But if you decide to keep that thing, here's a block of cheese and a check; and there's more where that came from, if you keep those votes coming for us. And make sure you don't have a contributing husband; or else no social assistance for you."[34]

Instead of Black Lives Matter calling to end Western-prescribed nuclear families, they should be encouraging family units to stay together. Instead of government programs incentivizing with subsidies the single-mother dynamic, the government should be encouraging cohesiveness in the family unit. The politician that finds a way to offer a "hand up" instead of a hand out while simultaneously encouraging the dynamics of a nuclear family will be worthy of all the accolades this society has to offer. Instead of cries to defund the police, Black Lives Matter should be shouting to defund Planned Parenthood. Any organization founded on the premise of eugenics should be denied social recognition in a country as sophisticated as the United States. The fact that federal money filters its way into this organization should be repugnant to everyone. Contrary to what Margaret Sanger said in 1921, eugenics is not the most adequate solution of racial, political, and social problems. In fact, abortions are responsible for the killing of no less than 62 million babies since the *Roe v. Wade* decision in 1973, and nearly nineteen million, of those babies, were black.

What is the number-one killer in the black community?

It's not the 3,591 deaths due to HIV.
It's not the 4,861 drug-induced deaths.
It's not the 7,903 homicides.
It's not the 13,435 deaths due to diabetes.
It's not the 14,135 accidental deaths.
It's not the 69,090 deaths due to cancer.
It's not the 73,095 deaths due to heart disease, or any of the 246,122 deaths from the top 15 leading causes, combined. It is the 259,336 deaths of black lives via abortion in one year.

Chapter Six:

Abortion

“I have to march because my mother could not have an abortion.”

—Maxine Waters (Pro-Choice March, April 25, 2004)

“The true measure of any society can be found in how it treats its most vulnerable members.”

—Mahatma Gandhi

The Emotional Lie

“‘My body, my choice’ is a slogan that is meant to represent the idea of personal bodily autonomy, bodily integrity and freedom of choice. Bodily autonomy constitutes self-determination over one’s own body without external domination or duress.”[35]

At a pro-abortion rally on March 4, 2020, Chuck Schumer proclaimed, “Women’s ‘reproductive rights’ have come under attack in a way we haven’t seen in modern history. From Louisiana to Missouri to Texas, Republican legislatures are waging a war on women, all women, and they’re taking away fundamental rights…

Let me ask you, my friends, are we going to let Republicans undo a woman's right to choose? No. We're going to stand together in one voice and take a stand on behalf of women and families throughout the country. We're going to stand against all these attempts to restrict a woman's right to choose, and we will win."

In a vain attempt to rationalize the acceptance of abortion as a means of birth control, some pro-abortion advocates have referred to the human fetus as nothing more than a "clump of cells." They argue that the human embryo is derived from the fusion of the fertile egg and a sperm cell. In their minds, regardless of what it will grow into or how far it develops later, there is a point at which the unborn human was completely unrecognizable as a person. Many of these women feel it is a great injustice for their entire being to be valued only as much as something so undeveloped. By dehumanizing the living being inside of them, it makes it easier to make a conscious decision to terminate the pregnancy.

The pro-abortion groups claim to be pro-choice. They will tell you that no one wants an abortion, but they also didn't want to get pregnant. As a self-proclaimed victim of circumstance, they have decided that they cannot, and will not, continue the pregnancy; therefore, they need this option to relieve them of this "mistake." They claim they don't want anyone to "need" an abortion and choices like this should be rare, but if that choice must be made, it should be safe and legal. In fact, they will tell you that all abortions should be safe, legal, and rare.

> "No one wants an abortion as she wants an ice cream cone or a Porsche. She wants an abortion as an animal, caught in a trap, wants to gnaw off its own leg."
>
> —Frederica Mathewes-Green

After *Roe v. Wade* was decided, Congress passed the first Hyde Amendment to be effective for the fiscal 1977 Medicaid appropriation. Introduced by Henry J. Hyde, the Hyde Amendment barred the use of federal Medicaid funds for abortion except when the life of the woman would be endangered by carrying the pregnancy to term. Basically, the Hyde Amendment is a provision that keeps taxpayers from paying for a woman's abortion.

Outraged that the Supreme Court had disagreed with *Roe*'s assertion of an "absolute right" to terminate pregnancy in any way and at any time, a coalition of activists, donors, and other pro-abortion advocates formed a group called the Planned Parenthood Action Fund. With the mendacity of a child, this collective has proclaimed themselves to be non-partisan. The Planned Parenthood Action Fund had this to say about the Hyde Amendment:

"For far too long, the United States has penalized low-income people seeking abortion—forcing those already struggling to make ends meet to pay the biggest portion of her income for safe, legal care.

Since 1976, the Hyde Amendment has blocked federal Medicaid funding for abortion services (since 1994, there have been three extremely narrow exceptions: when continuing the pregnancy will endanger the patient's life, or when the pregnancy results from rape or incest). This means Medicaid cannot cover abortion even when a patient's health is at risk and their doctor recommends; they get an abortion.

When insurance coverage provides for all pregnancy-related health care except abortion, it interferes with the private health decisions that are best left to a patient, their doctor, and their family. The Hyde Amendment is a dangerous and unfair policy that lets politicians interfere in people's personal health care decisions."

Another abortion advocacy group (paradoxically named) the Center for Reproductive Rights believes the Hyde Amendment is a restriction we must repeal to make abortion care available to all—not just to those that can afford it.

Perhaps one of the greatest emotional lies told by abortion advocates is the myth that Planned Parenthood performs a large variety of other clinical services for women including cancer screening, testing for sexually transmitted diseases, contraception, and prenatal services.

According to a consistent ten-year statistical breakdown of the affiliate medical services, Planned Parenthood has claimed that only 3 percent of its annual services have been dedicated to abortions. When Planned Parenthood released its latest annual report for the 2018–2019 fiscal year, it revealed that the number of abortions performed at its facilities had finally risen to 4 percent. Despite an overall national decline in the number of abortions performed, Planned Parenthood hit a new record for the most abortions ever performed in its facilities when they documented 345,672 abortions in a single year.

On the Center for Reproductive Rights' website, they speculate what would happen if the Supreme Court were to limit or overturn *Roe v. Wade*. In an article entitled "What if *Roe* Fell?" the Center for Reproductive Rights speculates that women would "lose access to safe and legal abortion along with a full range of other human rights, including the right to life, health, equality and non-discrimination, privacy, bodily autonomy, and freedom from cruel, inhuman, and degrading treatment."

In the same article, they cited: "The World Health Organization recognizes that in countries with restrictive abortion laws induced abortion rates are high, the majority of abortions are unsafe, and women's health and lives are frequently put at risk. Legal restrictions on abortion do not result in fewer abortions. Instead, they compel women to risk their lives and health by seeking out unsafe abortion services. According to the World Health Organization's safe abortion guidelines, in countries where induced abortion is highly restricted or unavailable, 'safe abortion has frequently become a privilege of the rich, while poor women have little choice but to resort to unsafe providers.' Conversely, the removal of legal restrictions on abortion has shifted clandestine, unsafe procedures to legal and safe ones, resulting in significantly reduced rates of maternal mortality and morbidity."

According to the Center for Reproductive Rights group, too many people are unable to access abortion care and are living in what they describe as a "No-Roe" reality. It is the opinion of this group that nine states have enacted unconstitutional pre-viability bans in 2019, including Alabama's total ban; the six-week bans enacted in Georgia, Kentucky, Louisiana, Mississippi, and Ohio; Missouri's eight-week ban; and the eighteen-week bans enacted in Arkansas and Utah. It is clear that the Center for Reproductive Rights believes that a woman should be able to undergo an abortion procedure at any time of her choosing and for any reason. Any restriction, in their eyes, is a human rights violation. Are they forgetting about the other human's rights in this equation, or do they really believe in this "clump of cells" mantra up until the day of delivery?

"There's no such thing as a safe abortion...in the end, someone always dies."

—Unknown

The Truth

Progressive Democrats and abortion advocates will step in front of any podium available and condemn Republicans for "waging war" against women. It is the battle cry of abortion advocates across the country that a woman has absolute control over her body, and only she can decide whether or not to keep the child growing inside of her. How would these same women's advocates respond if society expanded on that concept and concluded that the man responsible for creating the child could also unilaterally decide the fate of the child? How would the woman respond if the biological father of the child could force the woman to abort the child to avoid paying child support? Have these people considered the man who was diagnosed as infertile, only to find out that by miracle he had fathered a child? Is it really solely up to the woman to deny him his only opportunity to propagate his bloodline?

This is not the first time in history that progressive Democrats have taken it on themselves to determine who is and who is not "sufficiently human" to deserve rights. When these abortion advocates are complaining about "waging war" against women, have they forgotten that half of the babies aborted are women? Who's protecting the reproductive rights of those women?

This concept of personal bodily autonomy and choice is extended to the woman because it is her body, but think for just one second. This woman had choices before she got pregnant. She chose to have sex before she was ready to have a baby. She chose to have sex with a man she had no desire to raise a child with and/or could not afford. She chose to have unprotected sex. She chose not to use the morning-after pill. Perhaps these abortion advocates should explain why they are so adamantly defending this person's right to make *another* choice when it is clear that they have failed to make good choices at every turn before this choice?

Birth control is supposed to be proactive—not retroactive. And why do these progressives assume that all babies that are born, instead of being aborted, would need society to assume responsibility for the welfare and care of that child? By making this assumption, they have given society a false binary choice. They tell the rest of society to either pay for the abortion through federal funding or pay for the care and well-being of the child through tax-funded welfare programs for the rest of the child's life. They are in no position to force the rest of society to make a "lesser of two evils" choice that only benefits the pregnant individual to the detriment of the rest of society.

Chuck Schumer's assertion that limiting abortion rights is somehow denying a woman of her reproductive rights is absolutely absurd. Maybe Mr. Schumer knows this (then again, maybe he doesn't), but the fact that a woman is already pregnant means she was able to exercise her "reproductive rights." In fact, an abortion would put an end to those reproductive actions that she absolutely had the right to. Redefining terms is another tactic of the political left. In this case, redefining the term "reproductive rights" is essential to promote their political agenda. When Nancy Pelosi proclaims that she has to march for abortion rights because her mother could not have an abortion, it is hard to determine if this is an oxymoron or a statement being made by a moron.

The Center for Reproductive Rights is convinced that any pre-viability ban is unconstitutional, but what if the argument of "when is it too late to get an abortion" was compared to your "rule of thumb for not getting a speeding ticket"?

Everyone has their rule of thumb when it comes to driving in excess of the speed limit. Some people *never* exceed the speed limit, *ever*. In the abortion argument, these are the Christians that believe life begins at conception, and there is *never* a time to abort a living creature. These people will never get a speeding ticket.

There are the people who will travel along with the flow of the other drivers. These are the people who also believe that a heartbeat is the true indicator of life, and an abortion should not be performed after this indication of life. It is difficult to argue with this premise, as there is nothing on this earth with a heartbeat that isn't alive. There is a low incidence of speeding tickets to this particular crowd.

There are some that use the 10 percent rule. They never exceed the speed limit by more than 10 percent of the posted limit. These are the people that believe you shouldn't abort any time after the point of viability: where the baby can sustain life on its own outside of the womb. There are medical reports of premature babies being born between 17 and 23 weeks old and living.

There are still others that use the "10 mph over" rule of thumb. No matter what the speed limit is, they will drive ten miles per hour over the speed limit. This is the group of people that argue *sentience* is the true indication of life. It is impossible to prove either way if the fetus can or cannot feel, because there is no metric to determine this phenomenon. It is not likely that the fetus could talk or express the fact that it did or did not feel sensation, and conveniently there is no method of physically detecting this. Speeding tickets are issued frequently with this method, and it really depends on the mood of the officer that pulls the person over.

And finally, we have the "I will drive as fast as I want—it's my car and my license" crowd. These are the extremists that just don't care about morals or laws and believe it is appropriate to abort the baby at any time during pregnancy or immediately after the delivery. Almost everyone else agrees that these people are a menace and are not safe for society.

"The *Planned Parenthood* 3% lie has been debunked by a *Washington Post* fact checker, but the revelation has never stopped *Planned Parenthood* from using the inaccurate statistic.

"*Planned Parenthood* has downplayed its abortion services for years, claiming it is first and foremost a health care organization. Now, after firing its emergency room physician president D. Leana Wen for being too focused on health care and not enough on abortion, it seems it has to report that abortion has grown to account for four percent of its total services. With *Planned Parenthood* now committing 40% of the nation's abortions, it's clear that it is America's number one abortion provider and therefore the claim that abortion only makes up four percent of its services is a total misrepresentation of its statistics.

"To get away with the claim that abortion accounts for just four percent of its services, *Planned Parenthood* divides its total number of abortions by the number of services it provides. These services include packets of birth control, pregnancy tests, urine tests, STI testing, and more, which are likely provided for each woman who comes for an abortion. The abortion corporation is unbundling its services to make it sound like it's providing a lot of health services to people, but in reality, it is simply providing additional services to its existing abortion patients.

"As Rich Lowry pointed out in the *New York Post* in 2015, it is nonsensical for *Planned Parenthood* to claim abortion is such a small part of their business. He said that, for example, 'The sponsors of the New York City Marathon could count each small cup of water they hand out (some 2 million cups, compared with 45,000 runners) and say they are mainly in the hydration business.' Or, explained Lowry, 'Major League Baseball teams could say that they sell about 20 million hot dogs and play 2,430 games in a season, so baseball is only .012 percent of what they do.' *Planned Parenthood* can rearrange statistics to make them say whatever it wants. But they can't bury the truth or toss it in the medical waste bin. The truth is it doesn't even matter what the percentage of abortions done by *Planned Parenthood* works out to be, because by committing 345,000 abortions in 2018, *Planned Parenthood* killed one preborn child every 91 seconds."[36]

Abortion advocates' claim that the Hyde Amendment is an "unfair policy designed to let politicians interfere in people's personal health care decisions" is a lie that must have polled well in some focus group study. Regardless of what these people believe, abortion is not a form of pregnancy-related health care. In reality, the Hyde Amendment protects the American citizen from being held financially responsible for the poor personal health care decisions being made by other individuals. Without experiencing the physical pleasure of sex, the taxpayer should be protected from the financial experience of being screwed. The progressive left loves to pander to their constituents by promising the forgiveness of any and all consequences related to personal choices. The Hyde Amendment is a legislative reminder that some level of personal accountability must be maintained.

"*Roe v. Wade*, a legal case in which the U.S. Supreme Court on January 22, 1973, ruled (7–2) that unduly restrictive state regulation of abortion is unconstitutional. In a majority opinion written by Justice Harry A. Blackmun, the Court held that a set of Texas statutes criminalizing abortion in most instances violated a woman's constitutional right of privacy, which it found to be implicit in the liberty guarantee of the due process clause of the Fourteenth Amendment ('…nor shall any state deprive any person of life, liberty, or property, without due process of law').

"The case began in 1970 when 'Jane Roe'—a fictional name used to protect the identity of the plaintiff, Norma McCorvey—instituted federal action against Henry Wade, the district attorney of Dallas County, Texas, where Roe resided. The Supreme Court disagreed with Roe's assertion of an absolute right to terminate pregnancy in any way and at any time and attempted to balance a woman's right of privacy with a state's interest in regulating abortion. In his opinion, Blackmun noted that only a 'compelling state interest' justifies regulations limiting 'fundamental rights' such as privacy and that legislators must therefore draw statutes narrowly 'to express only the legitimate state interests at stake.' The Court then attempted to balance the state's distinct compelling interests in the health of pregnant women and in the potential life of fetuses. It placed the point after which a state's compelling interest in the pregnant woman's health would allow it to regulate abortion 'at approximately the end of the first trimester' of pregnancy. With regard to the fetus, the Court located that point at 'capability of meaningful life outside the mother's womb,' or viability."[37]

While dancing the fine line between acknowledging "a woman's right to privacy" and simultaneously denying the assertion of "an absolute right to terminate pregnancy in any way and at any time," the Supreme Court added more questions than answers and may have acted beyond its authority.

The Supreme Court was attempting to set a time limit on how late an abortion can legally be obtained when the Court described "approximately the end of the first trimester" as the time frame for when the state could begin to consider regulatory steps. Since the date of conception is typically speculative at best, the use of the word "approximately" in a legal decision has only served to muddy the waters on this topic. Likewise, the Supreme Court appeared to be tipping their hat at the definition of "personhood" when they mentioned "capability of meaningful life outside the mother's womb," or viability.

It is discouraging to hear that the Supreme Court chose to focus on the Fourteenth Amendment when hearing this case. By the Court's own admission, they agreed that the state shall not deprive any *person* of "life," liberty, or property, without due process of law. In their decision regarding this case, it is clear that the only *person* being represented would be the mother, despite their attempts to mention the fetus in afterthought. How could the United Nations Human Rights Committee, the International Covenant on Civil and Political Rights, and the United States Supreme Court all conclude that "the right to life includes the right to access safe and legal abortion"?

In reality, the Supreme Court should have denied the writ of certiorari (regarding *Roe v. Wade*) based on the Tenth Amendment. The Tenth Amendment states that "the powers not delegated to the United States by the Constitution, nor prohibited by it to the States, are reserved to the States respectively, or to the people." Since there is absolutely no mention of abortion anywhere in the United States Constitution, the powers to decide whether an abortion can be performed were to remain within the individual states. The founders wrote the Tenth Amendment specifically for issues such as abortion and marriage laws. The Supreme Court abused its authority by taking the abortion case to trial.

Based on the analysis of the Center for Reproductive Rights, if the Supreme Court were to limit or overturn *Roe*, abortion would remain legal in twenty-one states and likely would be prohibited in twenty-four states.

In 1998, having undergone two religious conversions, Norma McCorvey publicly declared her opposition to abortion. In the documentary *AKA Jane Roe* (2020), however, a dying McCorvey claimed that she had been paid by antiabortion groups to support their cause. Isn't it amazing what a person lacking principles will do for money?

The Solution

Abstinence from sex is the only form of pregnancy prevention that is 100 percent effective. Every other method of contraception has a risk of failure. Couples who practice abstinence are much less likely to experience emotionally volatile relationships and are better suited as parents when the appropriate time actually arrives. Studies have revealed a connection between low self-esteem and early sexual activity. A person who deliberately chooses to wait to have sexual intercourse is less likely to look to a relationship for validation and may be more self-reliant. Abstinence costs nothing, and there are no unwanted side effects as with so many other forms of contraception. Abstinence is only required for a four-day period out of an entire 30-day month. If they cannot refrain from the activity for 13 percent of the month to avoid an unwanted consequence, then the problem becomes their own. Unfortunately, this option requires a great deal of self-discipline to stave off social and peer pressure. With perpetual social messaging promoting a state of nirvana, in which there is neither suffering, desire, nor sense of self and the subject is released from the effects of karma and guilt, abstinence has become rare. In fact, the safe, legal, and rare qualities being called for by abortion advocates seem to be more descriptive of sexual abstinence. If a couple cannot have this kind of conversation before sex, then perhaps they aren't intimate enough to be having sex.

Dr. Dónal O'Mathúna wrote an article discussing this concept of personal bodily autonomy and choice, and this is what she had to say:

"The principle of autonomy has become widely respected, especially in health care. In general, this is good. I'm glad we are putting behind us the days of clergy running people's lives, husbands making all the decisions for their wives, or doctors telling patients what to do. But, in moving away from one end of the spectrum, we must avoid swinging to the other extreme. Self-rule is what the Greek behind 'autonomy' literally means. 'It's my body, and I decide what happens to it.'

"When applied to abortion, this supports freedom of choice. If a woman finds herself to be pregnant, and does not want a baby, this 'self-rule autonomy' declares she should be free from interference and have no limitations on her choice. That misses what ethics is all about; making decisions that are right and good. Self-rule autonomy only tells us who should make the decisions, not whether the decision is ethical. In many areas of life our autonomy is limited. We cannot and should not do everything we WANT. Choices about the unborn should be no different.

"The approach I advocate is called 'relational autonomy.' This holds that people should make important decisions about their lives, but we should consider the impact of those decisions on those around us. Relationships bring ethical responsibilities which can put limits on autonomy.

"Abortions involve a pregnant woman, but other relationships are involved. A woman may not want to give birth for many reasons, some highly complicated, some tragic, some less weighty—most relational. All these situations are difficult, and lead to decisions that cannot be made lightly. But pulling out autonomy as an ethical trump card, does not address the deeper issues.

"Even when the life of the woman is threatened by pregnancy, it's not just about autonomy. I believe it is ethical to save one life when two cannot live. Two lives can be intimately related and in conflict with one another.

"If only one can live, the autonomy of each and the good of each can give ethical justification for saving only one of the lives. Relational autonomy better expresses the pain of this tragic situation, rather than claiming it is about freedom of choice.

"One way to decide when autonomy clashes with other ethical principles involves the so-called 'harm principle': that people have the freedom to do what they want, as long as they do not harm others. This is precisely where the 'freedom of choice' argument breaks down in abortion. There is always, an 'other,' where abortion is concerned. And by definition, that 'other' ends up dead. Whatever opportunities, or potential opportunities, the unborn might have; they are terminated totally.

"The unborn are one group of humans least able to express autonomy. Yet if given the opportunity, they, with the same uncertainties we experience, can become autonomous and live their lives. Society has a duty to protect the most vulnerable among us, including the unborn.

"Relational autonomy goes beyond the right to choose; it includes the responsibility to choose rightly. If we get into bed with someone, we take on certain responsibilities whether we acknowledge them or not. Intended or unintended, a pregnancy may result. This is partly why becoming sexually active is such a momentous decision, with most societies urging that it be reserved until a committed, permanent relationship exists to welcome a child into society.

"This aspect obviously doesn't apply in rape situations. If a woman had no choice in becoming pregnant, why should she be responsible for the unborn? Rape is abhorrent, and my heart goes out to anyone who has been raped. But at the same time, the unborn had nothing to do with the harm inflicted. Why should they be the ones to have their chance at life terminated? If allowing the unborn to grow and experience life is the right thing in other situations, it does not matter how the pregnancy came to be. Certainly, after rape, this would be very difficult; heroic in many ways. Taking away the life of the innocent because of a man's crime will not relieve the pain or bring justice. Allowing life to come from a heinous crime can let some good come from something bad.

"Moving away from rape situations, the unborn come to be because of a relationship. Those relationships bring responsibilities, for the father and the mother. Both are autonomous. Both have choices. And in the middle is a new, vulnerable being, entirely dependent on the choices others make.

"They can exercise self-rule autonomy and end that life. Or they can choose to promote the good of that life, helping one another in a difficult situation and giving the unborn a chance of becoming autonomous. The length of that life, how able it is, or how it got started, makes no difference ethically. The ethical decision involves helping those in need when they depend on us...Building a society like this is not easy, but worth it."[38]

> "Every person has the right to have his life respected. This right shall be protected by law and, in general, from the moment of conception. No one shall be arbitrarily deprived of his life."
>
> —American Convention on Human Rights, Article 4, 1969

Before the responsible parties make any life-or-death decisions regarding a vulnerable being with no say in the matter, the parents of this child should be forced to listen to the video testimony of Dr. Anthony Levatino as he speaks before the Judiciary Committee on October 8, 2015. In fact, viewing this testimony should be mandatory in every sex education class in America. Here is the transcript of that testimony:

"Chairman Goodlatte and distinguished members of the committee, my name is Anthony Levatino. I am a board-certified obstetrician gynecologist. I received my medical degree from Albany Medical College in Albany, NY in 1976 and completed my OB-GYN residency training at Albany Medical Center in 1980. In my 35-year career, I have been privileged to practice obstetrics and gynecology in both private and university settings. From June 1993 until September 2000, I was associate professor of OB-GYN at the Albany Medical College serving at different times as both medical student director and residency program director. I have also dedicated many years to private practice and currently operate a solo gynecology practice in Las Cruces, NM. **I appreciate your kind invitation to address issues related to *Planned Parenthood* and late term abortion in general**. During my residency training and during my first five years of private practice, **I performed both first and second trimester abortions**. During my residency in the late 1970s, second trimester abortions were typically performed using saline infusion or, occasionally, prostaglandin instillation techniques. These procedures were difficult, expensive and necessitated that patients go through labor to abort their pre-born children.

"By 1980, at the time I entered private practice first in Florida and then in upstate New York, those of us in the abortion industry were looking for a more efficient method of second trimester abortion. The Suction D&E procedure offered clear advantages over older instillation methods. The procedure was much quicker and never ran the risk of a live birth. Understand that my partner and I were not running an abortion clinic. We practiced general obstetrics and gynecology, but abortion was definitely a part of that practice.

Relatively few gynecologists in upstate NY would perform such a procedure and we saw an opportunity to expand our abortion practice. I performed first trimester suction D&C abortions in my office up to 10 weeks from last menstrual period and later procedures in an outpatient hospital setting. **From 1981 through February 1985, I performed approximately 1200 abortions. Over 100 of them were second trimester Suction D&E procedures up to 24 weeks gestation**.

"Imagine if you can that you are a pro-choice obstetrician/ gynecologist like I once was. Your patient today is 24 weeks pregnant. At twenty-four weeks from last menstrual period, her uterus is two finger-breadths above the umbilicus. **If you could see her baby, which is quite easy on an ultrasound, she would be as long as your hand plus a half from the top of her head to the bottom of her rump not counting the legs. Your patient has been feeling her baby kick for the last month or more** but now she is asleep on an operating room table and you are there to help her with her problem pregnancy.

"The first task is to remove the laminaria that had earlier been placed in the cervix to dilate it sufficiently to allow the procedure you are about to perform. With that accomplished, direct your attention to the surgical instruments arranged on a small table to your right. The first instrument you reach for is a 14-French suction catheter. It is clear plastic and about nine inches long. It has a bore through the center approximately ¾ of an inch in diameter. Picture yourself introducing this catheter through the cervix and instructing the circulating nurse to turn on the suction machine which is connected through clear plastic tubing to the catheter. What you will see is a pale, yellow fluid that looks a lot like urine coming through the catheter into a glass bottle on the suction machine. This is the amniotic fluid that surrounded the baby to protect her.

"With suction complete, look for your Sopher clamp. This instrument is about thirteen inches long and made of stainless

steel. At the business end are located jaws about 2 ½ inches long and about ¾ of an inch wide with rows of sharp ridges or teeth. This instrument is for grasping and crushing tissue. When it gets hold of something, it does not let go. A second trimester D&E abortion is a blind procedure. The baby can be in any orientation or position inside the uterus. Picture yourself reaching in with the Sopher clamp and grasping anything you can. At twenty-four weeks gestation, the uterus is thin and soft so be careful not to perforate or puncture the walls. Once you have grasped something inside, squeeze on the clamp to set the jaws and pull hard – really hard. You feel something let go and out pops a fully formed leg about six inches long. Reach in again and grasp whatever you can. Set the jaw and pull really hard once again and out pops an arm about the same length. Reach in again and again with that clamp and tear out the spine, intestines, heart and lungs.

"The toughest part of a D&E abortion is extracting the baby's head. The head of a baby that age is about the size of a large plum and is now free floating inside the uterine cavity. You can be pretty sure you have hold of it if the Sopher clamp is spread about as far as your fingers will allow. You will know you have it right when you crush down on the clamp and see white gelatinous material coming through the cervix. That was the baby's brains. You can then extract the skull pieces. Many times, a little face will come out and stare back at you. Congratulations! You have just successfully performed a second trimester Suction D&E abortion. You just affirmed her right to choose.

"I want to make a comment on the necessity and usefulness of utilizing second and third trimester abortion to save women's lives. I often hear the argument late-term legal abortion is necessary to save women's lives in cases of life-threatening conditions that can and do arise in pregnancy. Albany Medical Center where I worked for over seven years is a tertiary referral center that accepts patients with life threatening conditions related to or caused by pregnancy. I personally treated hundreds of women with such conditions in my tenure there. There are several serious conditions that can arise or worsen typically during the late second or third trimester of pregnancy that require immediate care. In many of those cases, ending or "terminating" the pregnancy, if you prefer, can be life-saving. But is abortion a viable treatment option in this setting? I maintain that it usually, if not always, is not.

"Before a Suction D&E procedure can be performed, the cervix must first be sufficiently dilated. In my practice, this was accomplished with serial placement of laminaria. Laminaria is a type of sterilized seaweed that absorbs water over several hours and swells to several times its original diameter. Multiple placements of several laminaria at a time are absolutely required prior to attempting a suction D&E. In the mid second trimester, this requires approximately 36 hours or more to accomplish. **When performing later abortion procedures, cervical preparation can take up to three days or more. In cases where a mother's life is seriously threatened by her pregnancy, a doctor more often than not doesn't have 36 hours, much less 72 hours, to resolve the problem**.

"Let me illustrate with a real-life case that I managed while at the Albany Medical Center. A patient arrived one night at 28 weeks gestation with severe pre-eclampsia or toxemia. Her blood pressure on admission was 220/160. As you are probably aware, a normal blood pressure is approximately 120/80. **This patient's pregnancy was a threat to her life and the life of her unborn child. She could very well be minutes or hours away from a major stroke. This case was managed successfully by rapidly stabilizing the patient's blood pressure and 'terminating' her pregnancy by Cesarean section. She and her baby did well**. This is a typical case in the world of high-risk obstetrics.

"In most such cases, any attempt to perform an abortion 'to save the mother's life' would entail undue and dangerous delay in providing appropriate, truly life-saving care. During my time at Albany Medical Center, I managed hundreds of such cases by 'terminating' pregnancies to save mother's [sic] lives. In all those hundreds of cases, the number of unborn children that I had to deliberately kill was zero."[39]

If you can't hear the baby scream when the arm is being ripped off by the Sopher clamp during the abortion, is that because the baby can't "feel," or is it because nobody can hear the baby scream? Perhaps it is because the baby hasn't learned how to outwardly express its pain? Regardless of the reason, it is apparent that sentience is a preposterous metric for determining an acceptable timeline for an abortion. The pseudoscience of sentience gives the misguided impression that a green leafy plant has more "sensation" and therefore, a greater right to live than a human fetus with a heartbeat. It is tragic that people who weren't aborted are voting for others to be aborted. People in this camp love the idea of humanity but clearly hate human beings.

> "The debate is not about humanity, or life. It is about personhood."
>
> —Clare White

"Alabama Governor, Kay Ivey, signed what many consider the nation's strictest abortion law. The law makes any physician, performing an abortion, guilty of a felony in almost all cases. As expected, the national media have been critical of the Alabama law and have given little attention to the Alabama legislature's goal, which is to challenge the landmark 1973 *Roe v. Wade* Supreme Court decision by establishing personhood for a baby inside the womb. With personhood, the Constitution affords certain rights and protections. Senator Clyde Chambliss, the sponsor of the bill said, 'The way that this bill is drafted – it goes to ask the question of personhood.' He then added, 'The 14th Amendment gives people…a person…the right to life, liberty and property; but it doesn't say when a person becomes a person.' 'And so, we need some guidance,' he continued. 'We need some guidance from the Supreme Court. So, this bill has been drafted so that it goes directly to the Supreme Court to have that question answered.' The purpose of the law is to challenge the Supreme Court's 1973's *Roe v. Wade* decision by establishing a baby in the womb as a person."[40]

If for no other purpose than to challenge when personhood actually begins, the Alabama abortion law may be the single most perfect piece of legislature written in the last decade.

The lack of exceptions in the cases of rape and incest is what makes this piece of legislature so pure. "Adding the exceptions for rape and incest could possibly negate the argument that the baby in the womb is a person. How could you reasonably argue that the baby inside the womb is a person if conceived one way, but not a person if the baby was conceived in rape or incest? It was that type of reasoning that was used to make the *Roe v. Wade* decision: that the baby in the womb was not a person. The intention of the bill is to be a legal challenge to *Roe v. Wade* and force the court to rule definitively on the personhood status of the baby in the womb regardless of how the baby was conceived."[40]

Since the Alabama abortion law only makes it a felony for the abortion provider, there is virtually no legal jeopardy for the woman. Would this make it illegal for a provider to prescribe the morning-after pill, since one would only take that if they thought they were pregnant, and this bill makes abortion illegal from the moment a woman suspects she is pregnant? In short, the morning-after pill, as prescribed, is legally considered birth control and not a form of abortion.

"There has been considerable public confusion about the difference between the Morning-After pill and the Abortion pill. The Morning-After pill, also known as emergency contraception, helps prevent pregnancy if taken within five days of having unprotected sex. The Abortion pill, also known as medication abortion, is designed to end the pregnancy. Hormonal methods of contraception including: the Morning-After pill; prevents pregnancy by inhibiting ovulation and fertilization. The Morning-After pill will not induce an abortion in a woman who is already pregnant, nor will it affect the developing pre-embryo or embryo. Emergency contraception prevents pregnancy and helps a woman prevent the need for abortion."[41]

With a Democrat-run Labor, Health and Human Services, Education, and related agencies, there is an onslaught of new legislative abortion bills being presented. These new bills are calling for everything from legally killing a baby at any time during a woman's pregnancy for any reason at all and even (according to a bill in Virginia) up to the time when the mother is dilating, to repealing the current Hyde Amendment protections. The recent Democrat-controlled Appropriations Committee held a hearing on the Hyde Amendment, and they concluded that blocking direct taxpayer funding of abortion is somehow "racist and discriminatory." The truth is: 259,336 black babies aborted per year is a clear demonstration of who the real racists are. Pro-abortion politicians know that repealing the Hyde Amendment will line the pockets of their pals at Planned Parenthood, who will return the favor by funding their political campaigns to the tune of millions of dollars.

The abortionists are literally writing speeches for the Democrat Party. The abortionists are also coming to their defense when these politicians are confronted by the media, the American people, and even some members of their own party. When these politicians speak, they are reciting speeches from Planned Parenthood, the National Abortion and Reproductive Rights Action League, and massively funded groups such as the Arabella Advisors strategy company, which uses a web of fronts to push the interests of wealthy leftist donors. "The *Arabella Advisors* has been quietly behind key activism seeking to allow the use of federal funds to pay for abortions. *Arabella Advisors* is a centralized hub that runs nonprofit arms that in turn have spawned a nexus of hundreds of front organizations outwardly designed to appear grassroots, but actually working against ordinary people by expanding government control in the lives of Americans."[42] The bottom line is, more taxpayer funding for abortion means more abortion.

The blood money doesn't end there for Planned Parenthood. Video evidence has revealed a scandal involving the illegal sale of fetal tissues. Of course, Planned Parenthood claims that the tissues were shared legally. In fact, the undercover activist that blew the cover on this operation was prosecuted for trespassing and fraud. This is exactly the kind of protection that Planned Parenthood expected with its millions of dollars in political donations. Are fetal tissue sales being used as another financial incentive to destroy the most vulnerable among us?

In 1988 Congress passed a federal ban on fetal tissue research, but that ban was overturned by the Clinton administration in 1993. Fetal tissue is used in stem-cell research along with other research and testing to help find cures and treatments to diseases such as cancer and HIV. After a nine-month investigation by the US Department of Health and Human Services, the department said federal funding can still be granted to fetal tissue research, but there will be a stricter screening process and more scrutiny on the projects going forward.

It is time that the Supreme Court makes a legal ruling to define when personhood actually begins. Once this precedent is set, the states will have to adapt their individual laws accordingly. The time for ambiguity is over. This can no longer be allowed to stand as a political pawn to manipulate voters to one side of the aisle or the other. The 10th Amendment is clear: "The powers not delegated to the United States by the Constitution, nor prohibited by it to the States, are reserved to the States respectively, or to the people." Since abortion is not mentioned anywhere in the Constitution, it is up to the states respectively to make determinations on the legality or illegality of abortion procedures, and it is up to the respective states to determine when abortion violates the rights of the unborn person as determined legally and scientifically by the guidance of the Supreme Court of the land. Repealing *Roe v. Wade* would not prevent a woman from obtaining an abortion. It would simply limit her options to the states that approve of such procedures.

Furthermore, the Constitution protects property rights through the Fifth and Fourteenth Amendments' Due Process Clauses, and more directly, through the Fifth Amendment's "Taking Clause," which says: "Nor shall private property be taken for public use without just compensation." The Hyde Amendment follows the premise of these amendments, and therefore, any attempt to repeal the Hyde Amendment would be a violation of the private property rights of the citizens of this country.

These leftist idealogues claim that we need to import migrants to do the work because we don't have enough of a population to do the amount of work necessary, but they are the first to promote aborting members of our own natural workforce. While legislative policy can make a minor difference, the only thing that really drives the economy is procreation. Yes, sex is the answer to the economic puzzle. These millennials that are waiting until they are 30–35 years old before having children of their own will be the death of our economy. That is a 10–15-year gap in our economy that may be impossible to recover from. An average of 2.6 children per family is necessary to drive our economy. Apparently, nobody told the millennials that their children are going to be paying for *their* Social Security.

Bernie Sanders and Alexandria Ocasio-Cortez (and their climate alarmism) are also scaring people away from having children. Promoting their Gaia theories by talking about population control for the sake of the planet is a huge disservice to the country. From calling a fetus a "clump of cells," to falsely claiming abortion is "health care," the left has demonstrated a disturbing willingness to ignore the facts (and the science) when it is beneficial to their control of political power.

Chapter Seven:

Health Care

"The art of medicine consists of amusing the patient while nature cures the disease."

—Voltaire

"Poor health is not caused by something you don't have; it's caused by disturbing something that you already have. Healthy is not something that you need to get, it's something you have already if you don't disturb it."

—Dean Ornish

In virtually every instance encountered in life, the American person is infinitely better suited to manage his or her private affairs than the government. So why are so many politicians lobbying to control the American health care system?

"A survey in 2019 found that Americans trust Amazon more than the federal government. The most trusted entities were our military, Amazon, Google, local police, and universities. Congress came in as the least trusted, edging out political parties and the press. Bureaucratic incompetence and cronyism are not the only reasons we should be wary of government involvement in our medical care. The federal government has a checkered history when it comes to medical judgments.

"By the 1920s, thirty-three states had forced sterilization laws. Heads of psychiatric institutions were free to sterilize anyone they considered social misfits. We now cringe at the words of the revered Supreme Court Justice Oliver Wendell Holmes in the 1927 case *Buck v Bell* upholding Virginia's sterilization law for the institutionalized 'feeble-minded:'

'[Carrie Bell's] welfare and that of society will be promoted by her sterilization. It is better for all the world if, instead of waiting to execute degenerate offspring for crime or to let them starve for their imbecility, society can prevent those who are manifestly unfit from continuing their kind...Three generations of imbeciles are enough.'

—Justice Oliver Wendell Holmes

"In fact, Carrie's mother was a prostitute, but not feeble-minded. After Carrie's release, she maintained a job as a domestic worker and became an avid reader. Her 'feeble-minded' daughter was on her school's honor roll.

"With the third branch of the federal government on board, between 1909 and 1979 more than 20,000 government-funded forced sterilizations were performed. The last legal forced sterilization was in 1981. These went beyond the mentally challenged. Latinos and blacks were easy targets, particularly in the 1970's after Medicaid-funded family planning services offered sterilization. Some patients were bullied into consenting with threats of having their welfare benefits or medical care taken away. Sometimes patients were coerced into a tubal ligation immediately after their infant's delivery. At other times, tubal ligations were done during Cesarean sections unbeknownst to the patients.

These sterilizations were such an open practice in the South that they became known as a 'Mississippi appendectomy.'

"In North Carolina, an IQ of 70 or lower qualified a person for sterilization. Here, state social workers could file petitions for sterilization. One social worker sterilized her entire caseload.

"The Indian Health Service with its captive audience was worse. Between 1973 and 1976 some 3,400 Native American women—including minors—were sterilized without permission or with defective consent forms."[43]

It would be hypocritical to ridicule the progressive wing of the Democrat Party for ignoring progress away from past government indiscretions without noting that these heinous policies promoting forced sterilizations have since been corrected, but it must be noted that these incidents did occur. With leftist politicians threatening population control for the sake of halting climate change, will forced sterilization be making an ugly comeback in the near future?

"The 'Tuskegee Study of Untreated Syphilis in the Negro Male' lasted from 1932 to 1972. The U.S. Public Health Service used 400 mainly poor, illiterate, black sharecroppers with syphilis as lab animals. They were told they had 'bad blood,' but not that they were actually suffering from a serious disease. That was the extent of the 'informed consent.' In exchange for having their lives ruined, the men received free medical exams, free meals, and burial insurance. Although originally projected to last 6 months, the study actually went on for 40 years. The men were never given adequate treatment for their disease. Even when penicillin became the drug of choice for syphilis in 1947, researchers did not offer it to the subjects; nor were the subjects given the choice of quitting the study.

All subjects succumbed to untreated syphilis so our government could track the natural progression of the disease. Once the study became public in 1972, it took a nine-person panel appointed by the assistant secretary for health and scientific affairs to decide that the study was 'ethically unjustified.' A class-action lawsuit filed the next year resulted in a $10 million dollar settlement for the victims and their families."[43]

Additionally, "Operation Sea Spray" allowed for a bacterium known as S*erratia marcescens* to be experimentally sprayed by the US Navy over San Francisco. It was later learned that the US Army had also conducted 239 open-air tests of biological agents over populated civilian areas over a 20-year time span.

"The noted 19th century statesman and orator Daniel Webster said:

'Good intentions will always be pleaded, for every assumption of power; but they cannot justify it…It is hardly too strong to say, that the Constitution was made to guard the people against the dangers of good intention, real or pretended.'

"Given the government's track record, even the most jaded bureaucrat cannot justify such betrayals of patient's rights and the public trust.

"There is another theme between the lines: offer the people free stuff and then use it as a cudgel to keep the recipients in line. The helpless, the poor, and Native Americans were easy targets. Now 'Medicare for All' threatens to trap the rest of us in a system with no escape."[43]

The Emotional Lie

Bernie Sanders and the progressive arm of the Democrat Party say to the private health insurance companies: "Whether you like it or not, the United States will join every other major country on earth and guarantee health care to all people as a right. All Americans are entitled to go to the doctor when they're sick and not go bankrupt after staying in the hospital." They want to create a Medicare for All, single-payer, national health insurance program to provide everyone in America with comprehensive health care coverage, free at the point of service. In other words; they believe that health care is a human right, not a privilege.

They will tell you that the health of an individual is less about their personal behaviors and more about unfair economic circumstances. When Matt Hancock, the British health secretary, described "preventing ill health" as one of his main priorities rather than just "treating it," he was ridiculed. Hancock argued that "prevention is about ensuring that people take greater responsibility for managing their own health…It's about people choosing to look after themselves better, staying active and stopping smoking. Prevention is about making better choices; by limiting alcohol, sugar, salt and fat." In other words, he believed that people should take more responsibility for their own behavior by making more healthy choices and less unhealthy ones.

The progressives were quick to contest by saying:

"But decades of research show that health is not determined by our personal choices but rather the conditions in which we are born, grow, live, work, and age. Our access to these conditions is dependent upon our place in society. The poorer you are and the poorer the area in which you live, the less likely you are to have a stable job and control at work, a decent home, or an income to afford a healthy diet. All of these affect your health, either by restricting the healthy choices available to you, by leaving you in poor environmental circumstances (damp or cold housing affecting your respiratory health, for instance), or by affecting your psychosocial state (such as insecurity in work or a low position in the social hierarchy affecting your mental health).

Evidence has shown that approaches that try to change individual behavior may even make health inequalities worse, since those who take up the behavior changes are those who are most able to—those higher up the socioeconomic ladder, those who already have better health.

To improve life expectancy and narrow the gap between rich and poor, we need policies that nurture the conditions of a healthy life, like quality employment, adequate incomes, and good housing. Broccoli isn't the issue."[44]

These leftists will lie to you and tell you that Obamacare actually made health care affordable. They will bend every rule to convince the American people that the government is responsible for health care, and in fact, it was a Republican idea. And when those emotional lies aren't enough, they will use guilt as a tool to tell America that getting rid of Obamacare will strip 20 million people of their necessary health insurance coverage. Any Republican standing in the way of Obamacare just wants people to die.

"Incredibly, we spend significantly more of our national GDP on this inadequate health care system—far more per person than any other major country. And despite doing so, Americans have worse health outcomes and a higher infant mortality rate than countries that spend much less on health care. Our people deserve better."

—Bernie Sanders

The Truth

If Bernie is correct when he says that we spend significantly more of our national GDP on health care, then how is spending $57.4 trillion more going to help?

If there were no doctors in the United States, would health care still be a right? Is health care a right for the person that eats themselves to 400 pounds and becomes diabetic and then develops gangrene and has to have their toes amputated? To what extent is the government obligated to ensure that person's health? What about the person that refuses to quit smoking after developing lung cancer? How many lungs should we purge from others' who have lived clean lives to provide healthy lung transplants to those who make poor health choices? How many liver transplants are the taxpayers on the dole for; for the alcoholic that refuses to quit drinking? If health care is a right, these people can continue to make horrible choices about their health, and the government must provide them the care necessary to continue to live. Does this concept also nullify any living will? The person has expressed a right to die under certain circumstances, but what takes precedence if the government declares that health care is a right?

In a Senate Health, Education, Labor and Pensions subcommittee hearing on May 11, 2011, Rand Paul addressed this issue of health care as a human right by saying:

"With regard to the idea of whether you have a right to health care, you have to realize what that implies. It's not an abstraction. I'm a physician. That means you have a right to come to my house and conscript me. It means you believe in slavery. It means that you're going to enslave not only me, but the janitor at my hospital, the person who cleans my office, the assistants who work in my office, and the nurses.

"Basically, once you imply a belief in a right to someone's services... You're saying you believe in taking and extracting services from another person. Our founding documents were very clear about this. You have a right to pursue happiness, but there's no guarantee of physical comfort. There's no guarantee of concrete items. In order to give something concrete, you have to take it from someone. So, there's an implied threat of force.

"If I'm a physician in your community and you say you have a right to health care, do you have the right to beat down my door with the police, escort me away and force me to take care of you? That's ultimately what the right to free health care would be. If you believe in a right to health care, your belief is basically in the use of force to conscript someone to do your bidding."

The whole purpose of Obamacare was to make health care affordable. Government, particularly the Democrats, need to understand that health care is *not* the same thing as health insurance or insurance subsidies. Conflating the meanings of these terms is a disservice to the citizens of this country. The Band-Aid political approach needs to end. To make health care truly affordable we need to address the underlying problems that increase the actual costs of health care. By making a centralized, single-payer system that is subsidized or paid for by the federal government, they are creating just another entitlement program that ultimately becomes a monopoly ripe for corruption.

The 10th Amendment makes it clear that any governmental health care policies should be handled at the state and local levels rather than the federal level. Not only would these local governments be better suited to create such programs and negotiate cost solutions, but it would remove the federal government from any conflict of interest because it is the responsibility of the federal government to help protect the citizens against the creation of a monopoly.

The Marxists, desperately attempting to move this country into a socialist nightmare, are eager to centralize all of the decision-making power into the federal government. They will use every emotional trigger in their power to wrangle support for their historically failed ideology. They will show you a picture of a child with cancer and then (based on pure emotion) will tell you that we need to help that child via government-run health care. However, we can help that child now without ruining the current health care system. It is called charity, and that is a whole lot easier when the government is not ravaging your wallet with health care tax mandates. The Democrat Party has given up on the notion of compassion and generosity; that is why they feel the need to mandate generosity through government wealth redistribution programs. The problem with acting on emotion now is that ten years from now, after ruining health care and our economy, that emotion is gone—and we are stuck with the logical consequences of our actions.

When the Democrats tell the American public that 20 million people will lose their insurance if Obamacare is repealed, they neglect to disclose the fact that those are the same 20 million people that were forced to get the insurance or risk paying hefty fines for opting out of the mandates set forth by Obamacare. The proponents of the single-payer system also fail to mention the enormous price tag on this wealth redistribution scam. While supporters will claim a cost of $40.9 trillion over the next ten years, the actual cost will fall closer to $57.4 trillion after an, unaccounted for, increase in demand occurs. Even at the lowest estimate, the cost of health care will nearly double the annual fiscal budget of the federal government.

When pressed, even Bernie Sanders had to admit that income taxes on the middle class would have to go up to pay for universal health care. He errantly maintained that the savings in medical expenses would more than offset the tax hike. Without a single ounce of research or statistical evidence to back up his claims, Bernie purports to know more about the industry's bottom line than all of the actuarial scientists that work for those evil insurance companies.

"People who have health care under 'Medicare for All' will have no premiums, no deductibles, no copayments, and no out-of-pocket expenses. Yes, they will pay more in taxes, but less in health care for what they get."

—Bernie Sanders

But how does Bernie explain those increases in taxes to healthy people who seldom if ever utilize the health insurance? According to the Associated Press fact-checkers, taxes would significantly increase as "the Government takes on trillions of dollars in health care costs that were once covered by employers and individuals." How those tax increases would be divvied up remains to be seen, but you can bet that those in the middle class are going to be called upon to redistribute their wealth to those with an inability to pay.

"U.S. District Court Judge, Rosemary Collyer ruled that the Obama administration was unconstitutionally spending federal money to fund Obama's health care law. The Obama administration was unconstitutionally spending money to subsidize health insurers without obtaining an appropriation from Congress. She ruled that the administration was violating a provision of the law by paying promised reimbursements to health insurers who provided coverage at reduced costs to low-income Americans. The 38-page legal opinion highlighted the repeated complaint that Obama and his administration had ignored constitutional limits on their authority. The health care law said insurers who enroll eligible, low-income Americans shall cover the costs of their deductibles and co-payments, but promised the federal Government 'shall make periodic and timely payments' to cover those costs. The law was not entirely clear on where that money would come from."[45]

"The Democrats are pushing for Government controlled health care based on the 'quality of life' rather than God's 'sanctity of life.' In other words, a board will decide whether or not the quality of your life is worth Government spending money to preserve it.

If they decide you are too old to spend money on, or if you own a gun, the board will say no surgery for you. I'm talking Government death panels assuming the role of God; deciding who lives and who dies."[46] Lloyd Marcus, in the previous quote, is referring to the "quality-adjusted life years" system.

"One concern raised by critics of a government-run, single-payer health care system like 'Medicare for All' is that the government will start rationing health care to keep costs down. But some health care industry players are already trying to ration health care by using the 'quality-adjusted life years' system.

"Quality-adjusted life years were 'originally developed as a measure of health effectiveness for cost-effectiveness analysis, a method intended to aid decision makers charged with allocating scarce resources across competing health care programs,' according to the medical journal '*Value in Health*.' They are used by firms like the United Kingdom's National Institute for Health and Care Excellence and the United States' Institute for Clinical and Economic Review to guide drug pricing decision making.

"Sometimes these firms use quality-adjusted life years' analysis to pressure drug companies to lower their prices. However, they also are used to prevent drugs from going to market, or to discourage health insurance companies from covering costly drugs; which can prevent patients from receiving life-saving or life improving treatments.

"Here's how it works: if a person receives a quality-adjusted life years value of 0.5, that means they have 50 percent of the value of one year of life of a healthy person. The underlying principle is to mathematically quantify the quality of life for people with certain health conditions."[47]

"Quality-adjusted life year systems are a very crude measure, and typically fail to capture what matters most to patients...Using these crude assessments to argue well, maybe another couple, years of life aren't that important after all, and then putting a dollar on that... there's a lower dollar value placed on your extra year of life than for other people."

—Andrew Sperling

"Sperling said that the U.S. Medicare system already has other discriminatory problems, so he's worried that a Medicare for All plan would discriminate against anyone with a unique or chronic health condition. The 2010 Affordable Care Act banned Medicare from using 'cost-effectiveness research,' but the National Disability Council thinks the language is too vague and recently said Congress should explicitly ban the use of a quality-adjusted life years system across all federal programs (state Medicaid programs are allowed to use these systems). But the more pressing problem is that American drug companies and health insurance companies are already listening to the Institute for Clinical and Economic Review and allowing the quality-adjusted life years method to dictate how and whether or not patients get the drugs they need. 'In an effort to lower their health care costs, public and private health insurance providers have utilized quality-adjusted life year systems to determine the cost-effectiveness of medications and treatments,' the National Disability Council wrote in a letter to President Donald Trump. 'The lives of people with disabilities are equally valuable to those without disabilities, and health care decisions based on devaluing the lives of people with disabilities are discriminatory.'"[47]

Like so many of the utopian programs and policies presented by the progressive branch of the Democrat Party, the Medicare for All program comes with many hidden pitfalls. If the Medicare for All program had already been implemented, with the hidden "quality adjusted life years" provision, Ruth Bader-Ginsburg would not have been eligible for multiple cancer treatments that likely prolonged her life. Like so many Democrats who place "collective productivity" above all else, Ezekiel Emanuel summed up this Marxist ideology in an article he wrote in 2014. His article titled "Why I Hope to Die at 75" was his argument that "society, families…and you…will be better off if nature takes its course swiftly and promptly."

In the article Emanuel writes:

"I am sure of my position. Doubtless, death is a loss. It deprives us of experiences and milestones, of time spent with our spouse and children. In short, it deprives us of all the things we value.

"But here is a simple truth that many of us seem to resist: living too long is also a loss. It renders many of us, if not disabled, then faltering and declining; a state that may not be worse than death but nonetheless deprived. **It robs us of our creativity and ability to contribute to: work, society, and the world**. It transforms how people experience us, relate to us, and, most importantly, remember us. We are no longer remembered as vibrant and engaged but as feeble, ineffectual, even pathetic."

Of course, Ruth Bader-Ginsburg may have some dissenting opinions on his ruling.

Here is another myth-busting truth: Obamacare was not a Republican idea. When liberal Democrats couldn't get their dream of a single-payer system, they panicked. Then when Obamacare declined into one false promise after another, and with skyrocketing increases to the private cost of the insurance:

"The assembled denizens of the professional Left were scrambling in earnest to register their excuses with the public. Thus far at least, the award for the most creative contribution goes to former labor secretary, Robert Reich, whose paean to single-payer health care managed to combine all of the most dishonest talking points that have bubbled up…while constructing in tandem a counterfactual so dazzling that only the truest of apostles could be persuaded by it.

"In a column titled '*The Democrats' Version of Health Insurance Would Have Been Cheaper, Simpler, and More Popular (So Why Did We Enact the Republican Version and Why Are They So Upset)*' Reich claims that if 'Democrats [had] stuck to the original Democratic vision and built comprehensive health insurance on Social Security and Medicare, it would have been cheaper, simpler, and more widely accepted by the public.' And, he added for good measure, 'Republicans would be hollering anyway.'

"The underlying conceit here, that the Democratic party had the option of 'sticking to the original vision' of single-payer, but that it instead settled on Obamacare as part of some sort of grand compromise; is fairly popular among the law's apologists these days. Democrats, meanwhile, are presented as being too nice...for having elected to placate the Republican Party by forgoing pursuit of what they truly wanted: Medicare for All.

"Reassuring as this tale might be to those who are worriedly surveying the damage that Healthcare.gov has wrought upon their project; it remains self-evidently absurd. Obamacare was passed into law without a single Republican vote. It is a law that the Republicans actively opposed when it was suggested in a similar form by President Clinton during the 1990s.

"Reich's fantasy account of a 'restrained Democratic party' doesn't hold up either. There is a devastatingly dull reason the bulletproof Democratic majority of 2008 didn't build 'comprehensive health insurance on Social Security and Medicare,' and that is that it didn't have the votes. Indeed, with full control of the government, Democrats didn't even have the votes to set up a public insurance option, let alone take over the whole system.

"As for Reich's claim that a single-payer system would have been 'more widely accepted by the public:' is he joking? So acutely aware were the president and his allies in Congress of the fact that the vast majority of Americans did not want to lose their current insurance that, like so many traveling salesmen on the frontier, they just brazenly lied; promising things of their product that it could never possibly deliver...and assiduously playing down the scale of the chance that their customers were taking. Again, with Obamacare *as it is now*, the president was forced onto the defensive, provoked into repeating his mantra that 'if you like your health-care plan, you will be able to keep your health-care plan' and into reassuring voters that 'no one will take it away – no matter what.' One can only imagine what he would have had to promise if he had been peddling single-payer.

"As any good liar knows, it is the chaotic and amorphous opening days of any disaster that provide the opportunities for the most ambitious spin. Refusing to allow anything as prosaic as the truth to intrude upon their fantasies, progressives are engaged in an audacious attempt to blame their opponents for their signature mistake and, worse, to pretend that the solution to the havoc wrought by magical thinking is to commission even more magic.

"With Obamacare failing in precisely the ways that they predicted it would, conservatives have been given an extraordinary hammer. They must not let their opponents take it from their hands."[48]

"Health insurance plans available before implementation of the Affordable Care Act often provided more limited benefits and coverage than plans available after implementation of Obamacare provisions. Earlier plans did not have to meet Obamacare's 'minimum essential benefit' requirements and, in many cases, were not required to cover pre-existing medical conditions.

"According to *eHealth* (the largest private health insurance market in the United States), during the time period between 2013 and the first two months of the 2017 open enrollment period... average individual premiums increased 99% while average family premiums increased 140%."[49]

It was called the Affordable Care Act, but it was anything but affordable. Subsidizing the insurance created an entire cascade of problems. Most of those problems actually resulted in even greater health care costs. For instance, the lower financial responsibility to the patient empowered many doctors to increase their revenue by calling for more frivolous testing. Imagine a grocery store owner being told by the federal government that every customer in the store would only be charged ten dollars per cart, regardless of the contents of that cart. Then imagine that same federal government telling the store owner that the government would pay the remaining balance for anything over ten dollars in value. It would only be a matter of time before the store owner would be stopping customers at the register because their shopping carts were only half full. It would no longer matter if the customer could actually consume everything they were taking, or if they even needed those products. Waste, fraud, abuse, and corruption always accompany programs that are backed by a government's promise to pay. Health care providers were encouraging people to take more than they needed.

"The Congressional Budget Office released a report entitled, '*Key Design Components and Consideration for Establishing a Single-Payer Health Care System*,' which outlined many of the risks of establishing a one-size-fits-all health care system, much like the Democrats' Medicare for All. According to the Congressional Budget Office report, these risks could include:

"'Government spending on health care would increase substantially under a single-payer system.'

"'Shifting such a large amount, of expenditures, from private to public sources would require substantial additional government resources.'

"'Because the public plan would provide a specified set of health care services to everyone eligible, participants would not have a choice of insurer or health benefits, and might not address the needs of some people.'

"'By owning and operating hospitals and employing physicians, the government would have more control over the health care delivery system, but it would also take on more responsibilities.'

"'The transition would entail significant changes for providers, and those changes could lead to lower quality of care for patients.'

"'Setting payment rates equal to Medicare Fee-For-Service rates under a single-payer system would reduce the average payment rates most providers receive—often substantially; which means the care providers would actually earn less than currently.'

"'Lower payment rates, to the providers, would probably reduce the amount of care supplied and could also reduce the quality of care.'

"'Decisions about which new treatments and technologies would be covered would have a significant effect on innovations, as well as on the development of new treatments and technologies over time.'

"'In addition to its potential effects on the health care sector, a single-payer system would affect other sectors of the economy. Labor supply and employees' compensation could change because health insurance is an important part of employees' compensation under the current system.'"[50]

"As Congress voted on the Affordable Care Act, or Obamacare, in 2010, one of the bill's architects, Jonathan Gruber, told a college audience that those pushing legislation pitched it as a bill that would control spiraling health care costs even though most of the bill was focused on something else and there was no guarantee the bill would actually bend the cost curve...Gruber discussed how those pushing the bill took part in an 'exploitation of the lack of economic understanding of the American voter,' taking advantage of voter's 'stupidity' to create a law that would ultimately be good for them. In a series of videos, Gruber suggested that Obamacare proponents engaged in less-than-honest salesmanship.

"'Barack Obama's not a stupid man, okay?' Gruber said in his remarks at the College of the Holy Cross on March 11, 2010. 'He knew when he was running for president that quite frankly the American public doesn't actually care that much about the uninsured...What the American public cares about is costs. And that's why even though the bill that they made is 90% health insurance coverage and 10% about cost control, all you ever hear people talk about is cost control. How it's going to lower the cost of health care, that's all they talk about. Why? Because that's what people want to hear about; because a majority of Americans care about health care costs.' Gruber said attempts to control costs in a real way were politically untenable."[51]

Like spokes inside of a large health care "cost factors" wheel, there are many factors that contribute to the escalating cost of health care. Those factors include: education costs to the health care providers, loss prevention risks to health care providers, pharmaceutical companies gouging prices, skyrocketing malpractice and liability insurance rates for providers, the ever-increasing number of people on disability, patients with pre-existing conditions tainting the private insurance pools, minimum essential benefits requirements, cost sharing, the Cadillac Tax, a lack of free market insurance competition across state lines, Health Savings Account contribution limits, government-mandated insurance coverage for health care employees, endless raises in continuing education requirements, increasing corporate tax rates, frivolous lawsuits, diminishing health due to personal choices such as obesity, as well as cigarette and alcohol use, opioid drug addiction, the use of genetically modified organisms in our food, synthetic sweeteners in our food, illegal migrants using the emergency room as their primary care provision, as well as an increasing number of people (affected by these rising costs) suddenly becoming unable to afford their health care costs and falling into a situation of dependence on the government for their health care needs.

When Barack Obama said, "We are five days away from fundamentally transforming the United States of America," little did we know that every policy stance, every social reform, and every executive order signed was another step further and further in the direction of a completely centralized government that was hell-bent on feeding itself power while slowly eliminating individual liberties. Intentional or unintentional, the results have been a full-on progression toward socialism in the United States of America. Fueled by emotional manipulation and the promise of free stuff, the radical left arm of the Democratic Party has consistently moved in this direction. Of the eight levels of control that must be obtained before you are able to create a social state, number one on the list is health care. Remember, "Control health care, and you control the people." Despite the fact there is no mention of the word "health care" in the United States Constitution, the federal government is becoming more and more involved in the control and regulation of the health care system in America.

For an example of this government overreach simply look at the way the government handled the Covid-19 crisis. At every opportunity, the governors and many of our elected officials in Washington used a global pandemic to seize more regulatory power at the expense of personal liberties. In many ways they amplified and inflated this crisis in order to perpetuate fear. Then they used that fear to manipulate everything from the changing of election rules to picking winners and losers in the economy.

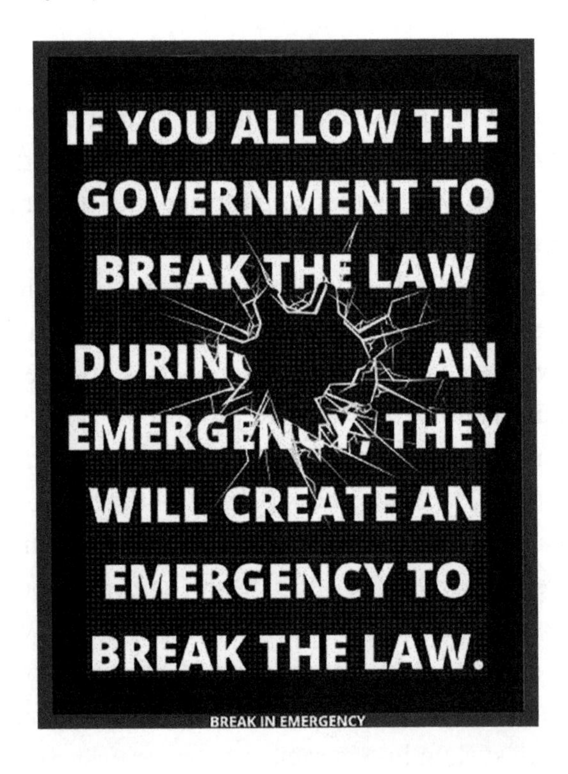

It is no secret that, under the guise of safety, the state and federal government was slowly picking away at the very liberties that so many have fought and died for in this country.

> "Any society that will give up a little liberty to gain a little security will deserve neither and lose both."
>
> —Benjamin Franklin

What was being propagated as a health and safety issue was really being used to oust a sitting president and to further divide a country. Democrat governors were using draconian measures to implement liberty stealing lockdown measures. These measures were used to cripple the national economy for the sole purpose of kneecapping an administration. These governors were quite deliberately punishing those that voted against them in prior elections. While liquor stores, marijuana dispensaries, and strip clubs were deemed essential, the gyms, restaurants, small mom-and-pop shops, and churches were closed. While common sense would tell us that attending the gym and praying would have benefits to a natural immunity against the virus, these governors were telling people to stay inside to avoid contact. Contrary to the known benefits of fresh air and sunshine against disease, these governors were issuing fines to those that found their way to the parks and beaches across the country.

With zero scientific evidence that paper masks or cloth face coverings would give any protection against a virus so small, these governors installed mask mandates. Social media sites were far too eager to aid in these divisive decisions. Anyone who dared to promote hydroxychloroquine, to oppose the use of a mask, or chose to be a conscientious objector regarding the use of an unproven and unapproved vaccine was met with the ire of a fact-checker and risked being banned from the site. The social media elites, the so-called journalists, the power-hungry governors, and many in Congress were anxious to use health issues as one more factor that they could use to divide the country.

"Supporters of socialism in the United States often point to nations with large social programs, such as Canada, the United Kingdom, and the Scandinavian states, particularly when it comes to health care. These are not true socialist countries; instead, they are highly taxed market economies with large welfare states. The problem for their argument is that, despite these extremely generous programs, some of these countries are seeing a steady growth of private health insurance.

"It's intriguing that while socialists in America would rush to nationalize the health care system, Norwegians, Swedes, and Danes are all gradually increasing their use of private health insurance. The growing European interest in private health insurance typically stems from dissatisfaction with the state-run systems, which often provide poor or incomplete coverage and long wait times. Most private insurance in Denmark is owner-based. The employer uses the private insurance as a perk of employment to entice top-tier employees to apply, because the private insurance gives shorter wait times and broader range of coverage with access to private health care facilities. In addition, the insurance company sells the product to employers with the notion that there will be less employee down-time due to illness, because care is rendered sooner rather than later. Private insurance plans even create value for the government, because it decreases public health expenditure."[52]

It should also be noted here that none of these Nordic countries are paying their fair share into NATO. Could they really afford this health care luxury if they were adhering to their financial commitment to their own national security?

The Solution

The 10th Amendment makes it clear that any governmental health care policies should be handled at the state and local levels rather than the federal level. These local governments are better suited to create health care programs and to negotiate cost solutions.

The solution to more affordable health care is to actually attack the areas that increase the costs of care and to minimize the need for medical attention in the first place. Throughout the entire existence of the United States government, there has never been an instance where the government has gotten involved and had the cost of a program actually become more affordable. Therefore, the first step toward making health care more affordable would be for Congress to pass a bill to repeal Obamacare 100 percent, as if it had never existed. The notion of replacing it with something else is a classic example of a false binary choice. The real choice is to eliminate government from the health care system.

The initial education cost to become a health care provider is becoming astronomical. With institutions implementing more and more general education requirements, it not only inflates the cost for classes but also delays the amount of time before these providers can begin to create an income to pay off their student loans. When each college elects to employ 17 diversity chancellors (at an average salary of $250,000 per year) for the purpose of giving the illusion that they are protecting students from some perceived injustice, they are wasting huge amounts of money and resources, and it drives the cost of education through the roof. When the state board of examiners consistently raises the continuing education requirements, they in turn add to the underlying costs to doctors, hospitals, and clinics, while reducing the amount of time a practitioner can actually be present to care for patients and create an income. These educational costs could easily be decreased by streamlining the general educational requirements to only those that are pertinent to the chosen occupation. Streamlining the curriculum would also serve to get doctors into the field more quickly so they can begin to pay off student loans even sooner. Eliminating the diversity chancellor positions at colleges would greatly decrease the cost of education.

When the government mandated insurance coverage for health care employees, it literally added to the cost of health care by increasing overhead expenses. Since most health care facilities, clinics, and private practices are incorporated to protect the personal liability of the care providers, increased corporate tax rates also serve to increase the overall cost of providing care. Again, whenever the government gets involved, program costs tend to increase rather than decrease.

Many service providers have provisions in place for "same day pay" pricing for those patients without insurance and those who wish to pay cash. Ironically, to prevent dual pay scales, the insurance commissioners will set limits on how low a service provider can discount a service. To set rigid restrictions on the doctor's fee schedule is self-defeating for the insurance company. Allowing cash paying patients and doctors to negotiate a fair price for eliminating many billing formalities should be a benefit to the insurance company in the long run, but service contracts oftentimes extend fee-setting jurisdiction to include even those patients that are not under an insurance contract. Likewise, there are governmental regulations and contribution limits for those who wish to open Health Savings Accounts. Oftentimes these high deductible "catastrophic" insurance plans are just as expensive as a regular insurance plan. Oftentimes the maximum allowed contribution is equivalent to the annual deductible. How does the consumer of this insurance handle a health care crisis in the first year, before they get an opportunity to accumulate growth in the product? The short answer is they can't. Similarly, the consumer of this insurance becomes a victim if they develop a chronic condition that also affects their livelihood. If the controlling agencies were truly interested in allowing individuals to move to a self-pay situation, then they would allow the consumer to contribute as much as they wanted annually to actually achieve health care independence.

Frivolous lawsuits and increasing liability and malpractice insurance rates are creating a cascading financial problem for hospitals, clinics, and individual health care providers. Why are "Good Samaritan" laws in place to offer legal protection to bystanders who give reasonable assistance to those who are, or whom they believe to be, injured, ill, in peril, or otherwise incapacitated but not extended to care providers? This protection is intended to reduce bystanders' hesitation to provide assistance for fear of legal repercussions should they make some mistake in treatment.

Additionally, actions must be taken to reduce the loss prevention risks to health care providers. As long as we have people abusing doctor visits and emergency room visits with no intention of paying for their care, the cost of medical loss prevention will run rampant. With an estimated $45 billion per year for unpaid emergency room visits, the problem has become an epidemic. When hospitals and clinics begin to factor in the "automatic" losses, they have to raise the prices for their services. This, in turn, creates a new generation of non-paying customers from a group that previously was able to pay but became "priced out" of that possibility. It becomes a perpetual motion machine that creates more and more non-paying customers. In addition, as the price goes up for the patient, insurance companies also have to pay the added cost of loss. In turn, the insurance companies raise their premiums and the consumer gets gouged twice. Currently, collection efforts favor the non-paying patient instead of the person who is owed the money. Society and legal provisions must be put in place to restore the provider with confidence that the patients are actually going to pay for their services.

There is currently a lack of free market competition across state lines. Obamacare literally created a monopoly by mandating that everyone buy insurance or pay a ransom. Then it allowed states access to only one or two companies that provide the product. What did the government think was going to happen to the cost of insurance in the absence of competition? It is, was, and will always be a ridiculous notion. That is why the insurance companies need to be able to bid across all state lines to create a competitive market in favor of the customer.

There was nothing about the Affordable Care Act that made health care affordable. It literally forced people to buy a product whether they wanted it or not, and it forced the paying customers to purchase aspects of coverage (for instance, mammograms for men, and prostate exams for women) that they themselves would never use. Those "essential benefits" were included in the cost for the express purpose of "redistributing" those coverages to those that were not paying for their own insurance. In other words, it was a government-mandated wealth redistribution scam. Rates increased by nearly 30 percent every single year for seven years, while young healthy people who opted out of the program were punished with penalties for making a personal choice. Insurance actuaries understand the common conditions related to gender and age ranges. The "essential benefits" mandates need to be lifted and replaced with an à la carte "minimum" package that is suitable for four or five age ranges. These basic packages should be obtainable for a minimal cost. Also, there must be a concerted effort by Congress to prevent the passage of an excise "Cadillac" Tax, which puts a 40% tax on high-cost employer-sponsored health plans.

Pharmaceutical companies in America are inflating their prices to the tune of 3,000 to 30,000 percent mark-ups on their pills, while the international market sells the same drugs for mere pennies on the hundreds of dollars. The answer is simple: allow international drug companies to compete in the American market. An open international free market for pharmaceutical drugs will create its own competitive pricing. Simultaneously, there must be transparency with regard to who is receiving kickbacks from the drug lobbyists and a public record of how these legislators are voting with regard to drug distribution and pricing.

The ever-increasing number of people on disability and making Social Security claims is alarming. With an open-ended interpretation of what a disability actually is, the redistribution of resources is spread too thin, and it hurts the willing payers. With the technological advances this country has made over the last couple of decades it would be difficult to define an injury that would prevent a person from being a productive member of society. While an individual may encounter a significant deviation, loss of use of any body structure or body function due to a health condition, disorder, or disease, that physical impairment may or may not preclude the individual's capacity to meet occupational demands. In other words, according to the American Medical Association's Guide to Physical Impairment, a person may be impaired but still able to function in an occupation. The health care system needs to undergo a disability determination and welfare reform. More emphasis needs to be placed on vocational rehabilitation and reeducation so people can be retrained to perform tasks within their physical capabilities for the purpose of creating a productive workforce.

As a physician, it should be noted that the term, "preexisting condition," is far too vague. It would be a challenge to think of an instance where a patient went to the hospital or sought care from a doctor without a condition for which they sought the care. It is this premise that prohibits a "preexisting condition" protection. Every condition is preexisting or they wouldn't seek care. Before any protections for "chronic conditions with no guarantee of resolution" can be made, the language needs to reflect the actual prognosis of the patient. In addition, a preexisting condition is a designation that is only used by insurance companies. Doctors do not give this designation. In fact, they don't even use the term.

To have a preexisting condition means that the patient was previously insured and then. by choice or by no fault of their own, they switched insurance companies. If the person chose to switch to another company after tainting their previous insurance pool, then that person deserves the financial consequences of their selfish act. When these people leave the insurance pool they are in, the remaining members of the pool do not receive a drop in insurance rates. Not all patients who have been labeled as preexisting are helpless victims. In fact, many of these people are knowingly changing insurance companies to seek cheaper rates for themselves after their physical condition was responsible for raising the rates for all the members in their original insurance pool. This would be the equivalent of crashing your car under the protections of one insurance company and then switching to a different insurance company and demanding that they fix your car.

Legislators allow this vague language to exist because protecting all preexisting conditions is an easy way to slide into a

Medicare for All system. We must seek first to understand the real problem and then seek a solution. Since every condition is technically a preexisting condition, there has to be greater levels of definition, or this gray area will be a point of contention in the future.

In the short term, anyone with a chronic medical condition that is unlikely to change with treatment or lifestyle choices should be placed into a high-risk pool that is subsidized by the state and local government with some federal assistance. This will be a one-time patient dump that will be subsidized until the people in this group are eventually eliminated from the pool. This short-term immediate fix should appease the population of uninformed people and those calling for socialized medicine, and it will still be a cheaper subsidy than Obamacare.

Then in the future, patients will be divided into two groups. There will be those with short-term illnesses or injuries and those with long-term illnesses or injuries. The long-term group will be further divided into two groups. These groups will consist of a congenital (no fault of their own) group and the other, a "lifestyle" group, which must hold some level of self-accountability. The congenital group will be eligible for subsidy as determined on an individual basis of need. The "lifestyle" group will have a greater financial responsibility until they change the poor habits that put them in the group. Each poor habit will bear a greater financial risk to the patient for coverage. A point system could easily be established, and this point system would determine the level of personal cost and/or government subsidy.

For example, a patient is 16 years old and develops diabetes. The condition is found to be congenital in nature. But the 16-year-old weighs 320 pounds and smokes half a pack of cigarettes per day and frequently uses marijuana. Is this a case where the state government should 100 percent subsidize the insurance coverage? The answer, of course, is no. However, if the patient was in the congenital group, there should be some level of subsidy, perhaps 50 percent. Then as the patient eliminates 120 pounds, stops smoking, and quits the illicit drinking or drug habit (as determined from blood and urine labs), the government subsidy would increase. Of course, we could argue that as the patient eliminates the bad habits, the need for care will inherently decrease and the subsidized cost would naturally go down. This high-risk patient will need to be subjected to follow-up lab work to determine if they are continuing with any bad habits that would jeopardize future government subsidy.

In place of the term "preexisting condition" we should be using phrases such as "acute with a chance of resolution" or "acute with no chance of resolution" and "chronic with a chance for resolution" or "chronic with no chance of resolution." These terms would be better to describe the patient's actual condition and prognosis. In the instances where the patient actually achieves resolution, they will be returned to their original pool. In the instances where the patient cannot achieve resolution, they will stay in the higher risk pool and pay the higher premium, which is subsequently subsidized by the state government. Once all the high-risk patients are eliminated from the public pools, the federal government can request that the insurance companies renegotiate rates for the insurance population that remains in the now "clean" pools.

Finally, there needs to be a merit-based pricing model for insurance coverage. While modern medicine has allowed Americans to live longer, there is no doubt that the Western culture has resulted in an overall decline in health during those living years. The coupling of a poorer quality of health with a longer life expectancy has created the staggering health care costs experienced by most Americans. Factors such as an obesity epidemic, opioid drug addiction, the use of genetically modified organisms in our food, rampant use of synthetic sweeteners, as well as cigarette and alcohol use have all contributed to the progressive decline in public health and the associated spike in health care costs. Matt Hancock, the British health secretary, was correct when he tried to make "preventing ill health" his main priority rather than spending billions to treat conditions that could have been avoided.

"Hancock argued that 'prevention is about ensuring that people take greater responsibility for managing their own health...It's about people choosing to look after themselves better, staying active and stopping smoking. Prevention is about making better choices; by limiting alcohol, sugar, salt and fat.' In other words, he believed that people should take more responsibility for their own behavior by making more healthy choices, and less unhealthy ones."[44]

"It is well known that obesity contributes to health conditions like arthritis, diabetes, heart disease and certain cancers. The health care costs reflect that. For people who are obese, even a small amount of weight gain may come with higher medical costs.

"A study (based on nearly 180,000 Americans), published March 24, 2021, in the journal *PLOS ONE*, revealed that health care costs for obese adults were nearly $1,900 higher each year; compared to their normal-weight peers. Not surprisingly, severe obesity carried an additional annual cost of $3,100, versus Americans with a normal Body Mass Index. As of 2018, more than 42% of U.S. adults were obese, according to the *U.S. Centers for Disease Control and Prevention*. Overall, it is calculated that adult obesity accounted for nearly $173 Billion dollars in annual medical expenses nationally.

"Efforts must be made to make fresh produce and other healthy foods more accessible to Americans; starting with our children. But it's also never too late for adults to make diet changes or to start exercising. For individuals to succeed, they need help. When healthier choices are made easier—a workplace with fruits and vegetables rather than vending machines full of junk food, for example—people will respond."[53]

The Democrats will tell you that addiction should not be criminalized. Instead, they argue that addiction is an illness. Keeping in line with their philosophy that no one should be accountable for their actions, they will tell you that people addicted to drugs are victims of some social constraint. In the case of many illicit street drugs, they are wrong. In many of those instances, the person knowingly partook in an illegal act when they took the drug for the first time.

However, in the case of opioids there is a "reckoning underway in the courts about the damage wrought by the opioid crisis—and who should pay for it.

"Thousands of cities and counties are suing drug makers and distributors in federal court. One tentative dollar amount floated to settle with four of the companies: $48 billion. It sounds like a lot of money, but it doesn't come close to accounting for the full cost of the epidemic, according to recent estimates – let alone what it might cost to fix it.

"Of course, there's a profound human toll that dollars and cents can't capture. Almost 400,000 people have died since 1999 from overdoses related to prescription or illicit opioids. Since 2016, the number of opioid deaths per year rivals or has exceeded the number from traffic accidents. These are lives thrown into chaos, families torn apart – you can't put a dollar figure on those things.

"But the economic impact is important to understand. The most recent estimate of those costs comes from the *Society of Actuaries* and actuarial consulting firm *Milliman* in a report published in October of 2019. The total number they came to was $179 billion dollars in just one year. And those are costs borne by all of society—both by governments providing taxpayer-funded services, and also individuals, families, employers, private insurers and more."[54]

For years the pharmaceutical companies and doctors (who follow an allopathic approach to pain) were watching patients fall into a void somewhere between therapy and surgery. Unwilling to concede those patients to more naturopathic approaches, they turned to a drug that is chemically similar to heroin.

"Opioids attach to receptors in the brain. Opioids are endogenous in nature; meaning they are created naturally in the body. Once attached, they send signals to the brain of the 'opioid effect' which blocks pain, slows breathing, and has a general calming and anti-depressing effect.

"Opioids can activate receptors in the brain, because their chemical structure mimics that of a natural neurotransmitter. This similarity in structure 'fools' receptors and allows the drugs to lock onto and activate the nerve cells. Although these drugs mimic brain chemicals, they don't activate nerve cells in the same way as a natural neurotransmitter, and they lead to abnormal messages being transmitted through the network.

"Opioids target the brain's reward system by flooding the circuit with dopamine. Dopamine is a neurotransmitter present in regions of the brain that regulate movement, emotion, cognition, motivation, and feelings of pleasure. The overstimulation of this system, which rewards our natural behaviors, produces the euphoric effects sought by people who misuse drugs and teaches them to repeat the behavior.

"Our brains are wired to ensure that we will repeat life-sustaining activities by associating those activities with pleasure or reward. Whenever this reward circuit is activated, the brain notes that something important is happening that needs to be remembered, and teaches us to do it again and again, without thinking about it. Because drugs of abuse stimulate the same circuit, we learn to abuse drugs in the same way.

"The purpose of Buprenorphine Treatment is to suppress the debilitating symptoms of cravings and withdrawal. This treatment enables the patient to engage in therapy, counseling and support, so they can implement positive long-term changes in their lives which develops into the new healthy patterns of behavior necessary to achieve sustained addiction remission. Some changes may be irreversible and for those changes, coping strategies need to be learned in order to deal with them successfully. Counseling, therapy and support, all help to guide the patient through this deliberate self-reconditioning process which is the actual recovery."[55]

This is why it is so important to avoid taking opioids in the first place. Education of our children and our medical providers is essential. It should also be noted that tolerance is not synonymous with love when it comes to addiction. The leftists, protecting people from the consequences of their own actions, are actually perpetuating the problem. Instead of tolerating the action and deeming these people as victims, there needs to be some tough sacrificial love to bring the problem to light.

The pharmaceutical companies (that knowingly released a drug with this level of addictive properties) need to be held accountable. And as a nation we must plead with our congressional leaders to stop the drug trafficking across our borders, particularly the porous southern border. Federal agents at the southern border say they've seen a 4,000 percent increase in fentanyl seizures over the last three years. And that does not include all the drug crossings that were not caught. In the first six months of 2021, agents have found 41 pounds of fentanyl. To put that into perspective, two milligrams of fentanyl can be lethal. In other words, 2.2 pounds is enough fentanyl to kill 500,000 people. This is why controlling our borders is so important. The following image illustrates the lethal doses of each drug.

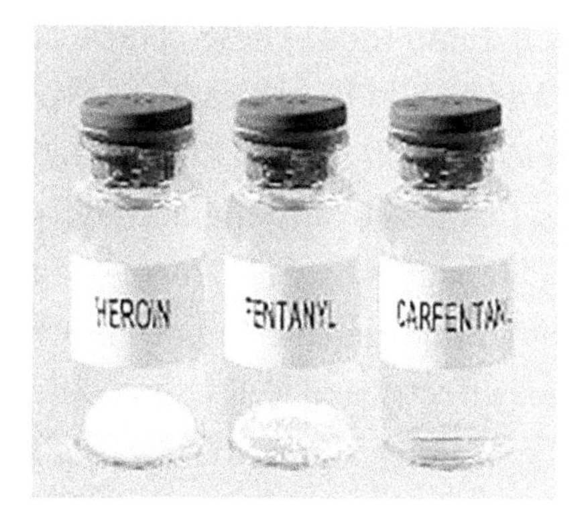

"A significant percentage of processed foods purchased today contain some genetically engineered food products. As a result, each day, tens of millions of American infants, children and adults eat genetically engineered foods without their knowledge. Consumers have no way of knowing what foods are genetically engineered, because the *U.S. Food and Drug Administration* does not require labeling of these products. What's worse, the agency also does not require any pre-market safety testing of genetically engineered foods. The agency's failure to require testing or labeling of genetically engineered foods has made millions of consumers into guinea pigs, unknowingly testing the safety of dozens of gene-altered food products.

"The FDA, in its response to a lawsuit filed by the *Center for Food Safety* in 1998, admitted in court that it had made 'no dispositive scientific findings,' whatsoever, about the safety of genetically engineered foods. In other words, the FDA has given the biotech industry carte blanch to produce and market any number of genetically engineered foods without mandatory agency oversight or safety testing and without a scientific showing that these foods are safe to consume.

"Genetically engineered foods are different from other foods. Genetic engineering allows, for the first time, foreign genes, bacterial and viral vectors, viral promoters and antibiotic marker systems to be engineered into food. These genetic 'cassettes' are new to the human diet and should be subject to extensive safety testing. Instead, in 1992 the *U.S. Food & Drug Administration* ruled, without any scientific basis, that genetically engineered foods present no different risks than traditional foods. FDA's own scientists ridiculed this unscientific agency view of genetic engineering. As result, some of the new 'unexpected effects,' and health risks posed by genetic engineering may include: toxicity, allergic reactions, antibiotic resistance, immune-suppression, cancer and a loss of nutrition."[56]

Many other countries disallow the use of these genetically mutated foods, but our government-led health and safety authorities are willing to sacrifice the health of our society for the sake of increasing the volume of production.

"In a 22-year landmark study published in *The American Journal of Clinical Nutrition* involving over 125,000 people, significant links were found between daily intake of aspartame and the development of leukemia and lymphoma.

"Annual consumption of aspartame in the United States is estimated at 5,000–5,500 tons and the most common product in which it is used is diet soda. Consuming only one 12-ounce can of diet soda per day increased the risk of lymphoma and myeloma; particularly in men.

"Aspartame (especially in liquids) breaks down into aspartic acid, methanol, and phenylalanine. When ingested, methanol turns into formaldehyde. Formaldehyde is a known carcinogen. Other studies show a direct connection between the methanol in aspartame and neurological disease. These synthetic sweeteners have been proven to be toxic to the brain and nervous system.

"Thirty years ago, a toxicologist from the *Food and Drug Administration* testified before the U.S. Congress on the subject of the safety of aspartame in the food supply:

"'...the cancer-causing potential of aspartame is a matter that had been established way beyond any reasonable doubt...Given the cancer-causing potential of aspartame, how would the FDA justify its position that it views a certain amount of aspartame as constituting an allowable daily intake or safe level of it? Is that position in effect not equivalent to setting a tolerance for this food additive and thus a violation of the law? And if the FDA itself elects to violate the law, who is left to protect the health of the public?' Aspartame poisoning, while not on most doctor's diagnosis chart, is disturbingly real."[57]

With federal agencies such as the U.S. Food and Drug Administration allowing genetically engineered foods, synthetic sweeteners, and cancer-causing agents such as acrylamide in the new vegetable burgers, why is everyone so anxious to let the federal government control our health care system?

It is time to move this country into a "Merit-Based Insurance Pricing" program that is spearheaded by the state and local governments. With a task force of actuarial scientists and years of insurance statistics we can determine an estimated "real" cost of health care over the lifetime of a patient. From those numbers we can determine what factors the patient can control and which factors the patient cannot control. By looking at the controllable factors, this task force can determine how those choices can influence the real cost of health care.

Clearly, people who don't drink, don't smoke, don't use illicit drugs, have good blood pressure, maintain a normal weight range, and keep their cholesterol low should be rewarded with discounted insurance rates.

A second task force would then determine the health costs at different stages of life (birth, infant, toddler, adolescence, adult, senior) and then determine cost averages at those times. That way, insurance rates could be end-loaded more toward the income earning periods in a person's life and lessened at times when income is less available. Fortunately, much of this data already exists:

> The average patient lives to be 85 years old.
>
> The average patient spends approximately $316,600 in medical expenses over a lifetime. That number divided by 85 years is $3,724.71 dollars per year, or $310.39 per month.
>
> Statistics show that 17 percent of those expenses occur between the ages of 0 and 18 years.

Approximately 33 percent of those expenses occur between the ages of 18 and 65 (wage-earning years).

Statistics show that 50 percent of those expenses occur between the ages of 65 and 85 (retired—no income).

If insurance premiums are locked at $100/month for the first 18 years, that adds up to $21,600.

If insurance premiums are locked at $200/month for the final 20 years, that adds up to $48,000.

That leaves an estimated $247,000 dollars in unaccounted health care costs over an individual's lifetime, which divided over 47 working years gives a premium of $437.95 per month.

If a person invested in a whole life insurance policy at a rate of $100 per month at 8 percent growth, the investment would provide a staggering $2,215,497 dollars for health care costs. This is just one example of how a private investment could prepare a person for health care issues far more efficiently than any health insurance product on the market or any government subsidized Medicare for All program. This same principle can be applied to paying for college and saving for retirement.

Finally, the state and local governments must eliminate as much financial risk to the health care providers as possible. Then these same entities must give the providers enough confidence to freeze their medical rates until new changes to the system can allow for financial markets to catch up.

Chapter Eight:

The Second Amendment

"The Second Amendment is only one sentence long; twenty-seven words that barely take up a full line on the Bill of Rights:

'A well-regulated Militia, being necessary to the security of a free State, the right of the people to keep and bear Arms, shall not be infringed.'

And yet, for years, those twenty-seven brief words have been the source of contentious debate...seen by some as an inalienable protection against tyranny; by others as a dangerous anachronism."[58]

The Emotional Lie

With the belief that the United States Constitution is an antiquated document that was only appropriate in its time, opponents of the Second Amendment will play semantic gymnastics with the meaning of the phrase "well-regulated Militia." Their entire argument is based on their belief that this "regulation" is to come from a centralized government. By those standards, they would argue that only a military formed by, and ran by, the government could possibly be "well regulated."

With visions of implementing more and more restrictive gun control laws, more intrusive background checks and threats of red flag laws that operate to enforce their own self-interests, these antagonists will declare, "There will never be enough deaths (for some Americans) to stop defending the right for mass murderers to have 'assault-style' weapons." They will take this stance even further by declaring defenders of the Second Amendment to be defending killers.

These hypocrites will declare that mass shootings, particularly from hate groups such as white supremacists, are on the rise, while simultaneously declaring that the violence is directly related to video game violence and inanimate objects such as bump stocks and magazine capacity. These propagandists will declare that "right-wingers are the greatest threat since the 9/11 attacks." They intentionally exclude any deaths associated with the attacks on the twin towers to make the numbers fit their narrative. To allow these fanatics to manipulate timelines and data, in an effort to propagate their misguided narrative, is a disgrace to those Americans who vowed to "never forget" the events that transpired on September 11, 2001. They cannot be allowed to cheapen that tragedy with their lies for the purpose of political gain.

The Truth

According to constitutional experts Jeffrey Rosen and Jack Rakove, "At the time of the American Revolutionary War, militias were groups of 'able-bodied' men who protected their towns, colonies, and eventually states. 'Well-regulated' in the 18th century tended to be something like well-organized, well-armed, or well-disciplined. It didn't mean 'regulation' in the sense that we use it now, in that it's not about the regulatory state. It means 'the militia was in an effective shape to fight.' In other words, it didn't mean the state was controlling the militia in a certain way, but rather that the militia was prepared to do its duty.

"The country had just fought a war, won its independence and was expanding west. There were plenty of reasons to feel unsafe, and so 'security' had a very palpable meaning. The principal defense provided by the militia was to protect local residents from attack and invasion. It also meant physical protection from government overreach. At the time, if government forces tried to take over land or overstep their boundaries, you'd have an institution in place—the militia—that would outnumber any army.

"Back at the birth of our nation, the framers believed that 'rights' are inherent, and not granted. The framers definitely believed in natural rights—that they are endowed by a creator.

'They believed we are born into a state of nature before we form governments and that we are endowed with certain fundamental rights.'

"It is fair to say the framers certainly recognized a natural right of self-defense. The legal consensus is that the Second Amendment applies to individual rights, within 'reasonable' regulations. The Supreme Court decided the rights outlined by the Second Amendment did apply specifically to possession of firearms for purposes of self-defense."[58]

These legal and constitutional premises put to rest any notion that Americans "don't need 30 round magazines to hunt for deer." There is absolutely no language in the Second Amendment that references hunting.

To put this into perspective, the first ten amendments to the Constitution are known as the Bill of Rights. This section of the Constitution explicitly explains the privileges, liberties, and rights of the American citizen, while defining restrictions that have been placed on the federal government. Put another way, not one single amendment in the Bill of Rights speaks of limiting your rights or taking your rights away. In addition to all of that, the Second Amendment is the only amendment that ends with the words "Shall not be infringed." There are absolutely no semantic games that can be played that can change the meaning of those words in the context of the Bill of Rights. To protect against the possibility of a tyrannical government, the regulation of an able-bodied militia was taken away from the federal government and placed in the hands of the citizens.

In fact, "It was the British 'gun-control' program that precipitated the American Revolution. In 1774 Great Britain put an import ban on firearms and gunpowder. From 1774 through 1775 Great Britain used violence to effectuate the confiscations of firearms and gunpowder. It was these events that changed a situation of political tension into a shooting war. Each of these British abuses provides insights into the scope of the modern Second Amendment.

"Furious about the December 1773 Boston Tea Party, the British Parliament in 1774 passed the 'Coercive Acts'. There were many provisions of the 'Coercive Acts' that were found offensive by Americans, but it was the possibility that the British might deploy the army to enforce them that primed many colonists for armed resistance.

'That in the event of Great Britain attempting to force unjust laws upon us by the strength of arms, our cause we leave to heaven and our rifles.'

"It was believed that any law that had to be enforced by the military was necessarily illegitimate.

"In an effort to stop Americans from organizing any resistance, the Royal Governor of Massachusetts, General Thomas Gage, had forbidden town meetings from taking place more than once a year. When Gage dispatched the Redcoats to break up an illegal town meeting in Salem, 3,000 armed Americans appeared in response, and the British retreated. Gage's aide John Andrews explained that 'everyone in the area aged 16 years or older owned a gun and plenty of powder.

'Military rule would be difficult to impose on an armed populace.'

"One response to the problem was to deprive the Americans of gunpowder. (Ironically, this same authoritarian quest to limit access to ammunition is still used by the Left today).

"Modern 'smokeless' gunpowder is stable under most conditions. The 'black powder' of the 18th century was far more volatile. Accordingly, large quantities of black powder were often stored in a town's 'powder house', typically a reinforced brick building. The powder house would hold merchant's reserves, large quantities stored by individuals, as well as powder for use by the local militia. 'Although colonial laws generally required militiamen to have their own firearms and a minimum quantity of powder, not everyone could afford it.'

"Consequently, the government sometimes supplied 'public arms,' and powder to individual militiamen. Public arms would often be stored in a special armory, which might also be the powder house.

"On September 1, 1774, the British Redcoats sailed up the Mystic River and seized hundreds of barrels of powder from the Charlestown powder house. The 'Powder Alarm,' as it became known, was a serious provocation. By the end of the day, 20,000 militiamen had mobilized and started marching toward Boston. War was initially diverted after accurate reports dispelled the initial rumors of violence in the streets. But the message was unmistakable:

If the British used violence to seize arms or powder, the Americans would treat that violent seizure as an act of war, and would fight.

"Shortly after, the Redcoats began general, warrantless searches for arms and ammunition. 'What most irritated the people was seizing their arms and ammunition.' On October 26, 1774, the Massachusetts Provincial Congress adopted a resolution condemning military rule, and criticized the British for 'unlawfully' seizing and retaining large quantities of ammunition in the arsenal in Boston.

"The Provincial Congress urged all militia companies to organize and elect their own officers. The famous 'Minute Men' were directed to 'equip and hold themselves in readiness to march at the shortest notice'. The Provincial Congress further declared that everyone who did not already have a gun should get one, and start practicing with it diligently."[59]

By contrast, the FBI (under the Biden administration) wasted no time listing "militia" groups along with violent extremism as part of their "Terrorism Reference Guide". In fact, they claimed these militia groups to be "anti-government/anti-authority violent extremists who seek to use or threaten force or violence to further their ideology in response to 'perceived' abuses of power by the government, 'perceived' bureaucratic incompetence, or 'perceived' government overreach especially in regard to suspected infringements on gun and land rights." The FBI goes on to say that these "militia groups fear the government is unwilling or unable to protect the United States from 'perceived' threats…and believe their actions are justified, given their self-appointed role as protectors of the United States Constitution—a responsibility they 'perceive' as consistent with a well-armed citizenry sanctioned by the Second Amendment. They hold a deep belief regarding the suspension of civil liberties, the internment of Americans, foreign invasion and occupation, and the end of constitutional government." Ironically, this authoritarian declaration against militia groups is, in fact, indicative of the end of a constitutional government.

In 1774, "King George III and his ministers blocked exportation of arms and ammunition to America by ordering, that sellers merely required a permit to export arms or ammunition from Great Britain to America. Of course, the British government insured that no permits were granted. Meanwhile, Benjamin Franklin was masterminding the surreptitious imports of arms and ammunition from the Netherlands, France and Spain.

"The patriotic Boston Committee of Correspondence learned of the arms embargo and promptly dispatched Paul Revere with the warning that two British ships were headed to Fort William and Mary to seize firearms, cannons and gunpowder. The New Hampshire patriots preemptively captured all the materials at the fort. A New Hampshire newspaper argued that the capture was prudent and proper, reminding readers that...The ancient Carthaginians had consented to 'deliver up all their Arms to the Romans' and were decimated by the Romans soon after.

"Derived from political and legal philosophers such as John Locke, Hugo Grotius, and Edward Coke, the ideology underlying all forms of American resistance was explicitly premised on the right of self-defense of all inalienable rights; from the self-defense foundation was constructed a political theory in which... 'The people were the masters and government the servant, so that the people have the right to remove a disobedient servant.'

"The British government was not formally attempting to abolish the Americans' common law right of self-defense. Yet, in practice, that was precisely what the British were attempting. First, by disarming the Americans, the British were attempting to make the practical exercise of the right of personal self-defense much more difficult. Second, and more fundamentally, the Americans made no distinction between self-defense against a lone criminal or against a criminal government. To the American, the right of self-defense necessarily implied the right of armed self-defense against tyranny."[59]

Yet here we are 247 years later, and certain members of our government are still attempting to stifle the American right to self-defense. And they are still using the same tactics.

"Patrick Henry's great speech on March 23, 1775, argued that the British plainly meant to subjugate America by force. Because every attempt by the Americans at peaceful reconciliation had been rebuffed, the only remaining alternatives for the Americans were to accept slavery or to take up arms. If the Americans did not act soon, the British would soon disarm them, and all hope would be lost.

'The millions of people, armed in holy cause of liberty, and in such a country as that which we possess, are invincible by any force which our enemy can send against us.'

—Patrick Henry

"Without formal legal authorization, Americans began to form independent militia. The militiamen pledged that 'we will, each of us, constantly keep by us' a firelock, six pounds of gunpowder, and twenty pounds of lead.

"The American War of Independence began on April 19, 1775, when 700 Redcoats under the command of Major John Pitcairn left Boston to seize American arms at Lexington and Concord. The militia that assembled at the Lexington Green and the Concord Bridge consisted of 'able-bodied' men aged 16 to 60. They supplied their own firearms, although a few poor men had to borrow a gun. Warned by Paul Revere and Samuel Dawes of the British advance, the young women of Lexington assembled cartridges late into the evening of April 18.

"When the British began to withdraw; things got much worse for them. Armed Americans were swarming in from nearby towns.

They soon outnumbered the British two to one. Although some of the Americans cohered in militia units, a great many fought on their own, taking sniper positions wherever opportunity presented itself."[59]

Advocates of gun rights often argue that in World War II Japan was deterred from invading the United States mainland by a fear of American citizens with guns in their closets. They frequently quote Japan's Admiral Isoroku Yamamoto saying, "You cannot invade mainland United States. There would be a rifle behind each blade of grass." While the quote has never been substantiated, that premise still holds true today.

Much like the FBI proclamation that militia groups are domestic terror groups, "On June 19, 1775, the British renewed their demand that Bostonians surrender their arms, and declared that anyone found in possession of arms would be deemed guilty of treason. On July 6, 1775, the Continental Congress adopted the *Declaration of Causes and Necessity of Taking up Arms*, written by Thomas Jefferson and the great Pennsylvania lawyer John Dickinson. Among the grievances were the efforts to disarm the people of Lexington, Concord, and Boston.

"Two days later, the Continental Congress sent an open letter to the people of Great Britain warning that: 'Men trained to arms from their Infancy, and animated by the Love of Liberty, will afford neither a cheap or easy conquest.'

"The Swiss immigrant John Zubly wrote a pamphlet entitled *Great Britain's Right to Tax*. In it he warned that... 'In a strong sense of liberty, and the use of fire-arms almost from the cradle, the Americans have vastly the advantage over men of their rank almost everywhere else.' Indeed, children were 'shouldering the resemblance of a gun before they are well able to walk.' 'The Americans will fight like men, who have everything at stake,' and their motto was 'DEATH OR FREEDOM.'

"They were all in arms, exercising and training old and young to the use of the gun. No person would go abroad without his sword, gun, or pistol...Every plain was full of armed men, who all wore a hunting shirt, on the left breast of which were sewed, in very legible letters, 'Liberty or Death.'

"The British escalated the war when they ordered that all seaports north of Boston be burned and Falmouth (today's Portland, Maine) was destroyed by naval bombardment.

"The next year, the 13 Colonies would adopt the Declaration of Independence. The Declaration listed the tyrannical acts of King George III, including his methods of carrying out gun control: 'He has plundered our seas, ravaged our Coasts, burnt our Towns, and destroyed the Lives of our people.' As the war went on, the British always remembered that without gun control, they could never control America. In 1777, with British victory seemingly likely, the British drafted a plan entitled '*What Is Fit to Be Done with America*?' To ensure that there would be no future rebellions, 'the Militia Laws should be repealed and none suffered to be re-enacted, and the Arms of all the People should be taken away, nor should any Foundry or manufacturer of Arms, Gunpowder, or Warlike Stores, be ever suffered in America, nor should any Gunpowder, Lead, Arms or Ordnance be imported into it without license...'

"To the Americans of the Revolution and the Founding Era, the theory of some late-20th Century courts that the Second Amendment is a 'collective right' and not an 'individual right' might have seemed incomprehensible.

"The Americans owned guns individually, in their homes. They owned guns collectively, in their town armories and powder houses. They would not allow the British to confiscate their individual arms, nor their collective arms; and when the British tried to do both, the Revolution began. The Americans used their individual arms and their collective arms to fight against the confiscation of any arms.

Americans fought to provide themselves a government that would never perpetrate the abuses that had provoked the Revolution."[59]

The public reaction to an authoritarian gun control plan can be explained by one of Aesop's Fables called "The North Wind and the Sun." The North Wind and the Sun had a quarrel about which of them was the stronger. While they were disputing with much heat and bluster, a traveler passed along the road wrapped in a cloak. "Let us agree," said the Sun, "that he is the stronger who can strip that traveler of his cloak."

"I can get his coat off more quickly than you can," the Wind said to the Sun. "I will let you try first," the Sun said to the Wind.

As the Wind blew harder and harder, the traveler clutched his cloak tighter and tighter. However; as the Sun's rays grew warmer and warmer the man took off his cap and mopped his brow. At last, he became so heated he pulled off his cloak and found welcome shade under a tree by the roadside. The moral of this fable, and there's always a moral, is that gentleness and kind persuasion win where force and bluster fail.

As overbearing government officials implement more tyrannical restrictions, they believe that gun owners will forget that their right to bear arms is to protect them from tyrannical government officials, and the more these officials use "force and bluster," the more the gun owners will cling to their guns.

"What are modern versions of such abuses? The reaction against the 1774 import ban for firearms and gunpowder (via a discretionary licensing law) indicates that import restrictions are unconstitutional if their purpose is to make it more difficult for Americans to possess guns. The federal Gun Control Act of 1968 prohibits the import of any firearm that is not deemed 'sporting' by federal regulators. That import ban seems difficult to justify based on the historical record of 1774–76.

"Laws disarming people who have proven to be a particular threat to public safety are not implicated by the 1774–76 experience.

In contrast, laws that aim to disarm the public at large are precisely what turned a political argument into the American Revolution."[59]

As equally unpopular as overly restrictive gun control laws; is the notion of a universal background check. "There are three basic problems with universal background checks: it will have no effect, the numbers don't prove the case, and the only way to make the scheme remotely effective is repugnant to the people.

"Most importantly is the fact that criminals disobey gun laws (and according to the Supreme Court, in their *Haynes vs. U.S.* decision, criminals are not legally obligated to). In a report titled 'Firearm Use by Offenders,' our own Federal Government noted that nearly 40 percent of all crime guns are acquired from street level dealers, who are criminals in the black-market business of peddling stolen and recycled guns.

"The same study notes that just as many crime guns were acquired by acquaintances, family members, friends or fellow criminals; who are equally unlikely to participate in 'universal' background checks. Totaled, nearly 80 percent of crime guns are already outside of retail distribution channels. Even if the law was enforced it would be nearly useless. These statistics show that 'universal' background checks would have an incomplete effect on guns used in crimes.

"To achieve any degree of success, the 'universal' background check system would require universal gun registration. Despite denials by some politicians, registration has already led to gun confiscation in the United States—in New York, California, Chicago, and the District of Columbia."[60]

Gun advocates and voters are wary of participating in a registration process that will give the government possible control over their means of self-defense. Voters are anxious and willing to control violence, but controlling guns doesn't control criminals and lunatics.

> "You cannot write a law...You cannot create a regulation...You cannot impose a tax...And you cannot say enough prayers to remove the evil that dwells in the heart of a man intent on doing evil."
>
> —Unknown

The concept of creating a red flag law is a perilous trap that must be avoided at all costs. Before any red flag legislation is passed, the originators of that bill must take a long, hard look into the future. Whenever a person's constitutional rights are in danger of restriction based on the subjective determination of another's judgment, we should all stop to question *who* will be making those determinations. Who decides what is considered a "mental illness" or what defines a "danger to society"? In a case where someone was determined to be too mentally ill to possess a firearm, how would those medical records be shared without violating the existing privacy laws? How will these arbiters be vetted to determine that they themselves are not corrupt or hyper-partisan? In the last decade, we have seen every aspect of our government abuse its power for the purpose of political gain. How long before one political party determines that anybody in disagreement with their ideology is considered to be unfit to carry a firearm? We have already seen a discrepancy in the way they treated protestors of George Floyd's death versus people on Capitol Hill to protest election results. The George Floyd protestors were handed bail money while the Capitol Hill protestors remained in prison a year later. These are not rhetorical questions. It is not a matter of "if" it will happen; it is only a matter of "when" it will happen.

"After the tragic events of El Paso, Texas, and Dayton, Ohio many took to social media and the airwaves to perpetuate the myth that the United States leads the world in mass shootings.

"The Crime Prevention Research Center compiled a study of mass shooting deaths from 2009–2015. The study showed that when it came to the annual death rate by mass shootings, the United States ranked 11th.

"The Crime Prevention Research Center took gun ownership and compared it to gun deaths, showing that places with fewer guns than the United States still had more murders, disproving the popular myth that more guns equal more gun deaths. Ironically, Socialist haven Norway leads the way with mass shootings per million people."[61]

"A lot of bad information can follow in the wake of such emotional events; clear, data-based discussions of mass homicides can get lost among political narratives. There are four common misconceptions about mass homicides and who commits them, based on the current state of research.

"Even President Trump, along with other Republican politicians, had linked violent video games to mass shootings. In 2018 the Trump Administration convened a School Safety Commission which studied this issue. The commission ultimately did not conclude there was sufficient evidence to link games and media to criminal violence.

"A 2017 public policy statement by the American Psychological Association's media psychology and technology division specifically recommended politicians should stop linking violent games to mass shootings. It's time to lay this myth to rest.

"The second myth is that of White Supremacy. Overall, the ethnic composition of the group of all mass shooters in the United States is roughly equivalent to that of the American population. Hateful people tend to be attracted to hateful ideologies. Most mass homicide perpetrators don't proclaim any allegiance to a particular ideology at all. Of course, mass homicides in other nations don't involve United States race issues at all."[62]

There was something about the El Paso shooter that the partisan media willfully chose to ignore. While the media and Democrats including Beto O'Rourke focused on the portion of the four-paged manifesto that referred to the attack being "a response to the Hispanic invasion of Texas," they completely ignored a whole host of his policy concerns that paralleled the interests of the Democratic Party. The El Paso shooter, Patrick Crusius, took Beto and Alexandria Ocasio-Cortez's climate change dooms day message seriously enough to actually take action. Rather than the media's depiction of a white supremacist, Patrick Crusius was an environmental extremist.

"He used the exact same talking points from radical environmental extremists, talking about 'the earth is being polluted, corporations are to blame, we need to depopulate the world.'

"From the manifesto, Crusius wrote, 'The American lifestyle affords our citizens an incredible quality of life. However, our lifestyle is destroying the environment of our country. The decimation of the environment is creating a massive burden for future generations. Corporations are heading the destruction of our environment by shamelessly overharvesting resources. This has been a problem for decades.'

"The rant ends with the shooter calling for population control. 'I just want to say that I love the people of this country, but god damn most of y'all are just too stubborn to change your lifestyle. So, the next logical step is to decrease the number of people in America using resources. If we can get rid of enough people, then our way of life can become more sustainable.'"[63]

"An entire paragraph of the manifesto is dedicated to environmental degradation and Malthusian claims about the need to 'get rid of enough people' to protect ever dwindling resources. The El Paso shooter cites the Christchurch shooter's lengthy manifesto, titled '*The Great Replacement*,' as inspiration, reiterating the paranoid fears of demographic shift and white decline. The

Christchurch shooter self-identified as an 'eco-fascist,' writing, 'there is no nationalism without environmentalism.'

"Eco-fascism is not new and finds its origins in Progressive-era linking of environmental preservation and eugenics. Eco-fascism's founding father, Madison Grant, was a renowned preservationist, hideous racist and an inspiration to Hitler. Grant was director of the *American Eugenics Society* and vice president of the *Immigration Restriction League*.

"The so-called deep ecology movement, claiming to argue for the intrinsic value of all living things, insists that the flourishing of nonhuman life is impossible without decreasing the human population. Deep ecologists like David Foreman in the 1980's welcomed famine as a means of depopulation; his fellow eco-fascist contemporaries saw a similar boon in the AIDS crisis."[64]

This is all reminiscent of a scene from the movie *The Kingsman: The Secret Service*. Samuel L. Jackson, playing the part of an evil villain named Valentine, is trying successfully to convince Arthur (the leader of the secret service) to join his evil plot to thin the herd. In the scene Valentine says, "When you get a virus, you get a fever. That's the human body raising its core temperature to kill the virus. Planet Earth works the same way. Global warming is the fever; mankind is the virus. We're making our planet sick. A cull is our only hope. If we don't reduce our population ourselves, there's only one of two ways this can go. The host kills the virus, or the virus kills the host. Either way...Arthur: The result is the same. The virus dies."

Unfortunately, this Gaia philosophy is alive and well in the world today, and fanatics are willing to kill for their deranged beliefs.

"As far as gender is concerned, it's true that most mass homicide perpetrators are male. And finally, whether mental illness is or is not related to mass shootings (or criminal violence more broadly) is a nuanced question. A U.S. Secret Service report identified mental illness—typically either psychosis or suicidal depression—as very common among mass homicide perpetrators.

Mental illness, such as psychosis as well as a mixture of depression with antisocial traits, is a risk factor for violent behavior. Mass homicides get a lot of news coverage which keeps our focus on the frequency of their occurrence. But using standard definitions, most data suggests that the prevalence of mass shootings has stayed fairly consistent over the past few decades."[62]

"The subject of The Desperate Cry of America's Boys is a difficult one. To point out that boys need their fathers is to shine a spotlight on divorce and single mothers, and that is admittedly, uncomfortable. But there's no way to address fatherlessness comfortably.

The fact is that divorce and family breakdown (the root of fatherlessness) is catastrophic for children. There's more than one reason why, but an obvious one is that in the majority of cases, divorce separates children from their fathers.

This is destructive to both boys and girls, but each sex suffers differently. Girls who grow up deprived of their father are more likely to become depressed, more likely to self-harm, and more likely to be promiscuous. But they still have their mothers, with whom they clearly identify. Boys do not have a comparable identification and thus suffer more from father absence. They also tend to act out in a manner that's harmful to others, where girls typically do not.

The root of fatherlessness rests in two things: our culture's dismissal of men as valuable human beings who have something unique to offer and its dismissal of marriage as an institution that's crucial to the health and well-being of children.

When boys don't have this model, they suffer. And when they suffer, society suffers. A majority of school shooters come from fatherless homes. And the saddest part is that most absent fathers aren't absent by choice. The deadbeat dad exists but not in large part. In many instances, women are divorcing perfectly good husbands in their search for what they believe will be a better match, which is a natural outgrowth of no-fault divorce laws. Certainly, women who are married to abusive or dangerous men should file for divorce. But such husbands and fathers cannot account for the seventy percent female-led divorce rate."[65]

The root of fatherlessness is deep and wide, but it ultimately rests in two things. The first is the cultural confusion created when we tell young men to man up and be strong while simultaneously telling them that manhood is synonymous with toxic masculinity. The second is the cultural dismissal of marriage as an institution that's crucial to the health and well-being of children. This comes from a long-standing opinion of the Democrat Party and cultural Marxists that society is responsible for rearing the youth of America, while they attack the dynamics of a patriarchal family.

> "Parents wonder why the streams are bitter, when they themselves have poisoned the fountain."
>
> —John Locke

The Solution

"Mass homicides are horrific tragedies and society must do whatever is possible to understand them fully in order to prevent them. But people also need to separate the data from the myths and the social, political and moral narratives that often form around crime."[62]

It's not the guns that are the problem. The problem stems from a combination of many other factors including:

1) The lack of fathers in the home due to a cultural breakdown of the family structure.

2) No consequences in schools and homes anymore.
3) The death of God and religion in modern society.
4) The growing feeling of self-importance and entitlement among the youth.
5) The isolating nature of social media.
6) The drug culture and its growing acceptance in modern society.
7) The way that the news media divides people and makes us hate each other.
8) The way the media glorifies the killers and keeps the stories active for weeks on end.
9) The lack of proper assessment of and treatment for mental illness.

It is offensive to equate the defense of a person's basic right of self-defense to that of someone who wishes to defend killers. The proposal to stop senseless murders does not lie within the object chosen to commit the murder. Cain killed Abel with a stone. It is not the weapon that is the problem; it is the evil intent of the person. It is illogical to blame an inanimate object for the actions of an evil person, but it is easier to regulate access to an inanimate object than it is to control the actions of an individual intent on doing harm.

The most radical leftists in politics would agree that a gun placed on a counter, with no influence from human interaction, would sit idly by for eternity without harming a single soul. And most defenders of the Second Amendment would concede their basic human rights immediately if that gun ever spontaneously discharged and took another's life.

These same radical leftists will argue that the "AR" in AR-15 stands for "assault rifle." Of course, they would be wrong. In 1956, ArmaLite designed a lightweight rifle, and designated it the Armalite model 15, or AR-15. There is no such thing as an "assault rifle." There are only rifles. What a person does with that rifle determines whether or not it is used for assault. If the rifle is used to kill a deer, it is a hunting rifle. If it is used to shoot the top off of a can, it is called a can opener.

The gun is a tool—only a tool. That tool was necessary to secure this country's independence from a tyrannical king. It still stands as the greatest deterrent against foreign invasion by any country against the United States. And if "we can look at the number of cases in the United States where a gun has been used for self-defense, estimates range everywhere from one hundred thousand uses to close to a million uses. Some organizations and some reporters only report on the ones where a gun was used and it actually resulted in the death of the perpetrator, but if you look at the ones where the mere presence of a firearm actually dissuaded the criminal from committing an act of violence, an act of rape, or an act of murder, the number skyrockets.

"So, when people on this side talk about the importance of the Second Amendment, please understand it is not just some base philosophical conviction we all have. It is rooted in the idea that, while we may be a post-enlightened society, the vast majority of horrible atrocities that have happened in post-enlightened societies have happened as a result of governments systematically disarming their citizens and claiming themselves to be the sole responsible party for their security and then turning on those same citizens and punishing them.

"If we are going to look seriously at school shootings and gun control, we would analyze things like…why do all mass shootings seem to take place in gun-free zones? Wouldn't it be reasonable to test whether or not the efficacy of gun-free zones has actually achieved what was intended?

"We would look at the fact that most of these shooters come from broken homes. What government policies have actually encouraged broken homes? You can look at left-leaning think tanks like the Brookings Institute who will actually say that some of it can be attributed to various cultural changes that happened in the sixties to include the abortion industry.

"Meanwhile conservative-leaning organizations will say the welfare state contributes significantly to dismantling the family, as families become more and more dependent on the government. And these policies incentivize single women to keep the man out of the household to be eligible for government benefits.

"We can look at areas within the United States with some of the strictest gun control measures and what their crime rates look like. Areas like Chicago, New York City, Washington, DC, and others, that have incredibly strict gun laws and yet, for some reason still have incredibly high rates of gun violence.

People on this side of the aisle hold the Second Amendment in such high esteem because we honestly believe that you have an inherent right to defend yourself, and your ability to defend yourself should not be excluded to your size and strength. Firearms are the great equalizer. They provide someone that is weaker and not as fast with the ability to actually defend against a stronger attacker."[66] Those claiming to be the great defenders of women should be sympathetic to this cause.

All of us agree that we need to make sure that our students are better protected when they go to school. One of the things we should look at is the arming of certain teachers. There is no harm in arming a teacher that is properly trained and is comfortable with handling a gun.

If controlling an inanimate object is the only solution amicable to the intolerant radicals claiming to be "tolerant," then there may be a multistep solution, and one of those steps does include an inanimate object. Wouldn't it be awesome if every school that declared itself a gun-free zone actually had a metal detector at the door to ensure than no guns ever made it inside? In addition, there should be paid security that is trained on what to look for from people who intend to do harm. Coltan Haab is a Parkland student who survived the mass shooting. He and a fellow ROTC student used Kevlar shields in a classroom to protect other students in the classroom. Imagine if the top of every desk was made of Kevlar shielding that could be detached and used to shield the vital organs during an attack. We have metal detectors and security guards at every Court House in America. While we protect attorneys, judges, and criminals, we don't have metal detectors or security guards at our schools to protect our greatest resources.

There should be a drill for this emergency situation. The schools have fire drills, tornado drills, and other emergency situational drills; we need to emphasize an "active shooter" drill along with other emergency reaction drills. As a society we need to reinvigorate the primitive parts or our children's brains and remove the mind-numbing electronic devices and the "safe environment" mentality to bring around an alert state of mind. An alert mind can be prepared for anything.

While on the subject of preparing our children for anything, let's have an honest discussion about how the indoctrination processes (built into our school systems) has created an animosity toward the very country these kids live in. Couple that with the protective bubble that mommy and daddy have put them in, and you have created an unrealistic expectation for how life is really going to treat you. In essence we are creating a new generation of narcissists that believe the world revolves around them. When these kids cannot hide behind the facade of an online personality, or when they enter into the real world, and people see them as a failure, a word they are unfamiliar with and unprepared for, they either implode and take their own lives or they explode and kill others—or they do both.

When sports programs provide participation ribbons for *everyone* because God forbid anyone ever have to experience a loss in their life, we have a problem. When reasonable parents teach their children that losing is an acceptable option, they create well-developed adults. This prevents twenty-year-old kids from freaking out when they enter the real world and realize that life is actually pretty hard and it requires compromise and sacrifice, and yes, some days you flat out lose. The final nail in the coffin is the fact that they get on some social media format and pretend for years to be someone they absolutely are not, and when faced with who they really are, they realize just how much they don't like that person—or any people. This disdain for oneself creates a whole onslaught of emotions, anxiety, and depression. When red flags of mental instability begin to rise, they are often ignored out of some societal duty to accept everyone as they are. Under the delusional premise of tolerance, we allow people to slip into an accepted mental illness.

The Parkland shooter was reported to the FBI multiple times, but the red flags were ignored for fear of upsetting some Obama-era "restorative justice" discipline program that was focused on prodding schools to reduce the number of suspensions and expulsions, especially for students of color and students with disabilities, to maintain some fictitious equity in discipline. Any policy seeking to achieve these goals requires basic common sense and an understanding that failure to report troubled students to law enforcement can have dangerous repercussions. Democratic policies create the problem by removing Christian beliefs and real discipline in schools and then blame the very thing they themselves took away. They take God out of the schools and then question how God could allow school shootings.

God disciplines his children. We should too; otherwise, we develop narcissistic children that become either the next mass shooter or the next suicide victim. If you leave the child in charge of deciding what's for dinner, you will eat candy and chips at every meal. Sure, it tastes good, but there is no substance and no nutritional value. Democrats don't understand that you can hold people accountable, demand results, and still display (tough) love. Stop allowing lawmakers to legislate policies that make the government the surrogate father to these children.

We need to teach our children to be humble in victory and gracious in defeat. Unfortunately, too many parents shield their children from loss. This protective behavior designed to protect their precious little ego prevents an important lesson from being learned.

> "It is easier to build strong children than to repair broken men."
>
> —Frederick Douglass

Another facet of this controversial subject is the news media. The media spends countless hours propagating narratives that divide every facet of this country. By dividing people according to demographics and core belief systems, they in fact create a natural animosity for those that don't think like us. This seed of hatred planted in the mind of a person with a mental instability can lead to devastating results. If it wasn't a gun, it would be a knife, or acid, or a bomb, but the media would be pleased to report on these stories of violence. "If it bleeds, it reads" is the mantra for most newsrooms. And they don't care if it was their newsroom that initiated the tragedy as long as it creates a headline.

If the media didn't glorify every shooting and run it nonstop for weeks, then maybe these narcissistic cowards wouldn't become so infatuated with "going out with a bang." As a society we should be tired of hearing, "This is the eighth worst mass shooting in history," as if they were setting the benchmark for the next killer. Of course, asking the media to participate in self-reflection on this subject would be as fruitless as asking Congress to enact term limits for themselves.

In a virtual State of the Union speech about guns, Bill Whittle had this to say:

"And now, I must turn to the issue of gun violence in America today, because mass shootings leave us all appalled and disgusted at the carnage. Now, some people, and that includes many of you in this room tonight...want to place the blame for this horror on things like: 30 round magazines, or semi-automatic rifles. We want to blame something...anything that we can control. But what we really want to ban is violence, and murder, and insanity. But we don't talk about that, because deep in our hearts each of us knows that violence, and murder and insanity are built into the human condition and likely always will be.

"You know, there are two kinds of animals in this world: predators and prey. No one watches a leopard chase down a gazelle and denies that the gazelle has a right to use its hooves and horns to protect itself from the predator. But there are people in this room tonight and all across the country who would deny that same right to self-defense to other human beings. Such people seem to think that the way to stop the leopard is to cut the horns off of the gazelle. Arguing that by somehow making it easier for the predator; the predator will simply go away. My friends, this is insane. When you make it easier for the predator you get more predators.

"So, let's start with the so-called assault weapons, more properly known as semi-automatic rifles. In 2011, the total firearm murders came to 8,583, according to the F.B.I. Now, during that time, the total murders committed by rifles, all rifles, not just semi-automatic rifles were 323. That's 3% of all murders. Hammers and clubs kill half again as many people as rifles. Hands and feet murder twice as many, and knives kill five times more Americans than all rifles combined. Preventable medical errors kill about 98,000 people per year. Medical malpractice kills more than 12 times as many people as are murdered in the United States each year. That's more than 300 x's the number killed by all rifles, not just the so-called assault rifles. And, yet, no one talks about limits on hammers, or knives, or doctors, or hospitals.

"No one does that, because the good we perceive from hammers and knives and doctors far outweigh their perceived harm, and yet, studies show that firearms prevent anywhere from 800,000 to over 2,000,000 violent crimes every year. The lowest estimate means that 100 x's more violent crimes were prevented with firearms than the total murders committed with firearms. That's 100 times as many!

"Now, in October of 2007 Amanda Collins was walking to her car after a night class at the University of Nevada at Reno. Amanda had a concealed carry permit for her 9mm Glock that she carried for self-defense. Unfortunately for Amanda, University of Nevada Reno is, like most college campuses, a gun free zone. So, like the law-abiding citizen that she is, she did not have her gun with her in this gun free zone when she was attacked by James Biela. Biela raped her on the UNR campus, less than 300 yards from the campus police office. He then walked away, and a few months later, this human predator went on to murder 19-year-old Brianna Denison. Amanda Collins went on to say, 'I know, having been the first victim, that Brianna Denison would still be alive had I been able to defend myself that night.'

"Therefore; I am directing the 'virtual' attorney general to aggressively challenge any gun control laws that violate Amanda Collins' right not to be raped. And Brianna Denison's right not to be murdered. You're not forced to abandon your first amendment rights when you enter Chicago or New York. Or your fifth amendment rights when you walk onto a college campus. As 'virtual' president, I will veto, on the spot, without hesitation, but with a great deal of pleasure any and all attempts to destroy any of the Bill of Rights of the Constitution of the United States of America. Because, when it's all said and done, the Second Amendment to the Constitution is there to protect more than our right to self-defense.

It is there to keep people from calling for gun control laws that at the stroke of a pen turn law abiding citizens into criminals.

"The Second Amendment is there to protect the American people from tyranny. The Second Amendment is there to protect the American people from politicians. The Second Amendment is there to protect the American people from us (the Government). Now, some politicians claim America deserves a vote on this issue. Ok, let's have a vote. Those of you advocating infringement on the right of the people to keep and bear arms need to go to the American people with the 28th Amendment, which would simply read 'the Second Amendment to the Constitution is hereby repealed.' That would, for the first time, give you the legal authority to do what you have been doing (and what you are trying to do now) in direct violation of your oath of office to defend the entire Constitution of the United States. Not just the parts you happen to approve of. So, go ahead, go to the American people and tell them that ultimate power is no longer to be vested in the people who can't be trusted with that power; according to you. Tell them, only the Government can have that power now. You go out there and try to convince the people of the 38 states that you're gonna need to get that Amendment passed, to agree with your opinion of them versus their opinion of you. I dare you.

"Twelve million unarmed men, women and children were unable to resist being murdered by their own national socialist government in Germany. Perhaps 50 million unarmed men, women and children were murdered by their own Union of Soviet Socialist Republics. Fifty million Chinese murdered by their own government under Mao; who also disarmed his people. More people killed in Cuba, and Vietnam, and in the 'killing fields' of Cambodia. Now, you say, 'That can't happen here'...you say, 'We're protected?' Protected by what? Protected by the Constitution that you are in the process of destroying? You are in violation of your oaths of office by even introducing this legislation, let alone passing it.

"My fellow Americans, the previous inhabitants of this chamber watched as 100 million people were murdered after being disarmed by their own governments. Every single one of those men, women and children were: real, precious and irreplaceable. And I tell you here and now, that I will be damned if I will let that happen to the American people."

"You are going to have a problem with so-called 'solutions' which infringe on people's liberty under the promise that the government will provide for the security, because ultimately in the Parkland shooting, we had a perfect example of government being engaged over 30 times and still failing to provide security for those students.

"You see, the problem with passing a couple of bills regarding background checks and banning bump stocks, is that quite frankly; nobody on this side of the aisle believes you when you say 'that's all you want to do.'

"Next it will be a different kind of background check. Then it will be national gun registration, then after that it will be the banning of other types of weapons. When those policies fail to produce, the results you are promising your constituents...you'll be back with more reasons why we have to infringe upon Second Amendment rights."[66]

Once all the guns are banned, what's to prevent the government from stealing other inalienable rights? Nothing—absolutely nothing!

Chapter Nine:

Climate Change

"The World Economic Forum is a forum for the rich and famous to gather at the world's most expensive winter resorts to discuss pressing issues about climate change. Ironically, the leaders who urge people to be more mindful about climate change seem to have done the opposite themselves. A recent study revealed that nearly 1,500 private jets flew in and out of Davos for the January 22, 2019, thru January 25, 2019, meeting."[67]

> "Rules for thee...But not for me"
>
> —Unknown

The Emotional Lie

The climate alarmists and their "climate experts" will tell you, for the forty-second time over the last 54 years, the world is going to end as the result of some environmental catastrophe. According to prediction number forty-two, if we don't do something immediately to stop the current warming trend, the planet will become uninhabitable within the next ten years. They will use scary terms such as "acid rain" and "acidification of the ocean" to invoke the greatest emotional fear possible. They will trot out a 16-year-old Swedish activist to spread prediction number forty-two because it is so much more credible when you are being shamed by a teenaged girl.

They will tell you that the only solution to the climate problem is a $16 trillion "Green New Deal" that completely eliminates fossil fuels within the next five years and replaces them with renewable energy. According to this plan, all jobs that are lost through the elimination of the fossil fuel industry will be replaced with higher-paying, more rewarding jobs in the up and coming (not quite here yet) green energy industry. With dreams of solar panels and wind turbines to replace oil and natural gas, these activists want to eliminate fracking, and they want to end oil and gas exploration and extraction on public lands. They want to ban nuclear energy because of challenges around nuclear waste storage. Meanwhile they ignore nuclear power as a zero-emissions alternative. They have also proposed the banning of plastic straws, the elimination of meat from the human diet, population control, adding carbon taxes, filing complaints with the United Nations about countries that don't comply, and reentering the United States into the Paris Climate Accord despite the fact that the United States is the only country in the world that has reduced emissions to the lowest level since 1992, while growing its economy.

Their reason for entering into this accord is simple: In their eyes, Americans are guilty of creating the majority of pollution around the world and should bear the lion's share of the financial responsibility necessary to clean up this mess, even if it means the de-industrialization of the United States economy, which would put millions of people out of work and lower the standard of living for everyone who lives in the country.

Of course, this will all be done in the name of "science," and they will justify their stance with claims of a 97 percent "scientific consensus." Anyone who disagrees with their assertions will be labeled a "science denier" and will be shamed publicly.

> "I would rather have questions that can't be answered than answers that can't be questioned."
>
> —Richard P. Feynman

The Truth

"For more than 50 years climate alarmists in the scientific community and the environmental movement have not gotten one catastrophic prediction correct. They have a perfect record of getting all forty-one previous predictions wrong.

"There is a reason people are skeptical of 'expert' prediction number forty-two, the one that says if we don't immediately convert to socialism and allow the government to control and organize our lives, the planet will become uninhabitable. Why would we completely restructure our economy and sacrifice our personal freedom for 'experts' who are 0–41? Sorry experts...sorry scientific consensus...only a fool comes running for the forty-second cry of wolf.

"Don't litter, be kind to animals, and stop feeling guilty. Go out there and embrace all the bounty that comes with being a 21st Century American...like Barack Obama, who says he believes in Global Warming with his mouth; but proves he doesn't with the $15 million he just spent on oceanfront property that we were told is doomed to flooding."[68]

These eco-fascists want to use emotional manipulation and guilt to coerce an entire society to bow to the restrictive regulations of their ideology but ignore how sinister some of their own proposals are. No, this claim is not in reference to the petty banning of plastic straws or even the ridiculous notion that cow flatulence will cause the demise of an entire planet. These people are actually talking about population control as a means to decrease carbon emissions. If you look at their policy proposals, many of them (including abortion) act along this premise.

Gaia "worship" is based on the hypothesis that life on earth has the capacity to regulate temperature and the composition of earth's surface. According to Nobel Prize–winner Ivar Giaever (a climate change skeptic), global warming has become a "new religion":

"Anyone who has studied the global environmental movement has no doubt heard the term 'Gaia.' Gaia is a revival of Paganism that rejects Christianity, considers Christianity its biggest enemy, and views the Christian faith as its only obstacle to a global religion centered on Gaia worship and the uniting of all life forms around the goddess of 'Mother Earth.' A cunning mixture of: science, paganism, eastern mysticism, and feminism have made this pagan cult a growing threat. Gaia worship is at the very heart of today's environmental policy.

"The United Nations has been extremely successful in infusing the 'Green Religion' into an international governmental body that has an increasing affect and control over all of our lives. The Gaia hypothesis can be credited to James Lovestock who worked for NASA. All of the lifeforms on this planet, according to Lovestock, are a part of Gaia—a part of one spirit goddess that sustains life on Earth. His theory presents Earth not as the rock that it is, but as a living being named Gaia, after the Greek goddess that was once believed to have drawn the living world forth from chaos.

"Gaia teaches that an 'Earth spirit,' goddess, or planetary brain must be protected. It is this belief that fuels the environmental movement, sustainable development, and a global push for the return of industrialized nations to a more primitive way of life."[69]

And in that more primitive time of windmills and burning cow dung, there were significantly less people on the planet.

Perhaps one of the greatest lies perpetuated on the American people is the 97 percent myth. In an effort to silence their critics, the climate activists will invariably cite the "fact" that 97 percent of all scientists agree with the ideological claims of the climate alarmists; therefore, any opposing argument must be rendered moot according to this consensus viewpoint. It is alarming that these so called "science observers" would consider a consensus "opinion" to be significantly more important than actual facts and statistics. But an even greater disappointment is the fact that their 97 percent claim is a statistical lie.

A scientific survey was sent out to 3,146 scientists. Of all the scientists surveyed, seventy-seven of those scientists declared themselves to be "climate experts." Seventy-five of the seventy-seven experts declared that humans (in their opinion) have an impact on climate. Seventy-five divided by seventy-seven is indeed 97 percent; however, they don't tell you that the 97 percent only represents 2 percent of the total survey responses. In fact, of all the scientists surveyed, only 64 percent believe that humans have some (not all) of the influence over our climate.

"Just as 16-year-old Swedish climate activist Greta Thunberg addressed the United Nations Climate Action Summit in New York accusing world leaders of robbing her of her future; more than 500 signatories consisting of experts in sciences, academia, economics, business, law and other fields were begging the United Nations to keep hysteria from obscuring facts.

"'Climate science should be less political, while climate policies should be more scientific,' the declaration stated. 'Scientists should openly address the uncertainties and exaggerations in their predictions of global warming, while politicians should dispassionately count the real benefits as well as the imagined costs of adaptation to global warming; and the real costs as well as the imagined benefits of mitigation.'

"The signatories underscored the importance of not rushing into enormously expensive climate action before fully ascertaining the facts.

"'There is no statistical evidence that global warming is intensifying hurricanes, floods, droughts and suchlike natural disasters, or making them more frequent,' they declared. 'However, CO2-mitigation measures are as damaging as they are costly. For instance, wind turbines kill birds and bats, and palm-oil plantations destroy the biodiversity of the rainforests.'

"'There is no climate emergency. Therefore, there is no cause for panic and alarm,' they note. 'We strongly oppose the harmful and unrealistic net-zero CO2 policy proposed for 2050.'

"In particular, the signatories criticized the general-circulation 'models' of climate on which international policy is currently founded as 'unfit for their purpose.'"[70]

In addition to these five hundred experts are thousands of scientists who have signed the "Global Warming Petition Project." To date, 31,487 American scientists have signed the petition; including 9,029 scientists with a PhD. This very large number of petition signers demonstrates that, if there is a "consensus" among American scientists, it is in opposition to the "human-caused" global warming hypothesis presented by the United Nations Intergovernmental Panel on Climate Change.

Patrick Moore is the co-founder of Greenpeace and the author of *Confessions of a Greenpeace Dropout: The Makings of a Sensible Environmentalist*. From his Twitter page he wrote: "Alexandria Ocasio-Cortez little twit. You don't have a plan to grow food for 8 billion people without fossil fuels, or get food into the cities. Horses? If fossil fuels were banned, every tree in the world would be cut down for fuel, for cooking and heating. You would bring about mass death."

In an interview he says, "The Green New Deal is a silly plan. She made up a proposal that is ridiculous and no one else did. She then rubbed me the wrong way when she claimed she was 'the boss.' And that is what is wrong with this. In fact, the whole climate crisis, as they call it, is not only fake news, but it is fake science (pseudoscience). There is no climate crisis. There is weather and climate all around the world. In fact, carbon dioxide is the main building block of all life. That's where the carbon comes from in carbon-based life...which is all life on land and in the sea."

When asked about other scientist's claims that Climate Change is real, Patrick Moore said, "Yes, of course Climate Change is real. It's been happening since the beginning of time. But, it's not dangerous and it's not made by people. Climate Change is a perfectly natural phenomenon, and this modern warm period actually began about 300 years ago when the Little Ice Age began to come to an end. There is nothing to be afraid of, and that is all they're doing is instilling fear. Most of the scientists who are saying it's a crisis are on perpetual government grants. On one hand they say the science is settled and people like me should just shut up, because 'they' know what's right. On the other hand, they seem to be studying it forever; as if there is something new to find out. And these two things are completely contradictory.

Carbon dioxide is actually a benefit to the world...Carbon dioxide is a benefit to the environment, to agriculture and forestry, and to the climate of the earth."

When asked why a founder of the Greenpeace organization would decide to leave, Patrick Moore said, "I was one of the founders doing a PhD in the late '60s early '70s in ecology. I was radicalized by the Cold War and the threat of all out nuclear war and the emerging consciousness of the environment...and we did a lot of good things. We stopped nuclear testing in Alaska and we stopped it in the South Pacific. We saved the whales and we stopped a lot of toxic waste being dumped into the ocean and the air. But, by the mid '80s after we gained a lot of notoriety and we began bringing in a lot of money; we were hijacked by the 'extreme left.' They basically took Greenpeace from a science-based organization to an organization based on sensationalism, misinformation and fear."

Patrick Moore went on to say, "The fact is, you cannot do agriculture for 8 billion people without fossil fuels; we don't have an alternative. It's one thing to have a battery powered vehicle for your family; it's another thing trying to get forty tons of food at a time into the cities."

Moore concluded by saying, "Eighty-five percent of the world's energy is derived from fossil fuels. The carbon dioxide that's being emitted from burning it was actually taken out of the atmosphere and the oceans millions of years ago; and stored in sediments. We are now releasing it back into the atmosphere where it can fertilize the life on Earth. Carbon dioxide and water are the two main constituents of all life: carbohydrates. Of course, fossil fuels are hydrocarbons; they are just missing the oxygen. When you burn them; the oxygen is recombined with the carbon to form carbon dioxide. People need to learn more about chemistry, because what the 'left' is propagating is fake science and it is driving a very dangerous movement on the energy front."

THE "GREEN" PART OF THE MELON REPRESENTS THE ENVIRONMENTAL CONCERNS

WHILE THE RED PART REPRESENTS THE SOCIALST AGENDA

Climategate

"It really doesn't matter in what order you read the 'Climategate' emails. You get the same result every time: a bunch of second-rate pseudoscientists bullying those who would dissent, accepting lavish grants, racking up air miles on conference freebies, cooking the books, manipulating evidence and torturing the data till it screams; in order to make man-made global warming look like a much more significant and well-understood problem than it actually is.

"The implicated scientists have come up with all kinds of excuses. They say 'It's a war on science conducted by the evil Big-Oil funded right wing.' Or they will say, 'It has all been taken out of context and that the incriminating emails don't mean what the deniers claim they mean; therefore, the Climategate scientists have been exonerated.' All lies.

"Meanwhile in the real world, no convincing evidence whatsoever has emerged to support the threadbare theory that anthropogenic CO_2 is causing the planet to warm in ways which are dangerous or unprecedented. Still, the theory rests entirely on computer models which, increasingly, appear to diverge from the actual observed data.

'Nature is on the side of the skeptic, not the alarmists.'

"Journalists have gone out of their way to publicize almost every alarmist claim the promoters of the scare could come up with, even after these had been shown to be without scientific foundations. They have consistently failed to explain the immense financial cost of those proposals and their enormous economic implications.

"The journalists have betrayed their obligation to be impartial, using the excuse that any dissent from the official orthodoxy was so insignificant that it should just be ignored or made to look ridiculous.

"Second, they have betrayed the principles of responsible journalism, by allowing its coverage to become so one-sided that it has amounted to no more than propaganda.

"Third, it has betrayed the fundamental principles of science, which relies on unrelenting skepticism towards any theory until it can be shown to provide a comprehensive explanation for the observed evidence.

'Man is prey when he becomes a victim of groupthink.'

"We now live in a world where everyone gets their lessons on global warming from a 16-year-old kid in pigtails who can see 'carbon' in the air, and an old, curmudgeon socialists who blames the Australian wild fires on climate change despite twenty people being arrested for arson; all courtesy of a propaganda institution that is shamelessly left-biased."[71]

"*Environment Canada*, the federal environmental agency in Canada has erased a century's worth of actually observed temperature data. They claimed that their modeled computer projections are 'more accurate' than the actual measured temperatures.

The reason for scrapping all observed weather data from 1850 to 1949 was, in their conclusion, necessary because there weren't enough weather stations to create a reliable data set for that 100-year period. In many cases the temperatures in the early 20th century were higher than they are today. This doesn't fit the narrative consistently pushed by green activists; claiming that the planet is warming at a dangerous rate due to man-made carbon emissions.

"*Environment Canada* is merely following the bad examples set by several other institutional climate gatekeepers including: NASA, NOAA, and the *Climatic Research Unit* at the University of East Anglia.

"The *National Oceanic and Atmospheric Administration* (NOAA), for example, has frequently been caught adjusting past temperatures downward and more recent temperatures upwards; in order to make 'global warming' look more dramatic. (If the data actually proved a warming trend, then why do they find the need to embellish the data?)

"During the Climategate scandal, scientists at the *Climatic Research Unit* admitted that they had thrown away much of their raw data, leaving only their revised data intact. Their excuse was that it had been done to 'save space' when they moved to a new building.

"It means that other academics are not able to check basic calculations said to show a long-term rise in temperature over the past 150 years.

"Others less committed to green activism might find it somewhat sinister that the international agencies charged with maintaining the world's temperature records are destroying them because the factual evidence doesn't support the global warming scare narrative."[72]

"Using complex statistical models, the *National Oceanic and Atmospheric Administration's* statisticians 'adjust' the data to reflect not reality, but their underlying theories of global warming.

"The key point here is that while NOAA frequently makes these 'adjustments' to the raw data, it has never offered a convincing explanation as to why they are necessary. Nor have they yet, explained how exactly their adjusted data provides a more accurate version of the truth than the original data."[73]

Climate alarmists hedge their bets with ten- and fifteen-year predictions of environmental catastrophes because they know that administrations are only in office for eight years. That way when they have spent $16 trillion of taxpayer money and the world doesn't end, they can claim a political victory and use that as leverage to impose greater tax burdens. And if the American people don't kowtow to the proposed taxes and the world still doesn't end, they will pretend like this alarmism never took place.

"The United Nations Intergovernmental Panel on Climate Change is misleading humanity about climate change and sea levels according to a leading expert on sea levels.

"In fact, 'it is more likely that sea levels will decline, not rise,' explained Dr. Nils-Axel Mörner retired head of the paleo geophysics and geodynamics at Stockholm University. A new solar-driven cooling period is not far off according to Dr. Nils-Axel Mörner.

"When Mörner tried to warn the United Nations Intergovernmental Panel on Climate Change that it was publishing false information that would inevitably be discredited, they simply ignored him. Dismayed, Dr. Nils-Axel Mörner resigned in disgust and decided to blow the whistle.

"Asked if coastal cities would be flooding due to sea-level rise caused by alleged man-made global warming, Mörner was unequivocal: 'Absolutely not.' 'There is no rapid sea-level rise going on today, and there will not be,' he said, citing observable data. 'On the contrary, if anything happens, the sea will go down a little.'

"The widely respected scientist, who has been tracking sea levels in various parts of the globe for some 50 years, blasted those who use incorrect 'correction factors' in their data to make it appear that seas are rising worldwide. 'That is just wrong,' he said.

"Indeed, even speaking of something called 'global sea level' is highly misleading, the expert explained. 'It is different in different parts of the world,' Mörner said, noting that sea levels can rise in one part of the world and decline in another depending on a variety of factors.

"Mörner's conclusion is that solar activity and its effects on the globe have been the 'dominant factor' in what happens to both the climate and the seas.

"Man's emissions of this essential gas, required by plants and exhaled by people, makes up a fraction of one percent of all so-called greenhouse gases present naturally in the atmosphere. 'Absolutely not,' Mörner said about the CO_2 argument, noting there was 'something basically sick' in the blame-CO_2 hypothesis. 'If it has any effect, the CO_2 effect is minute—it does not matter. What has a big effect is the sun.'

"'They just ignored what I was saying,' he recounted. 'If they were clever (if they had facts on their side) they could show that, but that is not the case. They just will not discuss it.'

"Instead of science, Mörner suspects that the behind-the-scenes promoters of the man-made warming hypothesis have dark, ulterior motives. 'I think the ultimate thing is that they want a government for the whole globe, and that is a weird idea,' Mörner said, criticizing the Rockefeller dynasty and global efforts to keep developing countries from developing under the guise of saving the climate. 'This is the hope of controlling everything. It is autocracy. Nobody should rule like that. This globalism is a dangerous thing.'

"'It is very simple for us to discuss climate change, because we really have the facts, they have their models; and facts are better than models,' Mörner said."[74]

Regardless of whether the problem is global warming, global cooling, or climate change, the extreme left wing's answer is always more government control, less personal liberties, and higher taxes. Most of their proposed solutions are shortsighted. For instance, when Alexandria Ocasio-Cortez calls for the elimination of fossil fuels, she in essence is calling for the burning of more wood. She is oblivious to the fact that burning trees for fuel would destroy our environment. Trees are the buffer for our environment. Burning them would literally release even more CO_2 into the environment, while eliminating the buffering system that captures the atmospheric CO_2.

These leftist politicians are repetitively calling for honest, open, and intelligent discussions regarding climate change, but the activists behind this nonsense are anything but honest, open, or intelligent. They fly their private jets from one climate summit to the next, leaving a carbon footprint larger annually than any one of us will leave in an entire lifetime. They will promote propaganda that is absolutely unfounded in the scientific community, other than the pseudoscientists working for government grant money. These "scientists" have been caught (multiple times) omitting, cherry-picking, adjusting, and readjusting the data for their "models." And every year their projections simply do not add up to what is really happening in the world.

"Early climate and weather models (constrained by computing resources) made numerical approximations on modeling the real world. One process, the radiative transfer of sunlight through the atmosphere, has always been a costly component. As computational ability expanded, these models added resolution, processes and numerical methods to reduce errors and become the earth system models that we use today. While many of the original approximations have since been improved, one—that the earth's surface and atmosphere are locally flat—remains in current models."[75] It is increasingly difficult to take these so-called scientists seriously when they use a flat earth model to demonstrate their climate projections.

Whistleblowers in the scientific community have exposed the scientists behind the Paris Climate Accord for breaking with their own data protocols, as they ignored data that did not fit their narrative. Real scientists don't ignore data that doesn't support their hypothesis; instead, they make all data relevant, and they follow the facts.

The fact is simple. We live on a large rock floating in space along no fixed axis. This rock spins at a speed of 1,000 mph and can wobble as much as 23° from center in any given direction at any given time, which means sometimes, one pole is closer to the sun, while the other pole is farther from the sun. While one pole experiences melting ice, the opposite pole experiences increased ice formation. As the earth orbits around the sun, the rotational path deviates from an orbit of perfect circularity. At the perihelion point of the orbital path the earth is 5 million kilometers closer to the sun than it is at the aphelion point of the orbital path. Charles Hapgood created the theory of "crustal displacement," which states that the entire crust of the earth is dynamic, and these crusts may shift upon the mantle. Large plate tectonics may shift enough to actually create a change in the orientation of the poles.

As the planet orbits around the sun, we experience varying phases of solar patterns that either increase or decrease the intensity of heat that we experience. Did "man's irresponsible behavior" cause the earth to tip as much as 23°or to orbit closer to the sun? Not one of these things could be prevented by taxing people for producing more CO_2, which by the way is the very molecule necessary for plant life to flourish. These fools with their regulatory proposals don't understand that CO_2 is either found in sediment or in the atmosphere, and it transitions from one to the other in a perpetual cycle. You cannot eliminate CO_2 on a planet with carbon-based life without upsetting the delicate balance of the planet.

As CO_2 levels rise in the atmosphere, the plant life on Earth begins to flourish and produces more oxygen for us to breathe, and that cycle continues until we no longer have a sun. Scientists have declared that over the past 4.5 billion years the sun has consumed 0.3% of its total mass, which suggests that the sun will be around for a lot longer.

Why should America shoulder the financial burden of paying for the Paris Climate Agreement, while allowing the largest perpetrators of global pollution (China, India, and Africa) to be exempt from the program for five years? All because some committee believes these countries should be exempt, while "growing their economies"? If climate change is such an immediate and existential threat to all of humankind, then why are certain countries exempt from participation? Either the existence of humankind is in immediate jeopardy, or it isn't.

The greatest immediate threats to humankind in this country are the politicians willing to put national security at risk while trying to make the lobbyists, and themselves, filthy rich because they invested in green energy. Meanwhile, how do they propose that America protects itself against missile and jet airplane attacks from our adversaries when we have no fossil fuels to fuel our defense mechanisms?

It is an arrogant man who believes that he can control the world that he lives in, knowing that the world will be here long after we are gone. The climate was changing long before humans or combustion engines ever existed. There is zero evidence that man is responsible for the climate on this planet. In fact, recent studies have revealed that annual global temperatures have actually gone down on two different occasions in the last twelve years. An even more recent study revealed that measuring empirical gases (rather than carbon core samples) is a more accurate method for measuring global temperatures. Those results show that we have only increased in global temperature by 0.3° Fahrenheit over the last fifty years. In other words, the temperature change is not scientifically significant, according to scientific protocol.

Meanwhile we live on a planet that is regularly being bombarded by debris floating in space that at any given time could collide with our atmosphere and cause Armageddon. When we finally lose our narcissistic arrogance as humans and stop worshipping Earth as some sort of separate God, we will realize how really insignificant we are on this amazing planet.

> "If you can't explain it simply, you don't understand it well enough."
>
> —Albert Einstein

These climate extremists must resort to hypothetical theories and a consensus of opinions because the science simply does not support their claims.

"The earth was formed roughly 4.5 billion years ago. Until 3.8 billion years ago it was a completely inhospitable environment with the surface being mainly molten lava. The earth eventually cooled enough for its crust to form. Land masses could then exist and, when it was cold enough to rain, the oceans formed. Around this time the atmosphere predominantly consisted of methane and ammonia, two extremely important greenhouse gases."[76]

"Earth is continually bathed in energy from the sun. A portion of the energy that arrives at Earth is reflected back into space, another portion is absorbed directly by the atmosphere, and the remainder moves through the atmosphere to the surface. Sunlight energy heats land and water at the surface, and in turn, they emit heat. This heat provides further warming of the atmosphere. The mix of these greenhouse gases in our atmosphere keeps some of the heat energy from escaping directly to space, similar to the way a blanket keeps warmth near your body. This process is the naturally occurring greenhouse effect, and it keeps Earth warm enough to support life.

"In accordance with the basic laws of thermodynamics, as Earth absorbs energy from the sun, it must eventually emit an equal amount of energy to space. The difference between incoming and outgoing radiation is known as a planet's 'radiative forcing.' In the same way as applying a pushing force to a physical object will cause it to become unbalanced and move, a climate forcing factor will change the climate system. When 'forcings' result in incoming energy being greater than outgoing energy; the planet will warm. Conversely, if outgoing energy is greater than incoming energy, the planet will cool."[77]

"Oxygen in the atmosphere was almost non-existent until approximately 2.5 billion years ago. The evolution of cyanobacteria, which produced oxygen as a by-product of photosynthesis, meant that oxygen levels dramatically increased. This rapid change in atmospheric composition caused widespread extinction of most of the previous anaerobic bacteria. This 'new' atmosphere made the earth much colder as there were no longer bacteria emitting 'radiative forcing' methane and carbon dioxide into the atmosphere.

"In the time between 250 and 65 million years ago, the evolution of aerobically respiring animals occurred. This meant the concentration of CO_2 increased and global temperatures increased again. We know that there was a sudden decrease in temperatures around 65 million years ago which resulted in the extinction of the dinosaurs. The most widely accepted reason for this is a massive comet hitting the earth sending huge amounts of matter into the atmosphere. This caused a global decrease in temperature due to an increase in the energy of the sun being reflected back into space; a phenomenon known as the 'albedo effect.'

"Records reveal that approximately 55 million years ago, during 'Thermal Maximum,' a massive warming of 5–8°C occurred in just 20,000 years. It is thought that during this time it was so warm palm trees could have grown at the poles. The direct cause is still disputed amongst scientists; however, it is generally agreed that a sudden release of carbon into the atmosphere caused the warming. This was probably in the form of methane from either the ocean bed or from within ice structures. It was after this period that mammals started to evolve.

"The 'Thermal Maximum' continued until around 35 million years ago when the earth cooled into the Ice Age. The theory behind this change in temperature is that a type of fern named *Azolla* became extinct. The *Azolla* then sank to the bottom of the ocean, taking with it much of the carbon absorbed as carbon dioxide; therefore, removing it from the atmosphere. With the carbon dioxide not present to act as a greenhouse gas, global temperatures decreased again. Unlike the last period of cooling, this time the earth had fully formed continents, including mountain ranges, and land mass at the South Pole, and this new land coverage helped to amplify the cooling via circulation.

"An ice age is defined as when a planet's poles are covered with ice, so technically we are still in one. Within an ice age there are periods of glacial and inter-glacials. Glacials are episodes of colder temperatures whereas inter-glacials are warmer phases. Both will last several thousand years. These changes in climate can be explained with the Milankovitch cycles."[76]

The fact that we continue to maintain ice at our planet's poles indicates that carbon dioxide levels are still low enough to keep this planet in an ice age of sorts.

"The planet seems remarkably stable. Continents and oceans, encircled by an oxygen-rich atmosphere, are capable of sustaining life. Earth and its atmosphere are continuously changing. Such constant change has characterized Earth since its beginning some 4.5 billion years ago. There have been long stages of relative warmth or coolness during the transition to modern geologic time. The paleoclimatic record has shown significant expansions and contractions of warm and cold periods in approximately 40,000-year cycles. This periodicity is interesting because it corresponds to the time it takes Earth to complete an oscillation of the tilt of its axis of rotation. It has long been speculated, and recently calculated, that known changes in orbital geometry could alter the amount of sunlight coming in between winter and summer by about 10 percent or so; and could be responsible for initiating or ending ice ages.

"Interestingly (about 600,000 to 800,000 years ago) these expansion and contraction cycles switched from 40,000-year intervals to 100,000-year intervals with very large fluctuations. The precise cause of the longer intervals, between warm and cold periods; are not yet understood. Volcanic eruptions may have played a significant role. It is remarkable that despite violent, episodic perturbations, the climate has been 'buffered' enough to sustain life for 3.5 billion years.

"Climatologists performed a complex statistical analysis involving some 112 different factors related to temperature, including tree rings, the extent of mountain glaciers, changes in coral reefs, sunspot activity and volcanism.

"The resulting temperature reconstruction model reveals there is considerable uncertainty in each year of this 1,000-year temperature reconstruction range. But the overall trend is clear: a gradual temperature decrease, over the first 900 years, followed by a sharp temperature upturn in the last 100 years.

"By studying the transition from the high carbon dioxide, low-oxygen atmosphere of the Archean to the era of great evolutionary progress about half a billion years ago, it becomes clear that life may have been a factor in the stabilization of climate. In another example (during the ice ages and interglacial cycles) life seems to have the opposite function; accelerating the change rather than diminishing it. This observation has led us to contend that climate and life coevolved rather than life serving solely as a negative-feedback on climate."[78]

"For more than 60 years, the National Aeronautics and Space Administration, (NASA) has known that the changes occurring to planetary weather patterns are completely natural and normal. But the space agency, for whatever reason, has chosen to let the man-made global warming hoax persist and spread; to the detriment of human freedom.

"It was the year 1958, to be precise, when NASA first observed that changes in the solar orbit of the earth, along with alterations to the earth's axial tilt, are both responsible for what climate scientists today have dubbed 'warming' or 'cooling,' depending on their agenda at the time. But NASA has failed to set the record straight.

"In the year 2000, NASA did publish information about the Milankovitch Climate Theory, revealing that the planet is, in fact, changing due to extraneous factors that have absolutely nothing to do with human activity. The truth, however, is much more along the lines of what Serbian astrophysicist Milutin Milankovitch proposed about how the seasonal and latitudinal variations of solar radiation that hit the earth in different ways, and at different times, have the greatest impact on Earth's changing climate patterns.

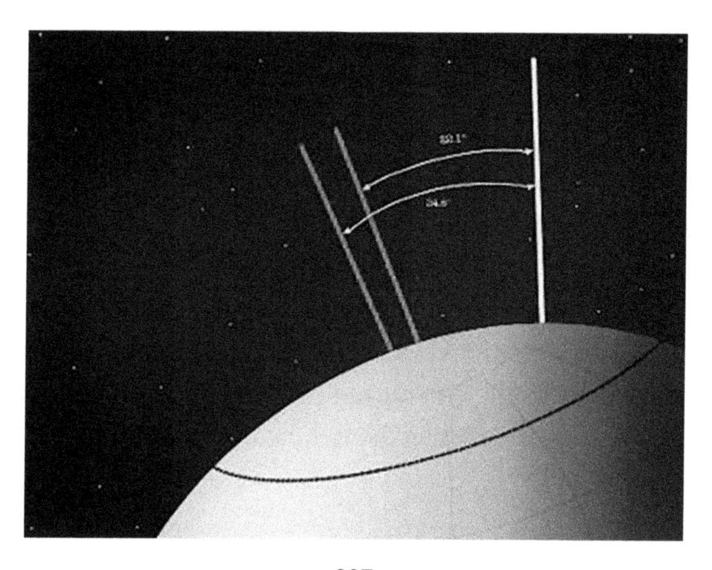

"The following image illustrates the massive change in distance that occurs between the earth and the sun, depending on whether it is at perihelion or aphelion. At the current eccentricity of .017, the earth is 5 million kilometers closer to the sun at perihelion than at aphelion.

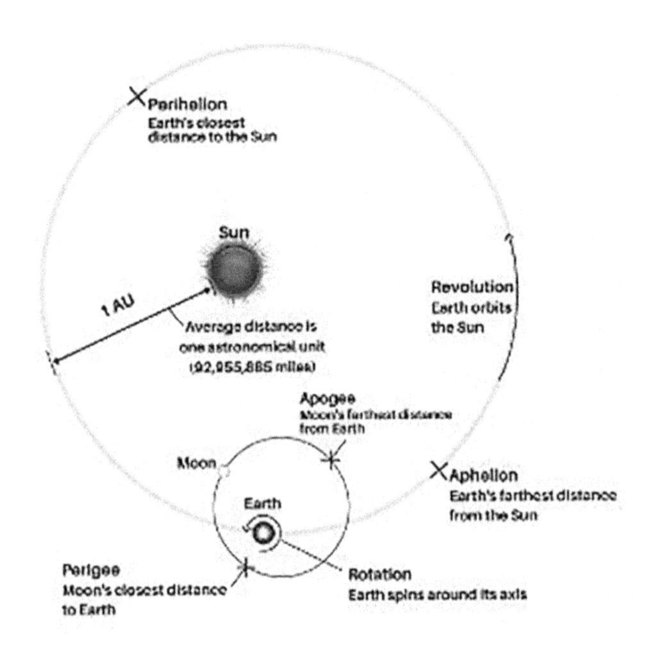

"The biggest factor affecting the earth's climate is the sun. As for Earth's obliquity, or its change in axial tilt, the below images (Robert Simmon, NASA GSFC) show the degree to which the earth can shift on both its axis and its rotational orientation. At the higher tilts, Earth's seasons become much more extreme. At the lower tilts the earth's seasons become much milder. A similar situation exists for Earth's rotational axis, which depending on which hemisphere is pointed at the sun during perihelion, can greatly impact the season extremes between the two hemispheres.

“Based on these variables, Milankovitch was able to come up with a comprehensive mathematical model that is able to compute surface temperatures on Earth going way back in time, and the conclusion is simple; Earth’s climate has *always* been changing, and is in a constant state of flux due to no fault of our own as human beings.

“In 1976, a study published in the journal *Science* confirmed that Milankovitch’s theory is, in fact, accurate and that it does correspond to various periods of climate change that have occurred throughout history.

“In 1982 the National Research Council of the United States National Academy of Sciences adopted Milankovitch’s theory as truth, declaring that:

“‘...orbital variations remain the most thoroughly examined mechanism of climatic change on time scales of tens of thousands of years and are by far the clearest case of a direct effect of changing insolation on the lower atmosphere of Earth.’

“If we had to sum the whole thing up in one simple phrase, it would be this: ‘The biggest factor influencing weather and climate patterns on Earth is the sun, period.’

"Depending on the earth's position to the sun at any given time, climate conditions are going to vary dramatically, and even create drastic abnormalities that defy everything that humans thought they knew about how the earth worked.

"But rather than embrace this truth, today's climate 'scientists,' joined by leftist politicians and a complicit mainstream media, insist that not using reusable grocery bags at the supermarket and not having an electric vehicle are destroying the planet so quickly that we absolutely must implement global climate taxes as the solution.

'The climate change debate is not about science. It is an effort to impose political and economic controls on the population by the elites.' And it's another way to divide the population against itself."[79]

"Earth isn't the only planet grappling with climate change, although this other orb doesn't have much in the way of fossil fuel emissions or a 97% of scientific consensus on global warming.

"Newly published evidence suggests Mars is experiencing global warming as it emerges from an ice age.

"The red planet, which moved closer to the earth than at any other time since 2005, has retreated from a glacial period according to a study published in the journal *Science*. The research was conducted using an instrument on board the NASA Mars Reconnaissance Orbiter that allowed an unprecedented examination of 'the most recent Martian ice age recorded in the planet's north polar ice cap,' according to a NASA press release.

"NASA attributed the changes to the planet's orbit and significant tilt. 'Earth has similar, but less variable, phases called Milankovitch cycles,' said NASA. Speculation about climate change on Mars has heightened since 2001. Photographs from the Mars Global Surveyor suggested that ice caps near the planet's South Pole were receding. A 2007 study by a Russian physicist concluded that the caps had been in decline for three summers in a row and attributed the decline to solar irradiance.

"The question of whether Mars is experiencing climate change has spilled into the global warming debates on Earth, fueling discussion over whether both planets are heating up as a result of solar activity.

"When a 2007 *National Geographic News* article claimed: 'most scientists think it is pure coincidence' that both planets are between ice ages right now; Russian physicist Habibullo Abdussamatov disputed that explanation.

"'Man-made greenhouse warming has made a small contribution to the warming seen on Earth in recent years, but it cannot compete with the increase in solar irradiance,' he told *LiveScience* in 2007."[80]

The Solution

It is time to lobby the United Nations to stop ignoring the carbon emissions and pollution being generated by China, India, and Africa, while ignoring the self-imposed mitigations efforts of the United States. While the United States continues to lower its global carbon emissions (without being mandated by some climate accord), "China, and China alone produces around one third of the ocean's plastic waste. China's CO_2 emissions are greater than the United States and Europe combined, and continues to rise.

"If these climate alarmists really believe that climate change is an existential threat to humanity, why are they proposing draconian and pointless curbs on the behavior of ordinary Americans? Why aren't they going after multinationals that continue to do business with the world's biggest polluter, without demanding any environmental commitments from them?

"The real reason they won't go after China is that they are now the party of global elites, and global elites are constantly salivating about the profits that can be made from China's market of 1.4 billion people. They look at America and see a dwindling middle class with a declining population. There's no money in that. As for the impact on the environment, the elites don't really care.

"There's a lot of misinformation out there about the climate. While I am skeptical of man-made climate change, natural climate change does occur. And even if you don't think climate change is a problem, that doesn't mean that the massive amounts of pollution generated by China is acceptable. Preserving the natural environment means preserving our heritage—a conservative goal."[81]

When Greta Thunberg and fifteen other children filed a complaint with the United Nations, the complaint did not name China.

When it comes to climate change, "People think the solutions are straightforward: solar panels on every roof, electric cars in every driveway, etc. They believe the main obstacles are political. A $300 billion dollar investment in renewable energy was proposed. The intention was to not only prevent climate change, but also create millions of new jobs in a fast-growing high-tech sector.

"The efforts were embraced by Barack Obama. Between 2009 and 2015, the United States invested $150 billion dollars in renewable and other forms of clean technology. But right away the program ran into trouble.

"Electricity from solar roofs costs about twice as much as electricity from solar farms, but solar and wind farms require huge amounts of land. That along with the fact that solar and wind farms require long new transmission lines, and are opposed by local communities and conservationists trying to preserve wildlife; particularly birds. Nearly one million birds are killed by wind turbines every year.

"Another challenge was the intermittent nature of solar and wind energies. When the sun stops shining and the wind stops blowing, you have to quickly be able to ramp up another source of energy. Despite what you've heard, there is no 'battery revolution' on the way, for well-understood technical and economic reasons. (And nobody addresses the issue of what to do with the batteries once they have to be retired. How do you dispose of the plastic and the acid?)

"Wind turbines are the most serious new threat to important bird species, because the rapidly spinning turbines act like an apex predator which big birds never evolved to deal with. Solar farms have similarly large ecological impacts. You have to clear the whole area of wildlife (and trees).

"There is no amount of technological innovation that could solve the fundamental problem with renewables. You can make solar panels cheaper and wind turbines bigger, but you can't make the sun shine more regularly or the wind blow more reliably. To know these limitations is to understand the implications of the physics of energy. In order to produce significant amounts of electricity from weak energy flow, you just have to spread them over enormous areas. In other words, the trouble with renewable energy isn't fundamentally technical; it's natural.

"Germany's carbon emissions have been flat since 2009. After an investment of $580 billion in a renewable-heavy electric grid; the result was a 50% rise in electricity cost. Meanwhile, France produces one-tenth the carbon emissions per unit of electricity as Germany and pays a little more than half for its electricity. How do they do it? They use nuclear power.

"It is reasonable to ask whether nuclear power is safe, and what happens with its waste? It turns out that scientists have studied the health and safety of different energy sources since the 1960s. Every major study, including a recent one by the British medical journal *Lancet*, finds the same thing: nuclear is the safest way to make reliable electricity.

"The uranium used as fuel in power plants and as material for bombs can create one million times more heat per its mass than its fossil fuel and gunpowder equivalents. Because nuclear plants produce heat without fire, they emit no air pollution in the form of smoke.

"Even during the worst accidents, nuclear plants release only small amounts of radioactive particulate matter. As a result, the climate scientist James Hanson and a colleague found that nuclear plants have actually saved nearly two million lives to date that would have been lost to air pollution.

"Thanks to its energy density, nuclear plants require far less land than renewable. Energy dense nuclear options require far less in the way of materials, and produce far less in the way of waste compared to energy-dilute solar and wind. In other words, the energy density of the fuel determines its environmental and health impacts.

"The Progressive Party believes that wind turbines are 'new.' Windmills have been around since before the combustion engine. Over the last several hundred years, human beings have been moving away from 'matter-dense' fuels towards 'energy-dense' ones. First, we move from renewable fuels like wood, dung and windmills, and towards the fossil fuels of coal, oil, and natural gas; and eventually to uranium.

"Energy progress is overwhelmingly positive for people and nature. As we stop using wood for fuel, we allow grasslands and forests to grow back, and the wildlife to return. And as we move from fossil fuels to uranium we clear the outdoor air of pollution, and reduce how much we'll heat up the planet.

"The problem with nuclear is that it is unpopular. It is a victim of a 50 year-long concerted effort by fossil fuel, renewable energy, anti-nuclear weapons campaigners and misanthropic environmentalists to ban the technology.

"What is to be done? The most important thing is for scientists and conservationists to start telling the truth about renewable energy and nuclear energy; and the relationship between energy density and environmental impact.

"It's high time that those who appointed themselves as Earth's guardians should take a second look at the science, and start questioning the impacts of their actions."[82]

You can be an environmentalist without being a climate alarmist.

While it is absolutely true that nobody should be buying into this 50-year climate hysteria, it is equally true that we should all agree not to defecate where we eat. Every single person on this planet has a duty to be a good steward for our environment. Eliminating toxins, pollutants, and waste from the air and water are essential for a healthy environment. We should recycle more and litter less. We should propose a national whistleblower program against littering, punishable with a $1,000 fine to the perpetrator and a $100 reward to the whistleblower.

It makes sense to plant more trees. Forest management that selectively removes trees to reduce fire risk can maintain uneven-aged forest structure and create small openings in the forest. Under some conditions, this practice can help prevent large wildfires from spreading. The deforestation created after these large fires is devastating to the natural buffering of our atmosphere.

Instead of giving *Time*'s Person of the Year award to Greta Thunberg in 2019, they should have given the recognition to a biology student named Morgan Vague who discovered and bred bacteria capable of eating plastic and potentially breaking it down into harmless by-products.

The microbes degrade polyethylene terephthalate, which is one of the most common plastics used in clothing, drinking bottles, and food packaging. While the microbes may not solve all of the world's plastic pollution problems, it certainly will be a large part of the solution.

And finally, we must tackle the issue of being eco-friendly even in death. It makes no sense to use our organic bodies to consume, consume, consume, and never return our gifts back to the earth to help complete the circle of life.

"Standard burial and cremation procedures take tons of energy and resources. Currently, when a person dies, we fill the corpse with toxic embalming fluid. This process drains the corpse of nutrients and prevents it from being eaten by bacteria in the ground. Then the bodies (shielded by a million pounds of metal, wood and concrete) are put in the ground annually in traditional cemeteries where they will be used for nothing else until the end of time.

"A single cremation requires about two tanks worth of fuel. If environmentalists are truly concerned about the future of our planet, then perhaps it is time to seek alternative, more environmentally friendly options for disposing of their bodies.

"For those who still want to be buried, a greener approach may include switching out the standard embalming fluids with ones made of essential oils. Instead of using a heavy wood or metal box that will take years to degrade, there are now biodegradable cedar caskets. Others are choosing to forgo the casket completely and opt for what's called a 'natural burial,' involving only a burlap sack buried in the woods.

"In some cities, bodies may soon be placed in an industrial sized compost bin, and turned over to create fertile soil. The pits are filled with carbon rich human bodies that microbes can decompose into compost. This process returns the remains into their natural place in the world."[83]

The realization that external factors have more control than we do over the environment we live in is frightening to most people. While there is little we can do about an asteroid or a comet colliding with Earth, there are some external occurrences that we can shield against to protect our current way of life.

It is time to awaken the sleeping giant known as "the silenced majority." There is no better time than right now to arm yourself with knowledge and to let your voices be heard. It was John Stuart Mill who said, "Let not any one; pacify his conscience by the delusion that he can do no harm if he takes no part, and forms no opinion. Bad men need nothing more to compass their ends than that; good men should look on and do nothing." I assure you this is not the last you have heard from me because *silence has consequences too*.

Bibliography

1. Jon A. Brake. November 23, 2017. "Beware of the Useful Idiots" Manhattan Free Press

2. Bill Whittle. March 17, 2016 "Here Be Dragons: How the 2016 Election is Shaping Up." *PJ Media* on YouTube

3. Saul Alinsky. 1971. *Rules for Radicals*

4. Frank Dux. April 5, 2018. "Beware of How Useful Idiots Attempt to Create a Socialist Deep State." *Artvoice*

5. John Milton. 2003. *Paradise Lost*. Penguin Classics. London England: Penguin Classics

6. Evan Sayet. July 13, 2017. "He Fights." *Townhall: Conservative News*

7. Yascha Mounk. October 10, 2018 "Americans Strongly Dislike PC Culture," *The Atlantic*

8. Bill Whittle, April 13, 2012"The Narrative: The Origins of Political Correctness." *PJ* Media on YouTube

9. Harry S. Truman, September 4, 1952. "Establishing the President's Commission on Immigration and Naturalization."

10. Michelle Garcia. April 25, 2019. "The Border Wall Isn't Just a Dividing Line—It's a Monument against Racial Progress." *The Guardian*

11. Shirin Ghaffary. February 7, 2020. "The 'Smarter' Wall: How Drones, Sensors, and AI Are Patrolling the Border." *Vox*

12. Paul Bedard. September 23, 2018. "Yale Shocker: 29.5 Million Illegal Immigrants, 3X Higher than Census Number." *Washington Examiner*

13. Andrew R. Arthur. April 1, 2019. "Unaccompanied Alien Children and the Crisis at the Border." *Center for Immigration Studies*

14. Curtis Florence. October 2016 "The Economic Burden of Prescription Opioid Overdose, Abuse, and Dependence in the United States, 2013." *Med Care 2016* Volume 54(10): 901-906.

15. Heather Higgins. June 19, 2019. "Border Crisis Puts Everyone's Health at Risk—Pandemics Can't become 'the New Normal.'" *Fox News*

16. Anna Giaritelli. May 18, 2019. "DNA Tests Reveal 30% of Suspected Fraudulent Migrant Families Were Unrelated." *Washington Examiner*

17. US Customs and Border Protection. May 3, 2019. "'Recycling' of Children in El Paso." Official website of the Department of Homeland Security

18. Mary Margaret Olohan. August 16, 2019. "Child Sex-Trafficking More Common in US Than People Realize, Activists Says. Here's What You Should Know." *The Daily Caller*

19. Anna Giaritelli. July 5, 2019. "Democratic Congresswoman Secretly Sending Staff into Mexico to Coach Asylum Seekers." *The Washington Examiner*

20. Aaron Bandler. October 22, 2016. "9 Things You Need to Know About Illegal Immigration and Crime." *The Daily Wire*

21. Michelle Malkin. September 9, 2019. "60 Terrifying Reasons Trump Is Right to Reduce Refugees." *Breitbart News*

22. Neil Munro. June 12, 2019. "Washington Post: Migration Crisis is Driven by Economics, not Crime." *Breitbart News*

23. Nina Totenberg and Hansi Lo Wang. June 27, 2019. "Trump Threatens Census Delay After Supreme Court Leaves Citizenship Question Blocked." *NPR*

24. Daniel Horowitz. June 11, 2019. "The Harrowing Pronouncement Scalia Would Make about President Trump's Authority to Secure Our Own Border." *Blaze Media*

25. Neil Munro. August 21, 2019. "DHS Issues Regulation Closing the Flores Catch-and-Release Loophole." *Breitbart News*

26. Home Office, "The Stephen Lawrence Inquiry: Report of an Inquiry by Sir William Macpherson of Cluny, Cm 4262-I, February 1999, para 6.34 (cited in Macpherson Report – Ten Years On in 2009); available on the official British Parliament Website.

27. John Nolte. August 16, 2019. "Nolte: New York Times Admits 'We Built Our Newsroom' Around Russia Collusion Hoax." *Breitbart News*

28. Henry Louis Gates, Jr. "Free Blacks Lived in the North, Right?" On *The African Americans: Many Rivers to Cross* website presented on PBS (Excerpt from Ira Berlin's book: *Slaves without Masters: The Free Negro in the Antebellum South*. 1974)

29. Henry Louis Gates, Jr. "The Truth Behind '40 Acres and a Mule.'" On *The African Americans: Many Rivers to Cross* website presented on PBS (Excerpt from Eric Foner's book: *Reconstruction: America's Unfinished Revolution,* 1863-1877) December 2, 2014.

30. John Miltimore. October 10, 2016. "Did LBJ Say, 'I'll Have Those N*ggers Voting Democratic For 200 Years'?" *Intellectual Takeout*

31. Dylan Gwinn. June 19, 2019. "WATCH: NFL Legend Burgess Owens Says Democrats Should Pay Reparations." *Breitbart News*

32. Bill Whittle. December 12, 2013 "Afterburner with Bill Whittle: The Lynching." *YouTube* video

33. Robert L. Johnson. December 12, 2018. "Reparations for Slavery are the Only Way to fix America's Racial Wealth Disparities." Johnson's transcribed speech from the Roosevelt Room of the White House. *NBC News*

34. AlfonZo Rachel. June 25, 2015. "The Reason Why Democrats Are the Party of Slavery and Victimization." *YouTube* video

35. The Sexperts. March 25, 2020. "My Body, My Choice." (Excerpt from "Bodily Autonomy" *SexInfo Online) Wikipedia*

36. Nancy Flanders. January 24, 2020. "Planned Parenthood Claims Abortion is Now 4% of its Services Instead of 3%. It's Still False." *Live Action*

37. The Editors of Encyclopaedia, and updated by Brian Duignan. Britannica. "Roe v. Wade, Law Case."

38. Dr. Dónal O□Mathúna. May 21, 2018. "Society Has a Duty to Protect the Most Vulnerable among Us." *The Irish Times*

39. Anthony Levatino, MD. October 8, 2015. "Testimony before the Committee on the Judiciary, U.S. House of Representatives, Planned Parenthood Exposed: Examining Abortion Procedures and Medical Ethics at the Nation's Largest Abortion Provider."

40. Jeff Poor. May 16, 2019. "Fact Check: 9 Things to Know about Alabama's Abortion Law." *Breitbart News*

41. Planned Parenthood. "The Difference Between the Morning-After Pill and the Abortion Pill." Cited from ACOG – American College of Obstetricians and Gynecologists (July 1998). Statement on Contraceptive Methods.

42. Tom Tillison. May 20, 2019. "Pro-life Dems Push Back Against Progressive Purge of Party: 'No, Enough!'" *BizPac Review*

43. Marilyn M. Singleton, MD, JD. June 8, 2019. "Can We Trust the Government with Our Medical Care?" *Veterans Health Administration Archives*

44. Daniel Button. November 8, 2018. "Take Responsibility for Your Own Health": Naivety or Convenient Excuse?" *New Economics Foundation*

45. David G. Savage. May 12, 2016. "Federal Judge Rules Obamacare Is Being Funded Unconstitutionally." *Los Angeles Times*

46. Lloyd Marcus. March 7, 2019. "What if Trump Loses in 2020: A Black Man's Perspective." *Unhyphenated America*

47. Kate Patrick. November 12, 2019. "Will Healthcare Be Rationed Under Medicare for All?" *Inside Sources*

48. Charles C.W. Cooke. October 29, 2013. "The Single-Payer Fantasy." *National Review*

49. eHealth. January 23, 2017. "Average Individual Health Insurance Premiums Increased 99% Since 2013, the Year Before Obamacare, & Family Premiums Increased 140%, According to eHealth.com Shopping Data."

50. CBO Report. May 1, 2019. "10 Risks of Establishing a One-Size-Fits-All Health Care System." *Budget House Republicans*

51. Jake Tapper. November 13, 2014. "Obamacare Architect Discussed Misleading Public in 4th Newly Uncovered Video." *CNN News*

52. Kevin Pham, MD. June 13, 2019. "'Socialist' Nordic Countries Are Actually Moving Toward Private Health Care." *The Heritage Foundation*

53. Zachary Ward, PhD, MPH, research scientist, Center for Health Decision Science, Harvard T.H. Chan School of Public Health, Boston; Marlene Schwartz, PhD, director, Rudd Center for Food Policy and Obesity, and professor, human development and family sciences, University of Connecticut, Hartford; *PLOS ONE,* March 24, 2021, online. "Obesity Costs the Average U.S. Adult Almost $1,900 per year: Study." *U.S. News & World Report*

54. Selena Simmons-Duffin. October 24, 2019. "The Real Cost of the Opioid Epidemic: An Estimated $179 Billion in Just 1 Year." *National Public Radio*

55. Center for Substance Abuse Treatment. Clinical Guidelines for the Use of Buprenorphine in the Treatment of Opioid Addiction. Treatment Improvement Protocol (TIP) Series 40. DHHS Publication No. (SMA) 04-3939. Rockville, Md: Substance Abuse and Mental Health Services Administration, 2004. *The National Alliance of Advocates for Buprenorphine Treatment*

56. "GE Food & Your Health." *Center for Food Safety*

57. American Journal of Clinical Nutrition. December 2, 2019. "Aspartame Is Linked To Leukemia and Lymphoma in Landmark Study On Humans." *Health News*

58. A.J. Willingham. March 28, 2018. "27 Words: Deconstructing the Second Amendment." *CNN News*

59. David B. Kopel. "The American Revolution against British Gun Control." Administrative and Regulatory Law News Vol. 37, no. 4, Summer 2012.

60. C.D. Michel. April 17, 2013. "Why Universal Background Checks Won't Work." *The Hill*

61. John Romero. August 5, 2019. "No, the U.S. Does Not Lead the World in Mass Shootings." *Media Research Center TV*

62. Christopher J. Ferguson. August 7, 2019. "Mass Shootings Aren't Growing More Common—and Evidence Contradicts Common Stereotypes about the Killers." *The Conversation*

63. Vivek Saxena. August 6, 2019. "Jesse Watters: Media Not Reporting El Paso Shooter is 'Environmental Extremist' Not Influenced by Trump." *BizPac Review*

64. Natasha Lennard. August 5, 2019. "The El Paso Shooter Embraced Eco-Fascism. We Can't Let the Far Right Co-Opt the Environmental Struggle." *The Intercept*

65. Suzanne Venker. February 19, 2018. "Missing Fathers and America's Broken Boys—The Vast Majority of Mass Shooters Come from Broken Homes." *Fox News*

66. Nicholas Freitas. March 2, 2018. "Gun Speech on Floor of House of Delegates." *YouTube* video

67. K.C. Archana. January 29, 2019. "Irony Just Died Because 1500 Private Jets Took World Leaders to Davos to Discuss Climate Change." *India Times*

68. John Nolte. September 20. 2019. "Nolte: Climate 'Experts' Are 0–41 with Their Doomsday Predictions." *Breitbart News*

69. Jeniffer Rast. August 30, 2019. "Gaia Worship—the New Pagan Religion." *Environment and Ecology*

70. Thomas D. Williams. September 24, 2019. "500 Experts Write U.N.: 'There is No Climate Emergency.'" *Breitbart News*

71. James Delingpole. November 20, 2009. "Climategate: the Final Nail in the Coffin of 'Anthropogenic Global Warming'." *The Telegraph*

72. James Delingpole. September 20, 2019. "Delingpole: Environment Canada Airbrushes 100 Years of Inconvenient Climate Data out of History." *WordPress*

73. *Investor's Business Daily*. March 29, 2018. "The Stunning Statistical Fraud behind the Global Warming Scare."

74. Alex Newman. February 12, 2019. "A United Nations Intergovernmental Panel on Climate Change Scientist Blows Whistle on Lies about Climate, Sea Level." *ResearchGate*

75. Michael J. Prather and Juno C. Hsu. September 9, 2019. "A Round Earth for Climate Models." *The Proceedings of the National Academy of Sciences*

76. Sarah Connors. August 3, 2013. "4.5 billion Years of the Earth's Temperature—MuchAdoAbout Climate." *WordPress*

77. National Oceanic and Atmospheric Administration. "Climate Forcing." *Climate.gov*

78. Claude J. Allgre and Stephen H. Schneider. October 1, 1994. "The Evolution of the Earth." *Scientific American.*

79. Ethan Huff. August 30, 2019. "NASA Admits that Climate Change Occurs Because of Changes in Earth's Solar Orbit, and NOT Because of SUVs and Fossil Fuels." *Natural News*

80. Valerie Richardson. May 31, 2016. "Mars Also Undergoing Climate Change as Ice Age Retreats, Study Shows." *The Washington Times*

81. Allum Bokhari. September 6, 2019. "Bokhari: If Democrats Cared about the Environment, they'd Talk About China." *Breitbart News*

82. Michael Shellenberger. February 27, 2019. "Why Renewables Can't Save the Planet." *Quillette*

83. Shannon Palus. October 30, 2014. "How to Be Eco-Friendly When You're Dead." *The Atlantic*

CPSIA information can be obtained
at www.ICGtesting.com
Printed in the USA
BVHW050340040522
635995BV00041B/2032